SOCIAL SCIENCE AND THE NEW SOCIETIES:

Problems in Cross-Cultural Research and Theory Building

SOCIAL SCIENCE AND THE NEW SOCIETIES:

Problems in Cross-Cultural Research and Theory Building

Edited by Nancy Hammond

Contributors: Erik Allardt, David E. Apter, Karl W. Deutsch, Max Gluckman, Alex Inkeles, Wilbert E. Moore, Manning Nash, Robert C. North, Peter M. Worsley

SS | SOCIAL SCIENCE RESEARCH BUREAU, MICHIGAN STATE UNIVERSITY
RB | East Lansing . 1973

TABLE OF CONTENTS

FOREWORD

As American social scientists increasingly recognize that parochial concerns with American society are not sufficient for developing new theories of human behavior, so, too, do they acknowledge that research in differing cultural settings, particularly systematic comparative research, poses difficult methodological and conceptual problems. The papers collected here contain some of the best current thinking about solutions to these problems. They also make major contributions to knowledge in such important substantive areas as the nature of modernization, the possibility of cultural convergence in industrializing countries, and the relationship between revolutionary ideologies and nation-building.

Planned originally to stimulate interest in and contribute to the solution of problems of cross-cultural and comparative studies in the social sciences, the first symposium was held at Michigan State University in 1967 and was sponsored by the Departments of Anthropology, Political Science, and Sociology; two more symposia followed, in 1968 and 1969. Altogether, nine distinguished scholars participated in these three programs, and their work is represented here. The National Science Foundation and the Michigan State University Center for International Programs provided grants that made these symposia possible. We gratefully acknowledge this support.

Iwao Ishino, *Chairman*
Department of Anthropology

O. Charles Press, *Chairman*
Department of Political Science

William A. Faunce, *Chairman*
Department of Sociology

Michigan State University
East Lansing, Michigan

I: Problems of Cross-cultural Research in Developing Areas

The papers in this section were presented at the first Michigan State University Symposium on Comparative Studies in the Social Sciences, May 25–26, 1967. The participants in this symposium discussed general conceptual and methodological issues in cross-cultural, comparative research. The level of generality of existing theories, problems of conceptual equivalence, and the appropriateness of standard research techniques and instruments are among the issues raised by this kind of research. The papers focus upon the nature of the modernization and economic development processes and upon problems in the study of these processes. They also contain some interesting observations on the history of social scientific concern with comparative studies.

David E. Apter is Professor of Political Science and Sociology at Yale University. He was formerly on the faculties of Northwestern University, the University of Chicago, and the University of California at Berkeley, where he was also Director of the Institute of International Studies. He has been a Fellow at the Center for Advanced Study in the Behavioral Sciences, a Guggenheim Fellow, and a Visiting Fellow of All Souls College, Oxford. He is an Associate Fellow of St. Antony's College, Oxford. A specialist in the comparative analysis of political systems, comparative theory and systems analysis, the politics of economic growth, and the development of political systems, Professor Apter has published extensively. His books include: *The Political Kingdom in Uganda, A Study in Bureaucratic Nationalism, Ghana in Transition, The Politics of Modernization,* and *Some Conceptual Approaches to the Study of Modernization.* He is also editor of *Comparative Politics: A Reader* (with H. Eckstein), *Ideology and Discontent,* and *Contemporary Analytical Theory* (with C. Andrain).

1

Max Gluckman is Research Professor in Social Anthropology, Victoria University of Manchester (England). He has been a Lecturer at Oxford, Director of the Rhodes-Livingstone Institute of Social Studies, British Central Africa, and, from 1949 to 1965, Head of the Department of Social Anthropology and Sociology at Victoria University. He now holds a Special Senior Fellowship from the Nuffield Foundation and is a Fellow of the British Academy and a Foreign Honorary Member of the American Academy of Arts and Sciences. Professor Gluckman has conducted extensive comparative research on problems of social organization, law, and change in South and Central Africa, and has directed research in Britain, in India, and, more recently, in Israel. His major publications include: *The Judicial Process among the Barotse of Northern Rhodesia, The Ideas of Barotse Jurisprudence, Custom and Conflict in Africa, Order and Rebellion in Tribal Africa, Analysis of a Social Situation in Modern Zululand,* and *Politics, Law, and Ritual in Tribal Society.* He has also edited *Closed Systems and Open Minds, Essays on the Ritual of Social Relations,* and *The Allocation of Responsibility;* and he has co-edited *Seven Tribes of Central Africa.*

Alex Inkeles is Professor of Sociology at Stanford University. For many years he directed studies in social relations at the Russian Research Center and studies on the non-economic aspects of development at the Center for International Affairs at Harvard University. Professor Inkeles has been a visiting scholar at the Russell Sage Foundation and at the Center for Advanced Study in the Behavioral Sciences, and has had considerable experience with cross-cultural research in both developed and underdeveloped areas. His major research interests are in comparative institutions, social psychology, and mass communications. His books include *Social Change in Soviet Russia, What is Sociology?* and *The Soviet Citizen: Daily Life in a Totalitarian Society.* He is presently directing a large-scale comparative study of the impact of the modernization process on the individual in Argentina, Chile, India, Israel, Nigeria, and Pakistan. The results of this work will be published, with David H. Smith as co-author, in *Becoming Modern: The Social-Psychology of Change in Six Developing Countries.*

NORMS, STRUCTURE, AND BEHAVIOR AND THE STUDY OF POLITICAL DEVELOPMENT*

DAVID E. APTER, *Yale University*

Political science today is going through an agonizing reappraisal—a period of major intellectual reform. To some extent, this reappraisal is a product of its recent history, namely, the attempt to deal with concrete issues of modernization. One consequence of the study of modernization is the modernization of the discipline itself. In my discussion, I will explain why political science has gone through a major change since the interest in developing areas became prominent after the war, and why this change cut to the heart of the discipline of political science in a way not true, I think, of sociology or anthropology.

First of all, one must recall that political science has had two main emphases, both intimately connected with the development of European and Western and American political institutions. The first concern in political science was to see to what extent specialized instruments of government, associated with European and American constitutional or legal practices, had universal significance. A kind of evolutionary notion existed in political science and continued through the period of Woodrow Wilson and well into the 1940s. It was assumed that the proper organization of equity would result in a proper mode of political behavior and civility leading to a sensible, intelligent, social life. Thus, a heavy emphasis was placed on the framework and the institutions associated with government. This intellectual emphasis had, in addition to certain evolutionary characteristics, a wider cultural

* This article was prepared under the auspices of the Politics of Modernization Project of the Institute of International Studies, University of California, Berkeley.

3

context embodied particularly in the notion that civilization and civility and culture all overlapped and found their highest expression in political instruments, particularly those associated with Western parliamentary institutions.

Secondly, there followed logically from the first an emphasis on reform. Especially for those interested in the moral basis of social life, which has always been a powerful, central concern in the study of politics, morality was to be realized through improving the relationships between the rulers and the ruled. Practical measures, which were to be preferred over global solutions, were the means by which some of the universal characteristics associated with specialized instruments of government could be established in places where they did not exist, or could be improved where they already did. So reform and the intellectual emphasis linked to the universalization of highly specialized instruments associated particularly with the practice of parliamentary government formed the core of the discipline. Underlying these ideas about formal aspects of government was also a shrewd, vulgar, Marxist explanation of why the world was the way it was, especially when observers noted that there was not a perfect fit between governmental institutions and the observable political behavior. This lack of fit was seen to be the result of some disproportionate or badly allocated set of power relationships. Since power was ultimately derived from economic activity, such dislocations as occurred were seen as flowing from an unequal access to economic power. This was also true on the intellectual side. The notion arose that the economics of distribution, equity, and constitutionality formed the basic model. Such a model was easily transformed into a reform tradition, such as embodied, for example, in anti-trust laws, or in creating the opportunity for those who were deprived or underprivileged to improve themselves by means of both economic and political weapons. Such an improving psychology, no matter its form, always had an undercurrent or a presumption of reality in the form of economics. Its normative and institutional characteristics were framed in the context of law and constitutions.[1]

So much for the tradition, which obviously has an uneven kind of history, even in the West. Certainly, for a long time this synthesis, this set of ideas, kept us in a position where totalitarianism, as in Germany or Russia, could be seen as aberrations resulting from faulty

1. For a more detailed discussion with relevant bibliographical references, see D. E. Apter and Charles Andrain, "Comparative Government: Developing New Nations," in Marion D. Irish (ed.), *Political Science, Advance of the Discipline* (Englewood Cliffs: Prentice-Hall, Inc., 1968).

or poorly framed constitutions and badly organized economic arrangements. So the notion that there was universality was mainly limited
not to *any* specialized governmental instruments but to parliamentary
and democratic institutions.

The same situation did not apply to the same extent in sociology
or anthropology. Many of the most significant kinds of issues that
political scientists, when they began discovering the rest of the universe, had painfully to contrive or discover for themselves were recognized at the birth of anthropology. The attempts to discover models
that were organismic or not, that were culturally deterministic or
not, that were functional or not, and so on, could hardly be separated
from that discipline, so that the emergence of anthropology as an
intellectual discipline was associated with major efforts to contrive
and establish theoretical constructs that were themselves not rooted
in any particular provincial set of institutions.

Such efforts, of course, created a very lively kind of discourse,
a discourse, it might be added, that was largely lacking in political
science—or at least lacking in modern political science ever since the
discipline lost its intimate connection with philosophy. When separated
from this wider analytical base, the discipline lost simultaneously its
innocence and its sophistication. Sociology differed from political science too because it remained intimately linked with that enormous
body of nineteenth and early twentieth century literature associated
with Marx, Weber, Durkheim, Tönnies, and Simmel, i.e., those who
dealt with the consequences of industrialization and the change from
agrarian social life to highly complex institutions. Here was a different
interest, in moral crises that these changes produced—a more analytical one. The role of religion, for example, was a continuous preoccupation. The significance of these changes, not to speak of a major concern
with the way people perceived themselves in relation to family, kinship,
tradition—all in the context of industrialization—articulated ways that
people defined their significance. Political science was largely oblivious
of these changes.

It was only when students of politics became interested in the
formation of new states that the old notions of the discipline were
found to be inadequate. The job of breaking through political science's
restricted view of the political universe and creating a different standard against which to measure success or failure of governmental
institutions is now in full swing. There is thus an intellectual crisis,
and it not only includes the old, traditional and well-worked categories
of the discipline itself, but exposes the ideology that lies behind it,

the rather gratuitous assumptions that long characterized the field and its simple pluralism and in which one did not have to pay much attention to behavior to find a good, normative, structural synthesis.[2]

In any event, political scientists now share the concerns that traditionally, and in more recent years, especially, have preoccupied sociologists and anthropologists: problems of innovation, of the changing role of religion, of the way in which tradition operates, of the consequences of complex, specialized instruments of particularism. Today, political scientists employ a wide range of categories in trying to discover how change occurs, why it occurs in an uneven fashion, what sources impede it, what instruments intensify it and make it readily acceptable—all have become political problems. It is no longer possible simply to segregate out specialized instruments of government and say, "These are traditional and these are modern and therefore we compare these." Rather, political scientists now study all of the problems of dislocation, problems that one finds when the congruence between the major dimensions of social action—from the most highly individualized level to the most structural and generalized to the most systemic—somehow loses its fit. In a very real sense, all have become subjects for political study because all of them present problems of control, of deviant behavior, problems of the mobilization of populations, problems, in short, of unpredictable consequences of predictable inputs. One finds, then, that a very different framework is necessary for the analysis of such complex events. Thus sociology or anthropology still occupies the center of the stage from an analytical point of view, while political science surprisingly enough does not. Nor will it until it reconciles itself to incorporating all the relevant materials or data that affect the balance among political norms, structures, and behavior. Therefore, the politically significant work of each of those in the other disciplines must somehow be known to a political scientist.[3]

This leads me to a second problem. If what I say is true, the burden on political scientists is overwhelming. First of all, the range of empirical information required is itself without good boundaries. We live in a universe exploding with data. We must be familiar with

2. When reading Professor Inkeles' chapter in this volume, one might well conclude that the shoe is completely on the other foot. He is concerned entirely with behavior. From his point of departure, structural materials are the less relevant and less significant data.

3. For a more analytical and fuller statement of these matters, see "A Paradigm for Political Analysis," in D. E. Apter, *Some Conceptual Approaches to the Study of Modernization* (Englewood Cliffs: Prentice-Hall, 1968).

a wide range of data just as a form of basic training, to gain a general understanding of the events, not only of our world, but that of others'. Moreover, as specialized theories develop new bodies of material, such data are added at a fantastic rate. An unbelievable additive process is at work and very little is sloughed off, so that the sheer accumulation of knowledge is in itself a strategic problem for a student. How can he find his way through this wealth of material gathered by people with diverse interests, with an extremely complicated and mixed-up set of categeories, without a consensus about the language of research, with each specialized discipline covering somewhat the same ground as every other but using different categories and some different models? The problem not only becomes a critical pedagogical process, but lends itself to an emphasis on technique that quite often is anti-theoretical or even anti-intellectual.

It is particularly difficult in the field of political science because the intellectual side was never so powerful or so weighty that one could not get most of it by reading a few good books. And if the boundaries of the discipline are flimsy and our original, rather basic map no longer serves as a guide, then—and this is, of course, what has happened—political scientists find themselves relying heavily on technique. Somehow the hardness of the data becomes a substitute for thinking. There seems to be a widespread belief that, even if you get only a good correlation, you'll get *something* anyway. This belief is silly if to begin with you lack good ideas.

This is a real problem. (There are a lot of silly people. But even those who aren't silly have done a lot of silly things.) But the crisis and the problem remain, and this reason gives some of us the temerity to try to sort out some different ways of conceiving of the major bodies of data by establishing a sort of map. I regard such a mapping operation not as ontologically "correct," but not purely arbitrary either, because it is linked to the general problem with which we have been concerned, namely, the problem of cross-cultural analysis (and, for me, of the formation of new societies, which I see as alternative and different systems of choice). Let me make this idea clearer by indicating the present point of departure. By defining politics in these terms, I see choice both as the strategic way of examining the significance of the study of cross-cultural units or societies and also as the main analytical device for sorting out categories, the main dimensions of theory, that are necessary. I am not specifying which theory or what particular approach one should opt for, nor, for that matter, the most critical or the most useful technique. Both of these questions—

technique and theory—are, I think, both objective in one sense, and terribly personal and idiosyncratic in another. A man does what he thinks he can do best. Professionalism is important, I think, in knowing the rules of the game and the limitations each theoretical approach imposes—both on the observer and between the various theories.

What are the different dimensions of choice as I see them? First there is the central theoretical tradition of political science, normative choice. Ever since Plato and Aristotle, this tradition has been the basis of politics, which is truly a moral discipline before it is a social science discipline. Political science is changing, but I do not think it can ever lose its moral origins. Those origins are a kind of beneficial original sin.

Secondly, I think that the normative aspect has two very different consequences. One of the consequences is simply to see what extent a normative or moral system lies behind the sense of obligation that binds people together in a community. What are the forms of obligation? What are the principles on which these forms are based? How are they integrated in some fashion? What are their ideological or religious expressions? These are part of what can be called a normative level of discourse, and this normative pattern is sometimes identified as central values or key operating ideas or modal beliefs, but they share one thing in common. They all represent some higher virtue, some sense of meaning, a dimension of meaning, through which individuals relate themselves to others in the community and have some means of evaluating the consequences of their own actions on the actions of others.

Although this normative dimension represents a very old tradition in the study of politics, it requires the student of developing areas to do some rather interesting things. He is called upon somehow to break through the limitations of his own normative set and comprehend the meaning of others. At one level this task is sometimes simple and at another level it is very difficult indeed. So far, what has been lacking, despite our sensitivity to the problem, is a set of rules to the normative game. That is, although normative theory has a good deal to say about the way in which norms are observed and the observations generalized, rarely are the following questions about the normative dimension put directly: "What is the appropriate dimension or the mode of observation and what is the mode or method of generalization?"

The answers are complex. For example, an observer who has never wrestled deeply with his own normative position will never understand the norms of others. That is why, I believe, political science can never lose its normative base. Those who become political scientists are somehow troubled or concerned by the moral meaning of the universe in a directly political sense. That is to say, they see this meaning as crucial to the relationship of politics. Participant observation, which is the answer to the first question, is, I would say, very much in its beginning stages. Just as normative observation begins in participation, so its mode of generalization is through a dialectic of meaning, a reciprocity of moral terms. In a manner of speaking, no one understands a good Catholic like a good Lutheran. The dialogue doesn't really mean anything unless the participation in that pattern of belief has become dialectically significant. Similarly with political ideologies. Many of us who were interested, for example, in African nationalism went to Africa, not wholly for good scientific reasons, but because we felt somehow that a new moral dimension was being created or framed there, and it was attractive, it was interesting, it had universal significance, perhaps, and we could, by observing it, participate in it and translate that meaning into more general terms.

Now obviously there are enormous pitfalls in this method, and the question of how you generalize in a legitimate way from self to society, from individual perception to something more objective, is an exceptionally difficult thing indeed. (Some of the people who have been interested in the sociology of knowledge, as have Marxists, for example, will blithely tell you that a good Communist, no matter what his social class, can break through its limitations with some higher perception to see the universal significance of the role of the proletariat in the future of history. How this man is able to do so is never quite made clear, especially if he has, like Lenin, middle-class origins.) The normative discourse should be seen more directly as essentially a dialectical one. To set up an opposite by virtue of identifying that which is meaningful to you creates a method of approach. And, in the constant flow of argument and debate about these things on a self-conscious basis, one then begins to develop some useful set, some recognizable range, of normative meanings, which begins with what the observer knows and may—though not necessarily—wind up well beyond what he knows.

In the second category, and one that I think is especially important for political science as it changes its categories, is what I have called the structural dimension. The structural dimension deals with sets of roles in social systems. The structural dimension, as traditionally used in political science, tended to be centered almost entirely on what could be called concrete structures, membership units, and the inferred properties that I spoke of earlier, such as the properties of political parties, the properties of two-party systems, the properties of single-member constituencies, of plurality voting, of the separation between church and state, judicial review, a separate and well-defined civil service, etc. All of these are concrete units that have become the substance of the categories of political analysis. In breaking through those categories by working in other areas, where none of these terms has the same connotations, where the fit is faulty, we must ask, "What do you replace them with? Where do you go in order to examine different kinds of structures which, if they have familiar names, are names in another language and indeed a language that sometimes is very hard to learn?" If we are not to accumulate a new set of concrete structures for old ones, tribal councils for parliaments, chiefs for presidents, with all the misleading inferences of such substitution, a more analytical approach is required. First, one fundamentally changes the role of the observer from the one employed at the normative level. Whereas the participant observer tries, in a certain sense, to become part of the social system in which he is involved, the structural analyst does the opposite. He tries to remove himself from the environment and become an external, or, if you will, a theoretically omniscient, observer. Now, the dangers here are obvious. So far, the number of successful, theoretically omniscient observers has been noticeably small and, in any event, it is not so evident to the eye of the beholder that they are as omniscient as they are supposed to be. But just for the sake of argument let us accept this as an idea and for this reason: One is concerned with trying to map a range of relationships in a unit, and one can use the membership unit, like a new society or a new government or a particular kind of association, a church, the separatist movement, the nationalist movement, a burial and lending society, and so on, and see it as it relates to some larger and more analytically defined set of properties of which the system is composed. So if we begin with a concrete unit, we begin to ask, "What are the things that bind it together? What are the implications of the membership groups? What are the activities that they perform?" And if we cluster these activities, if we analyze them, if we begin to put them into typologies at the first or most basic level of abstraction by saying, "This is a Class A, this is a Class B, these are services, these are kinds of activities of a more instrumental nature," for example, or "These are less serviceable in that sense but seem to provide emotional and psychic rewards and benefits; these are things that lead to some pattern of motive or solidary activities," then, it seems to me, we shift the ground entirely to asking, "What is the functional consequence of the activities observed by an outside observer?" Some of these consequences will be categorical, and some will be what could be called functional. But both are based on some perceived definition of social need. Hence, the basic method of generalization in structural analysis is a functional one, and the kinds of theories that one develops relate to the functioning of whole systems and their sub-systems. One moves from the most general level down to the particular, as well as from the particular to the general.

Essentially an emphasis on deductive generalization, it is particularly useful for dealing with large-scale or macro-units. By working "down," one can repeat this process in order to find out the more specialized characteristics of sub-units. This is a methodological procedure that can be either quantitative or qualitative, but it has so far been less quantitative than it should be. But with the development of computers, with the clarification of language, with the organization of techniques that are emerging now, I think it will be possible to make very rapid gains in structural analysis, away from a sometimes sterile categorization to more useful generalizations about differentiation, size, centralization, decentralization. For politics, the specialized characteristics of political systems will be analytically defined not as democratic or totalitarian in some direct sense but according to process variables that indicate some predictable or hypothetical solution to the kinds of issues with which they are confronted.

Finally, I think there is a third dimension of choice, which is different from the other two. The first two, the normative and the structural, embody, as far as I am concerned, a set of limitations on behavior. They represent analytically distinct, although not concrete, sets of boundaries, so that they should, with a proper and effective analysis of both normative and structural dimensions, make clear what it is we want from behavior. And when I say "want" from behavior, I mean that we will be able to ascertain its normative and structural limits. However, this is hardly the whole story. Whereas norms and structures determine the limits of choice, they cannot specify what within those limits people will opt for, what they will perceive, how they feel about these things, what motivates them, what socializes them. Here are all the questions of perception, socialization, and innovation. The behavioral dimension is the one with the most analytical promise for the future. Moreover, the other two dimensions, normative and structural, can be seen behaviorally. That is to say, if you want to see what behavioral consequences the normative dimension may have, you look at socialization, the intensity of feelings and attitudes, the conditions under which people will shift from one set of norms to another.

Similarly with structure. Political systems are themselves translated into real things: into membership units that people accept or reject, participate in or not, are apathetic towards or possibly alienated against; or they may find them useful and perceive in them some mode of effective participation for themselves. So the true question, the true pay-off, is, in my mind, in the behavioral dimension. But—and here I think the problem of modernization is a severe one—it is very difficult when working in unfamiliar areas to do meaningful work at the behavioral level until one knows a great deal about the normative and structural levels. The minute one leaves familiar ground and the presumed balance among norms and structures and behaviors lacks congruence in some readily understandable way, then it is extremely difficult to make very much sense out of behavioral responses. Indeed, I think I would go further and say that, unless made very specific, both norms and structures have a looseness and flexibility that make possible a wide variety of behavior, even in what may appear at a casual glance to be closed situations. Take attitudes towards tradition, for example. No matter how effectively surveyed they will show perhaps very persistent and interesting patterns of response. But, in fact, tradition will do anything that people want it to do. I noticed that Professor Inkeles uses the word "schizophrenia" in reference to people caught between traditions. I remember that Everett Hagen also implies a notion of a kind of schizophrenia and the marginality it produces because of the terrible normative choices that people in traditional societies undergoing modernization need to make when these choices become translated into behavioral consequences.[4] Yet is this really such a behavioral problem? From my experience in West Africa, the nearest approximation of this excruciating kind of psychological result that I could see was in the eye of the observer. He was the one who suffered the schizophrenia, whereas the people quite happily seemed to splash around in a number of quite inconsistent patterns of life, which seemed to widen their choices rather than to restrict them.[5] What I am suggesting, too, is that the

4. Everett E. Hagen, *On the Theory of Social Change* (Homewood, Illinois: The Dorsey Press, 1962).

5. See David W. Brokensha, *Social Change at Larteh, Ghana* (Oxford: The Clarendon Press, 1966), p. 269.

techniques appropriate to behavioral analysis, when really applied well, can contribute to the most important level of analysis we can develop, but only after an enormous amount of work has been completed on the structural and normative dimensions of theory.

Now a great many interesting questions arise in my own mind about this approach. First of all the normative, structural, and behavioral dimensions are the ingredients for a map. Since this is a map, it is too schematic for use as such. Moreover, there are obviously other ways to figure out norms than through participant observation, just as there are other ways to seek functions than through the theoretically omniscient observer. And there is a variety of ways to do behavioral analysis, quite apart from tough-minded, quantitative, and experimental studies. But there is a certain amount of confusion, it strikes me, when one moves around between these methods of observation and methods of generalization without recognizing what the consequences are. And a great deal of slipperiness emerges when structural analysis is done, for example, on the basis of participant observation, where one makes a "jump" at an analytical level because one may feel strongly or have a certain pattern of commitment about certain kinds of institutions. Similarly, it is very difficult to jump from participant observation to behavioral conclusions without a real sense of inadequacy—as when psychoanalytical theories are applied to new nations.[6]

Now let me return to developing areas. When one goes to a new nation, or an alien cultural environment, and gets off the airplane, he has a certain sense that everything is known and everything is familiar, and yet a certain sense in which everything is strange. Certainly, with any historical depth at all, one knows roughly that the kinds of problems being confronted in the area in which he intends to work are not altogether dissimilar from the changes that took place in the nineteenth century in Europe or in relatively recent years in the shift from rural to urban America. All of this is as much a pitfall and a snag as it is a comfort and assistance, because the meanings of all these things remain different and obscure. They are obscure

6. We have, for example, someone at Berkeley who is very much concerned with the continuing Berkeley crisis because of his very direct and personal interest in the revival of the kind of radicalism that perhaps reminded him of his youth (which had somewhat passed him by all too suddenly). He is experiencing now the kinds of feelings he had then. He has a real identification with the very normative demands and generalized behavioral principles centering on the problem of "identity." With this set of observations he now teaches what could effectively be called elementary alienation, advanced alienation, post-graduate work in alienation, with special studies in Berkeley. This is the sort of absurdity that can arise, it seems to me, when one shifts these levels too easily.

not only to the observer but quite often to the participant, especially when the change is radical, and where he is involved. The participant's own recognition of events is distorted as much as the observer's. The problem of this lack of fit, the lack of congruence, between norms and norms, structures and structures, behaviors and behaviors, as well as norms, structures, and behaviors, is that it gets to be fairly formidable. It imposes a strategy of research within the confines of the "map." As I see it, the best method of approach is to select for analysis a fairly tight, immediate, concrete unit, like a local government, or a local civil service organization, or a burial society, or a religious body; and simply by working through that unit in normative, structural, and behavioral terms it becomes possible to explore the larger political universe. Gradually, if the concrete unit selected is strategic enough, it will be possible to uncover the different layers and points of contact between role sets. Moreover, since these are never structurally limited to the unit with which you begin, the more generalized societal norms will be found to some extent within that unit, and behaviorally can be observed in what people do and their attitudes and feelings about these norms and structures. That is one way of doing it, and I think that, perhaps, at the present time, now that the more general work has been done in most hitherto "exotic" areas (and the easiest parts or the tops of the icebergs have already been uncovered), that is the way one must work.

Concretely and strategically, then, one should not begin with the largest possible concrete unit on which he can work. I say this while fully aware that I prefer to begin with the largest concrete unit. Perhaps to some extent one always does both, just as he tries historically to read over the materials, to see what the sequences have been, and then to focus on a structural problem in order to establish its normative implications and significance and identify its behavioral options. My own work, as it develops, is beginning to focus on certain intermediate concrete units for comparison, although it is within the context of a seven-country study involving four West African and three Latin American cases. I have spent several years working at various times on the four West African cases, which, as I see them, are in the early stages of modernization, and I am now getting started on the Latin American ones. I have tried to define modernization, not as Professor Inkeles does, as a set of identifiable characteristics in a general way, but rather according to the roles that have developed in an industrialized setting without an industrial infra-structure. And therefore I can locate indicators that to me demonstrate the spread

of those roles as a measurement device, as a way of indicating modernization, quite apart from attitudes or feelings or the ways of thinking
about it, while locating particular strategic elite groupings as intermediate units on which to concentrate.

In treating the comparison of modernization in this way, I view
the four West African cases as the earlier stages of modernization,
and each of them represents a different political set. The kind of
systems I have taken, in my own peculiar language, represents several
different structural types. The three Latin American cases are in
varying degrees of transition to major industrialization, and they also
represent different structural types—indeed the structural types kept
changing as I observed them. (I was in Argentina when the *coup*
occurred.) Although I am primarily concerned with the structural
boundaries of the political systems types with which I work, I am
also concerned, for example, with such problems as the types of traditions and the complications that occur when a Spanish, as distinct
from an English or a French, kind of colonial input is involved. In
other words, there is a historical dimension that can be examined
normatively and structurally (but not really behaviorally at all). This
dimension makes possible the formulation of certain hypotheses about
what happens when particular, traditional, structural types with particular, normative characteristics meet and are linked into particular
forms of colonial input. This is not really *the* source of innovation;
rather the combination is seen to produce innovation. From there
it is possible to operationalize the research in such social structural
categories as those related to stratification (the functions of an elite,
different patterns of coalition, etc.) and the way in which the political
community or the political systems respond to them, in order to make
some generalizations about how both innovation and some stable pattern of control occur, and what each political system type tries to
do when it responds to the kinds of tensions and conflicts produced
by this pattern of innovation.

That very briefly is simply a way of identifying an emphasis.
I start with the notion that there is an imbalance between the normative
and the structural. My concern then is to see how and by what means
I can identify what these imbalances look like. I then try to translate
them into a political problem. They become the central concern of
any government that exists concretely. I try then to see the government
as a normative and structural combination, a type, in order to
generalize to some extent about the problems likely to be encountered
by the type and, more particularly, where the type will fail.

Now let me give you just one example. The relationships with which I am concerned, ultimately, deal with coercion and information, so that certain types of systems for me are more likely to use coercion than others. When they do, what are the consequences? If they don't, what are the consequences? Here we have some very interesting, concrete illustrations. In the countries in which I have been working, Ghana, Guinea, Mali, and Senegal, where in differing degrees there has been a self-conscious application of a structural device, coercion, the loss of information is extremely important politically, and it can be measured. The consequences are that the more governments coerce, the less information they have at their disposal, while the more the government is isolated, the less capable it is of handling the problems of this lack of fit among norms, structure, and behavior.

I have attempted to link together several broad themes. First of all, there are the problems of the discipline. The explosion of the discipline away from its ethnocentric categories has affected its ability to handle much more generalized problems. In order to do so, those in the discipline must immediately confront the very serious issue of what categories to use and how to employ models and ideas and data that come from other disciplines in order to see them in a useful political frame. To do this, however, it is necessary to think not only of the dimensions of theory, but also the ways in which different layers of observation lead to different layers of meaning, which can be sorted out and put together more or less at the discretion of the observer. His skill and his particular genius then is to solve the Humpty Dumpty problem.

Secondly, I have tried to translate these problems into a concrete concern with the countries on which I am working in early and late stages of modernization; here is just a bit of an idea of the kinds of structural concerns that preoccupy me. My colleagues and I, in studying the seven countries, will be working our way through this long-term research project by focussing on a behavioral unit, that is to say, the behavior of real actors, namely, bureaucrats and technocrats. We are hoping that our structural findings will square with our behavioral ones, and by this means we will be able to make some generalization about the uneven processes of development, the increased pace of development, and the kinds of political systems most suitable for containing both.

SOCIAL ANTHROPOLOGY IN THE STUDY OF DEVELOPING COUNTRIES

MAX GLUCKMAN, *University of Manchester*

Let me say at once that I am convinced that social anthropology has a specific contribution to make to the study of social life, in all social fields, whether of subsistence societies or highly developed industrial societies, whether at the microscopic or the macroscopic level. In his *Foundations of Social Anthropology,* Nadel wrote:

> The human sciences, too [like the natural sciences], appear at first sight to embrace a homogeneous field, divided fortuitously and conveniently into different levels of analysis: man is the same whether he is studied by sociology, psychology, or physiology, and reveals different aspects of his being only in conformity with the agreed depth of analysis. Thus, every social fact, that is, every human action in respect to other humans is, *at any given moment,* a complex of psychological processes (by which I [Nadel] mean mental events, such as seeing, hearing, thinking, desiring), physiological processes (movements, muscle-tensions, innervations), and innumerable other processes on yet deeper levels of analysis, and can be broken down to these events and processes. It is merely convenient to handle the phenomena and their relations, on a given level, in the less completely analyzed form and to frame them in the corresponding "shorthand" concepts.[1]

I would agree with Nadel that there are not specific differences between the specialized disciplines of sociology and social anthropology and political science in the types of problems they tackle, how they formulate these problems, or how they use concepts in framing hypotheses and what are the hypotheses they frame. (Differences

1. S. F. Nadel, *Foundations of Social Anthropology* (London: Cohen and West, 1951), pp. 210-211.

are at least as great within each of these disciplines.) Still, we should ask, I think, first whether Nadel is correct when he speaks of the human sciences as being divided "fortuitously and conveniently into different levels of analysis. . . ." Is it fortuitous only, and merely convenient, that we are divided into sociologists and psychologists and physiologists, and, beyond this, that social scientists are divided into at least sociologists and social anthropologists and political scientists? Are these divisions and subdivisions, as some argue, merely accretions of academic history that have created vested interests, so that practitioners of each discipline remain separate to serve themselves? Alternatively, do these divisions and subdivisions correspond with differing types of relations between the events that, in their passage through space–time, make up the observations from which we scientists start our work?

It is usually safer, in considering a problem of this kind, to assume that the answer to all questions is "yes." The division of disciplines is an accretion of academic history, and each of us does have a vested interest in maintaining that separation or, sometimes, in trying to overcome it. But the divisions also usually correspond to differing types of relations between the passage of events through space–time, which is reality as we know it. I am here defining the disciplines not by the events that they study and that, after observation, become their factual raw material, but by the types of relations between those facts that each of us seeks to establish.[2] Each human action, as Nadel says, is enormously complex; but if we are to understand human actions, we have to destroy that complexity by dissection and analysis. And we can show how a human action is related to other events in the functioning of the human body—that gives us physiological relations—or we can show how that human action is related to other actions of that human being as a person, and to actions of others and the outer world as internalized—that gives us psychological relations. (Let me emphasize that I am here using "psychological" to refer to statements in the science of psychology, and I do not take it as equivalent to emotional or mental, in short, to psychical.)

Finally, we may try to relate the one human action of one person to the actions of other persons in the same region of social life, and to the material world—that gives us sociological or social anthropological relations. These sets of relations, which examine the influences

2. For a fuller exposition of this point, see Max Gluckman (ed.), *Closed Systems and Open Minds* (Chicago: Aldine Publishing Company, 1964), Ch. 1.

of other events (and the sun, for example, is an event, a very durable and permanent one) on the event we are examining, are of quite a different type, as Durkheim demonstrated in *Les règles de la méthode sociologique* (1895) when, in an out-of-date epistomology, he argued for the uniqueness of social facts as "things" that are external to, greater than, and constraining on individual actors. To this extent then the divisions between the human sciences are not fortuitous and convenient but are essential for our attempt to understand the regularity of relations between events in reality. And I would find it difficult to argue that we can use the concepts of psychology and physiology in a social-anthropological analysis, even though I know that the findings of psychologists and physiologists (and of other types of scientists) are essential if we are to understand the whole complexity of any human action. Fortunately, we do not as theoreticians have to attempt that complete understanding.

I consider that there are also differences between social anthropology, on the one hand, and sociology (or political science) on the other, differences that equally reflect different types of relations between real events. Social anthropology is an outgrowth of general anthropology, which developed as the study of man within the animal kingdom, of the differences between types of men as organisms, of the material objects made by men at lower levels of technology, and of the culture (the customs) of men, particularly of tribesmen and peasants. In time it became clear that, for an adequate study of man within the animal kingdom and for the comparative study of different kinds of men, intensive training in the biological sciences (wider than physiology) was essential. Physical anthropology specialized out: It is now taught in only two universities out of sixteen in Britain where students are trained in anthropology. For, correspondingly, to become a social anthropologist concerned with the relations between events in a postulated social system, one had to associate with other social sciences—sociology, political science, jurisprudence, economics, history. Still, correspondingly, as some anthropologists became interested in the cross-societal and cross-cultural study of personality, they had to become expert in certain branches of psychology, psychiatry, and even physiology. All this is clear if one looks only at the kinds of bibliographical references that occur in works by these different kinds of anthropologists. There remained, as the core of the old, general anthropology, what we call "cultural anthropology"—the analysis of patterns of culture, of value orientations, and so forth. For we recognize that, in modern industrial France, Britain, and the United States, and increasingly in the U.S.S.R., the basic pressures of industrial organizations are associated with certain similar patterns of social relationships, which differ in radical respects from social relationships in, say, tribal societies. We recognize too that human personalities everywhere, despite differences, have similar structures. I remember Fortes' saying to me that he felt that among Tallensi in Ghana he met the same kind of people as he had in England and, he thought, in the same relative numbers. But he added that there was something different about a Tallensi, as there is a difference between Englishmen, Americans, Frenchmen, and Russians. This difference we call "culture"; and it has to be studied.

Our historical origin as a subject was largely in the study of culture, and cultural anthropologists carry our traditional banner. But we social anthropologists still march partly under it; we cannot escape allegiance to our past. Here I consider we remain, as a discipline, very different from sociology and political science, with their different origins. We are fascinated by culture in a way that they are not, and we remain deeply interested in customs. In fact, we love the little chaps. We are always, in the end, trying to explain the significance of culture, of customs, within social relationships, and their influence on social relationships; and this fascination with custom keeps us linked to cultural anthropologists and also to psychological anthropologists, who seek the relations between variations in custom and variations in personality. In our analyses we accept still that there are interdependencies between customs, and these interdependencies affect social relationships: hence the number of our studies that include cross-cultural comparisons of customs as setting frames for social behavior.

Together with Professor Ely Devons I have argued that to some extent we can define social anthropology, perhaps all anthropology, as the study of "custom and the logic of the irrational."[3] I cited the manner in which Evans-Pritchard made sense of the apparent absurdities of Azande witchcraft beliefs, showed the internal logic of this system of beliefs, and opened the way for developing research into how they are connected with the varying incidence of accusations of witchcraft in different types of economic and social situations. Beyond this, out of an analysis of this set of, for us, exotic beliefs, he advanced general theories about the structure of systems of social thought, of ideas of morality and responsibility, and of society with its internal and external conflicts. Similarly, we have worked on taboo and ritual and law, on feud and settlement of dispute, on varieties

3. *Ibid.*, pp. 254-255.

of kinship terminology, etc. Shifting our attention to modern society, we have put into perspective the so-called restriction of output by industrial workers;[4] analyzed why in some London families spouses share domestic duties and in others they segregate these duties;[5] why in British villages the villages allow the upper class to run recreational activities;[6] how peer groups of young men in London develop an apparently anti-heterosexual culture to bridge the gap between adolescence and adulthood;[7] how the Tristan da Cunha-ites, brought to Britain after a volcanic explosion on their island, used teasing, in the pattern of joking relationships, to prevent any of their members from being renegades and agreeing to remain in Britain instead of pressing for return to their barren homeland.[8] All these analyses used culture as customs, in the setting of an examination of social relationships. But the distinctiveness of the anthropological dimension is apparent in all.

Given our distinctive contribution (and we should be proud of it), it seems always to me to be a pity when social anthropologists are so captivated by the new ideas that can be brought to our subject from sociology and political science that they drop the cultural dimension. Of course, as individuals they are right to go where their problems and ideas lead them; but they then become political scientists or sociologists and cease to be distinctive as social anthropologists. I consider that, for example, when Fallers worked on Soga bureaucracy and phrased his problems after Weber in terms of a conflict of the particularistic ethic of chiefs towards kinsmen and clients, as against the demanded, universalistic, bureaucratic ethic of the British administration, he in practice eliminated many of the cultural factors that influenced both chief and British officer: how far did varying knowledge of the Soga language, varying capacity to interact with Soga, etc., affect the manner in which chief and British officer in practice handled affairs?[9] In short, by drawing a hypothesis from sociology, Fallers illuminated the situation, but he did not, from my point of

4. Tom Lupton, *On the Shop Floor* (Long Island City: Pergamon Press, 1962); and Sheila Cunnison, *Wages and Work Allocation: A Study of Social Relations in a Garment Workshop* (New York: Humanities Press, 1966).

5. E. Bott, *Family and Social Network* (New York: Humanities Press, 1957).

6. Ronald Frankenberg, *Communities in Britain* (Baltimore: Penguin Books, 1957).

7. D. Allcorn, unpublished Ph.D. dissertation, Manchester University (U.K.), 1953.

8. J. B. Loudon, "Teasing and Socialization on Tristan da Cunha," in P. Mayer (ed.), *Socialization: The Approach from Social Anthropology*, A. S. A. Monograph No. 8 (London: Tavistock Press, 1970).

9. Max Gluckman, "Inter-Hierarchical Roles: Professional and Party Ethics in the Tribal Areas in South and Central Africa," in Marc Swartz (ed.), *Local-Level Politics* (Chicago: Aldine Publishing Company, 1968).

view, continue sufficiently to operate as a social anthropologist deploying information on customs as interwoven with action and behavior.

I consider that this has to some extent happened also to my colleagues Swartz, Turner, and Tuden in writing their introduction to the recent symposium on *Political Anthropology*. Insisting that political life, all social life, is in flux, they write,

> In the diachronics of political field analysis, it is possible to arrest the flow of events at any given point in time and abstract a "still." We are then confronted by a set of co-existing parts that can be conceptualized as structured, or as having position relative to each other, and therefore as occupying a type of space—analogous to Kurt Lewin's notion of the *life-space* of an individual. Although such a still deprives us of the time dimension, it allows us to enumerate, with some accuracy, the political entities engaged and the type, kind, and intensity of their inter-relations, and to attempt to estimate the sources of support held by them severally or in varying combinations.
>
> But this creates an erroneous impression of stability and balance. In fact, the passage of time always reveals instability and imbalance in power relations, although the extent of stability and the speed with which it will be revealed is [*sic*] highly variable among political fields. . . .[10]

Given this over-all view that delineations of stability and balance are at best useful ideas of positions conceptualized relative to one another but are misrepresentations as far as reality is concerned, it follows that the importance of culture has to be played down and only due obeisance made in its direction. For culture is inherently stabilizing and conservative: It tends to operate against change and development out of its very nature as external to and constraining on the individual. Of course, cultural elements do change. What I am saying is that the cultural structure of a social field inhibits change just as the physical environment does, by deploying redressive and readjustive containing mechanisms,[11] which are part of the cultural environment. Thus, when persons within the field try to achieve change, they run against difficulties and obstructions, hazards and barriers, which are not anticipated. They may not consciously be opposed by other persons in the field (these others may be in favor of the development proposed); but customary structures and beliefs and attitudes and values assert themselves against both the proposers of developments and the subjects to whom proposals are made, to

10. M. J. Swartz, V. W. Turner, and A. Tuden (eds.), *Political Anthropology* (Chicago: Aldine Publishing Company, 1966), pp. 27-28.

11. *Ibid.*, p. 346.

influence and rechannel action in directions other than those that were envisaged. Moreover, those who propose changes have to draw on some cultural equipment to formulate their propositions, so that even in the new there is present the old culture, constraining the paths that developments can follow.

In proposing this point of view, I remember many discussions with British and South African administrative and technical officials, who were occupants of positions, armed with some coercive power, who were attempting to change certain modes of action among Africans. Some of their proposals were technically sensible, most were moved by good will; but always they ran into barriers, often not of people, but of customary practice. Eventually, one officer said: "Our trouble is that we are attempting to make a revolution without having a revolution, and it cannot be done." But developments even after revolutions show that the cultural past continues to exert a constraining influence.

Culture is thus on the whole conservative. And therefore it follows that all anthropologists tend to describe and analyze a continuity. This emphasis on continuity is deeply built into the anthropological disciplines, and arises, I believe, partly from the fact that we are interested in customs, not as single items (as earlier anthropologists were), but as they are linked into institutions, or into cultural patterns, or into syndromes influencing the development of individual personality. But, speaking for social anthropologists who are interested in the study of institutions, we have to cope with the fact that each institution has a time-scale built into it; and it is impossible to analyze an institution as a set of linked customs save in its time-scale. Let me give two brief examples to clarify this bare statement.

If I want to analyze a day in the life of the British House of Commons, I must see what is happening on that day in relation to a period of at least 15 years: For activity in the House of Commons is influenced by at least the two preceding elections, the prospects of the coming election, and the five years between elections. Thus, our House of Commons has what I shall call, following a suggestion made to me by John Barnes, a basic structural duration of 15 years, at least. It may be longer at particular periods of history, but it cannot be shorter. Within that basic structural duration, there are other durations internal to the parliamentary system. They are set by Budget Day debates, as well as by other debates, the various stages through which a bill has to pass, and so forth. Similarly, the institutions of the family can nowhere be analyzed unless within a basic structural duration of four generations: For each family contains within itself, at any one moment, its derivation from an earlier parental pair, each of whom had parents, and the growing up of children to become parents themselves. In some societies it may be wiser to use a basic duration of more than four generations. But as the House of Commons contains within its rules and the way it operates at least two previous elections and, in anticipation, the next election, so the rules of the family and the way a family operates encapsulate grandparents (even if dead), parents, children, and the anticipation that those children will marry and have children. This duration, I stress, is contained in the rules, the customs, themselves.

If this idea is correct, it follows that as soon as we attempt to analyze an institution we have to "throw" it into its structural duration. We have to analyze it as if it were operating through a far longer period than the actual period during which we observe it or its parts. This rule is commonplace, but it is fundamental. The failure to bear this elementary methodological principle in mind when reading an analysis of institutions may give the reader the false impression that the writer believes that the institutional system he analyzes has endured in exactly the same form from far in the past and will thus endure into the future. This failure to comprehend what is being done is fairly frequent; and it is expressed in a tendency to insist, in contrast to this method of analysis, that all real societies are always changing and have always changed—without specifying what is changing, how far the changes go, and what the changes are, as against what remains constant. Studies of the structure of institutions, therefore, often appear to be studies of systems that appear to be in equilibrium—i.e., studies of systems *as if* they were in equilibrium.

Leach, for example, uses the concept of "as-if" systems because he

> recognized the great power of this type of equilibrium analysis and the difficulty of evading it within the general framework of current sociological theory.... In brief, my argument is that, although historical facts are never, in any sense, in equilibrium, we can gain genuine insights if, for the purpose of one analysis, we force those facts within the constraining mould of an *as-if* system of ideas, composed of concepts which are treated *as if* they were part of an equilibrium system.[12]

It is here that Leach and I part company. For he argues that the idea of equilibrium has great power in making a set of logical

---

12. E. A. Leach, *Political Systems of Highland Burma*, 2nd ed. (London: Bell, 1964), Introduction.

constructs in the anthropologist's mind, while I argue that the idea has great power, because, in the mathematician's phrasing, it "maps reality." Its power comes from the fact that it enables us to understand the systematic structure of any institution as it exists, by working out the interdependence between its part in its own structural duration or time-scale. In conditions of relative stasis, it also enables us to understand the limits which that institution's structure sets on the choices and capacities for free action of actors within the institution.

We can examine too the redressive and readjustive mechanisms that come into force when a person acts to commit a breach of institutional tenets or to change the institution. In a social field where the total structure, each institution, and the relations between various institutions are in relative stasis, the *as-if* equilibrium model enables us to analyze actual historical situations. We can penetrate deeply into the structure of the field and make sense of continuity and stability, despite movements of individuals and groups through the institutions as the generations come and go, as people make their livings, as people cooperate and clash, as people compete for political power, and so forth. For the dominant characteristic of such a field is that, while changes of personnel and distributions of resources and power between persons and groups go on continually, the pattern of institutions changes but little. We are certainly dealing here with what may be called change, but it is what has been termed variously repetitive change, recurrent change, or situational change.

Various writers have asserted, as Leach apparently does, that there is always change in the system of institutions themselves. I concede that theoretically this assertion may be true: Even the most infinitesimal change may in the long run produce a major alteration of pattern. But up to the present we have been able to handle this problem only with the old dialectical contention that changes in quantity accumulate gradually until suddenly there is a change in quality—a radical amendment of the institutional pattern. I believe, on the basis of everything I have observed and read, that this contention again "maps reality"—this is in fact the way institutional change goes, by sudden leaps, not by crawling steps. Hence, I maintain that the *as-if* equilibrium analysis is essential for understanding any period except the brief period during which a leap occurs.

Given adequate information over a long enough period, we can see and map the process of accumulating quantitative change within our equilibrium analysis. But we must also accommodate the problems arising from the occurrence of changes of different types. I believe that it can be done if we adopt, in the terms of the concept of the social field, a relative point of view. In studying the history of Zulu-land,[13] for example, only by looking at the total area of the field can we see that, if the dispersed, small changes in population that were occurring continued long enough, they were bound to make continuance of the system of small tribes impossible. Meanwhile, temporary changes in the land-population ratio produced particular struggles that were solved in the continuing pattern of small tribes. At the same time, of course, ships bearing goods in the trade between Europe and the East around the Cape of Good Hope were passing the coast; in 1652 the Dutch established their resting-station at the Cape. These events presaged an end to the isolation of this whole system. Mariners were shipwrecked on the coast: We have records of African reactions, and of the absorption of some Europeans and Asians into the African system, and we can show how they did not disturb its pattern. Ultimately, clash had to come from the expansion of Europe; and first Boers, then British, defeated the Zulu. Here again we have to adopt a relative view of fields. From the point of view of the Zulu, these defeats, and ultimate conquest by the British, were unique. Within the British and even the Boer systems of relation-ships, they were repetitive changes, connected with the steady expan-sion of the total system of Europe and the United States, over Africa, Asia, the Americas, and Australasia. Similarly, we propound our *as-if* equilibrium analyses for relatively defined periods of time, and not forever.

I have argued so far that the specific contribution of social anthropology to the study of developments in social relationships, where such developments occur, is at least partly to note where those changes are, so to speak, slowed down and stabilized into customs, which as they become set in institutionalized links engender new pat-terns of stasis analyzable in a form of equilibrium. Does this mean that we as social anthropologists cannot cope with radical change at all? Not inevitably. Rather, in our discipline we cope with change in a limited, although, in my judgment, an illuminating, way. Nor need we be afraid of being limited; because all scientific analysis is by definition limited in what it can do and because no scientific analysis can hope totally to explain any complex reality, we should be abstinent enough to leave some work for colleagues in other sciences to do. This too we should accept.

For change can be seen in many ways. If we wish accurately

13. Max Gluckman, *Analysis of a Social Situation in Modern Zululand*, Rhodes-Livingstone Paper 28 (1958).

to record what happens in reality, to note every change, we are compelled to produce an elaborate historical narrative. I take it this would be as true of natural scientists as it is of social scientists. But we have to try to generalize and to assess, by simplifying and distorting reality. In our discipline, we seek for some kind of structural generalization that will "make sense" for us some relations incapsulated within a particular complex piece of changing reality. We seek for some general forms in many particulars. The more accurately we record every change, the less we know how far it is repetitive change and how far it is radical change. We must have some structural standard to assess change; and in setting up that standard structure for our assessment, we necessarily lose sight of changes within that structure. This is our dilemma. We have not yet solved it, and it may always be with us.

My contention here is that an understanding of change in institutions, that is, the study of a real, radical change of structure, as against a repetitive change of personnel within the structure, is developed almost necessarily against an analysis of the structural durations of certain other institutions, held constant in *as-if* equilibrium analysis. Thus can we formulate laws of structural change. Evans-Pritchard's studies of the rise of the Nuer prophets also emphasized that they were "foreigners" to the Nuer groups they united, as the Sanusi order were foreigners to the Bedouin. This is a phenomenon we know from many other eras and regions: Joan of Arc was a woman and a peasant, yet she united the squabbling noblemen of France against the English. In South Africa, commoner, and again sometimes female, prophets united the divided tribes of what are now Ciskei and Transkei against the encroaching Whites when they could not ally themselves together. The equilibrium analysis of disunity between groups in different kinds of segmentary systems enables us to understand why leaders must be in some sense "outsiders."

There are of course situations within which radical change proceeds so rapidly that any student, whatever his discipline, is virtually forced into a detailed narrative. Here we can attempt to generalize as between similar and divergent situations about processes of rapid change of various types. But again it is often profitable to look at what happens in these periods against an *as-if* equilibrium analysis of the period just before the rapid change began. In this way, we can assess the changes that have occurred in an institutional setting, and we can examine what new institutional arrangements begin to emerge.

Setting of the Problems

Any of you who have read my general studies, or my studies of Barotse law, know that I believe that any particular investigation has to be set within a general morphological view of the main stream of societal development. The views that have been most fruitful for me personally are Durkheim's view of the movement from mechanical to organic solidarity, Marxism, to a lesser extent, Weber, and very much indeed Maine's dictum that the movement of progressive societies has hitherto been a movement from [familial=kin group] status to [commercial] contract. On the basis of this wider morphology, I develop a corresponding morphology of the nature of states in Africa, within which I would set any specific investigation.

For example, I affirm that Zululand in the 1930s exhibited a high degree of cohesion[14] at many levels and in many situations; and it still does as far as I know. This cohesion arose from the different types of conflicts of allegiance of both Zulu and Whites as they pursued often mutually inconsistent goals and lived by discrepant values.

Research in Central Africa supports these earlier conclusions. Rural Africans became involved in the developing mining and industrial economy because they had to earn money for taxes, for goods, and for services like education. Most of the tribesmen had to earn this money by migrating for longer or shorter periods to work in enterprises, owned by the Whites, mainly in the towns. But they thought that they had little security in their industrial life, and industrial life did not give to many of them the ultimate satisfaction they sought from life. Housing and other difficulties, as well as sentiment, led them to dislike rearing children in the towns, although increasingly many settled in the towns. Houses in towns were often tied to jobs, particularly in Central Africa. There was no provision for unemployment; sickness and accident compensation was very low; and there was an inadequate provision of work, or alternatively of pensions, for the old. This insecurity of town and industrial life had been emphasized in the depression of the 1930s as well as in many other situations. Without security in towns, many, so long as there was land,

---

14. Since the terminology is always centrally necessary for my analysis, I have reproduced it in several papers. I refer readers of this paper to my paper in Kuper and Smith's *Plural Societies in Africa* (Berkeley and Los Angeles: University of California Press, 1969), where I have set out some of the reasoning behind this terminology and the processes by which I amended it to meet comments at the Los Angeles and Manchester seminars where I presented this paper. I am grateful to the members of those seminars for their comments. Dr. Martin Southwold kindly helped me with a written paper on this terminology.

clung to their tribal affiliation and the security of land to fall back on. In order to have access to land in rural areas and to "raid the town for money," as Watson has phrased it for the Mambwe,[15] Zulu maintained their association within groups of kin, some of whom went out at any one time to earn money, while others remained at home to cultivate the soil and care for cattle as well as wives and children. Some tribes seem to have organized this deployment of men more successfully than others. But all regarded the land as their ultimate security and support.

Land here was not an individual item of land that a man owned for himself and by himself. He secured his rights to land in two ways. First as a citizen of the tribe he was entitled to some arable and building land and to the use of commonage. Second, in all tribes except the widest shifting cultivators, he obtained his rights through membership in a group of kinsmen, a village, or both. That is, a man's right to land in his tribal home depended on his accepting membership in a tribe, with all its obligations, as well as its rights. This membership involved his participating in a working system of social relationships, economic, political, and domestic.

It has to be stressed that the migrant laborer moves not only between two places with different modes of production, consumption, etc., but also between two distinct types of social systems. The tribal system is one that has its own goals and values, even though some are radically changed from those from the traditional past. Here the migrant laborer on his return home becomes again, more than in the towns, a man with a variety of roles, with clear affiliations to others, and with culturally approved goals. He can marry, raise children, and acquire satisfaction and prestige there. He can seek prestige within the tribal political system, or in other domains of its total system. All anthropologists must have had something like the following experience. Once, after I had visited Johannesburg from Zululand, I drove back accompanied by two young Zulu ricksha pullers. They came with their bundles and were dressed in rags. One lived in the village that was my base. That night, after we arrived, he sat in my hut, with all his father's wives and their children, and other distant kin. He boasted of his adventures in the town, including brushes with the oppressive police. But his proudest moment came when he unpacked his cases and began to distribute his gifts to his father,

---

15. W. Watson, *Tribal Cohesion in a Money Economy* (Manchester: Manchester University Press, 1958).

mother, mother's co-wives, and his full and half siblings. He brought out the money he had earned and discussed its allocation with his father: so much for this purpose and for that, and above all so much towards the marriage-payment for the bride he would seek. Next day he dressed in war dress and went dancing over the hills seeking for that bride; he had moved into a system of social relationships full of satisfactions.

That system can offer satisfaction of this kind provided that two sets of circumstances continue. The first clearly is that there continue to be enough land to support the migrant laborer and his family. The second is that expansion of the industrial sector allow him to migrate there to earn money.

If the land lasts and is sufficient, the tribal system as an organized set of political and social relationships can endure and provide satisfaction; and the White administrators and technical officers and missionaries, and even traders and recruiters, can be drawn into the several levels of consensus in the social field. The migrant laborers brought money and goods back into the system in return for having their claim to its land, and thereby to a position in its society, preserved. Hence it is not surprising that (according to a survey I made first in 1943), as land became short, the right most emphasized in these societies was the right of every subject to some building and arable land. The right of members within smaller groups to some of the land of those groups was similarly emphasized. As pressure on the land increased with the increase of population, following often on restriction of tribal territory as land had been taken for White settlers, chiefs tended to take over unused, already allotted land, which was not being worked, after a short period of rest. At this stage, land was becoming short under the prevailing system of cultivation. The ultimate end of the process was found in Basutoland where each married man was entitled to only three small fields. Most of these developments were reported from South Africa and the British Protectorates, but I detected the germs of similar developments in a few scanty reports in Northern Rhodesia. But I overlooked a statement by Hilda Kuper in her *Uniform of Colour* about Swaziland that "pressure on land aggravates antagonism within a principality. A chief who did not distribute his land with equity, but retained the best plots, even though they were not used, for his family and favorites, was publicly censured by his council. Many chiefs endeavor to be fair, and are guided by the opinion of their advisor."[16]

16. Hilda Kuper, *The Uniform of Colour: A Study of White-Black Relationships in Swaziland* (Johannesburg: Witwatersrand University Press, 1947), p. 11.

Similarly, Professor Monica Wilson concludes that, in both the Xhosa and Nyakyusa tribes, "the attitude ... is still that the use of land for cultivation and grazing is a right to which every man is entitled and in practice they criticize any individual who lays field to field and leaves his brother landless."[17] In the Xhosa tribal reserves the area of land for each man is officially restricted by the village headman and the White native commissioner. Where some families had been settled many years ago on freehold and quitrent farms, they or their descendants have tended to accommodate landless relatives; but the lending and leasing of land, and particularly share-cropping, are widely practiced. The Xhosa's main source of income is labor migration.

The Nyakyusa have developed cash-cropping on richer land in ancient craters, but even this land is not yet leased or sold, although Wilson believes that these transactions will soon become common. Wilson says that the effect of land shortage has been to stop the redistribution of land periodically as new villages of coevals were established, and to make all land inheritable in the agnatic line, as the rich crater land always was. Men are more tied to old villages, there is less movement, and, whereas formerly villages tried to attract new members, they now no longer do so. Land is not so freely lent. Quarrels can no longer be settled by having sections of villages or individuals move away. But generally the stress is still on the rights of all men, and presumably women, to land for their support, although not necessarily to land that will carry the cash crops. Migration of men to labor centers keeps the system going.

In Xhosaland, in South Africa, many married men cannot obtain fields and are left landless. Basil Sansom, who studied a similar situation in one Pedi chieftaincy in the Northern Transvaal, has allowed me to summarize his findings of a type of social development not reported from any other tribe. The chief has endeavored to maintain the principle that each married woman is entitled to a tract of land to produce food for her household. But the chief has not been able to ensure that a second category of land, in which title is held by men, is equitably distributed. Technically, title to land cannot be gained or relinquished without the chief's approval. However, wealthy men "borrow" and work the land of poorer tribesmen. A poor man in debt to a wealthy man may virtually surrender his land to his creditor. In this way some men in the chiefdom are able to build up large

17. Monica Wilson, "Effects on the Xhosa and Nyakyusa of Scarcity of Land," in D. Biebuyck (ed.), *African Agrarian Systems* (London: Oxford University Press, for the International African Institute, 1963), pp. 374–391.

holdings in "men's land" to the detriment of the holdings of others. They emerge as a set of "land brokers," manipulating debts and land as much for social power and prestige as for monetary gain, since the main source of Pedi income is labor migration. No traditional authorities have entered into these pursuits, and the chief apparently turns a blind eye towards them.

Only one study, by Jaspan in the mid-1940s, of a small tribal reserve in southern Natal in the Republic of South Africa, suggests that a chief tried to gain land at the expense of his subjects. Jaspan reported that the chief early began to compete with his subjects for land. (He already possessed more livestock than any of his subjects.) Eventually some brought a suit against him; they claimed that he had used his official position unlawfully to monopolize the grazing rights in a government-trust farm where grazing is restricted by proclamation. "Part of the reaction of the Chief to this unprecedented act of opposing him at a supratribal level was to accuse the leaders of the 'opposition' and their sympathizers of attempting to destroy him by sorcery and witchcraft. The chief has for many years steered clear of this district in which the 'opposition' is centered; he neither eats nor drinks, nor attends any ceremonies or meetings there." Jaspan's implicit contention seems to be that land shortage in this reserve has reached a point where the whole traditional system must break down. The chief cannot begin to meet his obligations to his subjects, because the reserve is so severely denuded of fertility that in many respects it is a reserve residence for men working in towns, and most men are absent at any one time. The chief, facing the competition of better educated men for prestige, maintains his wealth at the expense of his subjects. It is the only report of which I know of a chief's acting thus. In short, so long as there is land, the tribal system can work and give satisfaction, drawing Whites in the area into the achievement of those satisfactions. If the land becomes too short, the tribal system will break down, and with it will disappear the satisfactions it grants. An increasingly amorphous mass of peasants, akin to those described for Southern Italy by Carlo Levi in *Christ Stopped at Eboli*, will emerge. The peasants will begin to develop new forms of association, and will either form political groups pursuing their interests or enter more chiliastic forms of religious cults.

The second change in circumstances that will alter this type of cohesion, and the relationship between the tribal area and the town, is if the central government forbids tribesmen to move from the relatively impoverished areas into the richer industrial sector to earn money. The rural area alone probably can no longer give adequate satisfactions. I am analyzing in the symposium edited by Turner (*Profiles of Change* ...) my own full view of how I would conceive of the sociological problems of plural societies. Here I must say, all too briefly, that I think that, although sociologists, political scientists, and anthropologists recognize as basic the cohesion that arises from economic development, some of them nevertheless tend to lose sight of its implications. For example, South Africa's relatively high economical development, in comparison with the rest of Africa, gives it far more cohesion, and hence greater what we may call stability of personnel in political offices (even if force is more manifestly repressive), than newer African states seem to have. There is an inherent instability in any society in which vertical divisions between territorial or ethnic segments or both are inadequately crossed by the development of links of organic (in Durkheim's sense), utilitarian, economic interdependence. Without that interdependence, civil war is endemic in the system. In simpler organizations, before the development of the state, civil war may take the form of permanent states of feud between segments, and in segmentary states a similar situation, emerging from simple tools of production, simple consumption goods, simple means of communication, and simple weapons, is marked by the eruptions of segments out of the state or by rebellious war around the kingship. As the economy develops in more highly stratified systems, with the development of more varied standards of living, larger capitals emerge with greater trade and the development of a city aristocracy. Then two other forms of strife are found. First, there may be peasant risings in addition to the struggle of aristocrats for power. Second, some of the peasants are attracted to the cities or proto-cities and form a city mob, whose support the competing elites have to woo. Not all "riots" start from the city mob, but it is a recruiting ground for rioting and can aggravate protest marches, etc. We know this situation from classical and medieval times. It will tend to develop in modern times wherever there is a numerous, relatively poor peasantry and the city economy does not develop rapidly enough to absorb the influx from their ranks. The South African government has prevented this development with draconic measures and ruthless application of the law: Since 1938 only those Africans who are necessary for the urban economy have been allowed in the cities. The employed are committed to the industrial system. Mitchell analyzed how the African population in a Central African town is woven into a kind of society by the intricate ties, as well as by conflicts of loyalty, between various members,[18] and Kuper analyzed a similar situation in South Africa. He also brings out that:

> The races do not confront each other as solid antagonistic blocks. Cooperation and interdependence are more marked than conflict and separation. Social relationships extend across racial barriers, weaving complex and varied patterns of interracial contact and creating common interests transcending those of race. Even the policy of racial segregation, by virtue of its inner contradictions, forges new links and new mechanisms of integration.
>
> Shared privileges and common domination do not guarantee the unity of the rulers. There is an uneven distribution of power among the members of the ruling White group. . . .[19]

The major danger to political stability probably resides in the unemployed and the unemployable. If the cities cannot continue to provide for the migrant laborers from the tribal areas, I believe that this lack of opportunity will be a major cause of political disturbance, and if it is added to increasing land degradation in the tribal areas, they are likely to be the foci of major discontent. Consensus and cohesion within them will weaken, and their links to the total system will disappear. Only force will be left. Urban African workers may well form an elite against the poor peasants of their own ethnic group, even though urban Africans will provide leaders resisting the domination of the Whites, as elites everywhere provide some leaders in revolts. But these leaders will be a small proportion of all urban Africans, just as some Whites out of the whole White population side with the Africans.

We can now look at the other African states by contrast. Their inadequate industrial development will leave them as unstable polities, in terms of personnel in office, even after the withdrawal of the colonial powers. Despite high consensus arising from the struggle for independence, cohesion will be inadequately developed. These governments cannot be as ruthless with their own peasants who come into the cities as is the South African government. There will be city mobs (restricted in numbers in South Africa) who consider themselves underprivileged, and who are likely often to be the unemployed. The mob will be an effective force, which will have to be cajoled by the military who control the other form of forceful power, since

18. J. C. Mitchell, *Tribalism and the Plural Society* (Cape Town: Oxford University Press, 1960).

19. L. Kuper, *An African Bourgeoisie: Race, Class, and Politics in Africa* (New Haven: Yale University Press, 1965), pp. 5-7.

weapons are now complex. In South Africa and in colonial regimes, the military and police were necessarily loyal to their government; in independent African states they are potential competitors for power with the governments. The rural areas will remain underdeveloped and be foci of discontent as in South Africa. Because of the demand for high consensus in the state and the party, representatives of the party and the state are less likely to become representatives of the interests of rural areas against the center than was even the South African native commissioner. The ethic will be that of the party and not of the profession. Because consensus is high, slight deviations will be regarded as criminal, for, as Durkheim said, the more sensitive the collective conscience, the less venial are acts of non-conformity. Those who deviate are likely to be severely reprobated under Simmel's principle that the renegade, traitor, and heretic are more hated than the open enemy. This principle applies with sharpening cleavage in South Africa. Again, consensus may appear to be high, while cohesion in local areas will not be well developed.

These examples, and my own research on Zululand, illustrate a type of analysis which I hope brings out the complexities of interaction in an area of a total politico-geographic field where ultimate articulation depends on force, but where there are many other collaborative, and hence cohesive, alignments. I emphasize that, when we approach the study of a society of the South African type, or other African type, we must take full account of these complexities of interaction and the complicating articulations which produce them and which they in turn establish. Up to the point of radical adjustment or revolution, it is important to study why such adjustment or revolution does not occur, or why attempts at it fail, as well as to stress the long-term course of deepening cleavage. I believe that the idea of taking a series of cross-sections in time as if they were in relative stasis, and analyzing them by using equilibrium models, enables us to penetrate into institutional structures in all their interdependence with cultural patterns. Further, we can then assess radical as against repetitive change. We can detect elements that are stabilizing and lead to continuity, as against elements that are likely to be productive of radical change. In the next section, with this general background, I propose to try to formulate the kinds of processes we should try to detect, in the combination of social and structural movement with culture. This task again involves me in drawing on my own work, including work long published, which has not been taken up, since younger anthropologists, including my own pupils and colleagues, have swung largely against the structural-functional approach that, as Leach says, has great heuristic value in analysis.

Social Movements and Cultural Forms

The movement in social anthropology toward the study of histological processes of competition and cooperation has been encouraged by certain very illuminating ideas in social anthropology, sociology, and political science, concerned mainly with what I may describe as "small-field" research. The influence of sociometry, of a book like Homans's *The Human Group,* of Goffman, and of others working on detailed interaction has fed into ideas developed within social anthropology, of which one of the most fruitful has been Barnes's conception of the "network," taken up in several different forms, with an added set of conceptions like "action sets,"[20] and so forth. Situations examined in this way often seem to allow greater control of the variables than do studies of larger, more diffuse situations. I find all this work most stimulating. But when some argue that this small-field analysis is the only profitable one, I am far from being persuaded. Above all, I do not agree that studies of "small fields" can ever explain major structures to us; for I do not believe that the whole is ever explicable as a larger-scale version of the parts. A major lineage is a kind of unit quite different from a minor lineage. Parish-pump politics are parish-pump politics, and not national politics—even if detailed interaction within national politics has some few of the characteristics of parish-pump politics. This is not to say, of course, that ideas illuminating at one level are not also illuminating at another.

Major structures, both in social relationships and in cultural elements, have a tendency to endure. Again, I take my example of the small tribes in the early history of Zululand. I have suggested that the increase in population of men and cattle was beginning to upset the land–population ratio, and tribes were splitting and coming into struggle in their search for new land, between the mountains and the sea. A radical change of pattern was bound to occur eventually. I have further suggested that, when we look at a social field of this type, we must examine what is happening by constantly shifting our point of view, in space and time. When we look at one zone in the field, or at one period of time in its existence, social life is full of

20. A. C. Mayer, "The Significance of Quasi-Groups in the Study of Complex Societies," in M. Banton (ed.) *Social Anthropology of Complex Societies,* A. S. A. Monograph No. 4 (London: Tavistock Press, 1966), pp. 97-119.

disturbances that cannot be solved by repetitive movement back to the former equilibrium. Individual families break up when children mature. But if we look at a wider field, the major pattern endures.[21] When we are dealing with changes that are, on a wider view, accumulating to render previous forms of collaboration impossible and to prevent repetitive solution of conflict, I think it advisable to say that we are dealing with "repetitive deviance." Over a certain range of space–time, the pattern is being duplicated: movements are repetitive. On a wider view, there is an emerging deviance within the apparent repetition.

The concept of repetitive deviance is more important if we are trying to understand what happens when two social fields interpenetrate, as when the British assumed rule over Zululand, or if we try to understand what happens when a revolution occurs, or what will happen when the field of independent national organization comes to reorganize tribal areas. Here the short-term, isolated, repetitive movements produce increasing deviance, until they ultimately build up into a new, large-scale, repetitive movement, working out with a full structural duration. When I worked in Zululand from 1936 to 1938, this movement had not yet occurred, since all the playing off of political authorities against one another had not solved ultimate conflicts involved in the color-bar. Hence deviance continued within the largely repetitive processes, and it took two forms. First, there was increasing differentiation, in that, for example, the independent Zulu churches, trade union leaders, etc., had emerged. Chiefs had to come to terms with them as had the native commissioner. This was qualitative deviance. Secondly, there was quantitative deviance. There was a change in the numbers of Zulu adhering to mission and Zulu churches; there was an alteration in the prestige and strength of the Zulu kingship as it regained some of its former stature; while on the other hand people increasingly went to the commissioner for certain purposes. So that I found in this situation both repetitive, or oscillatory, movements, and also deviance. Although I still found it profitable to carry out my analysis in terms of repetition and oscillation in structural durations, I had also to allow for the deviance, which was occurring in chronological, or historical, time, with its complex of many, actual, variable events and processes. The welding together of these two types of analysis is a major problem, which can be solved only in analysis, not in theory.

Repetitive deviance also works through custom; and, as it occurs,

21. Max Gluckman, *Custom and Conflict in Africa* (Glencoe: The Free Press, 1955).

custom becomes established with all its exaggerating functions. It occurred in both the political and the religious affiliations of modern Zululand. Because the chief was seen by his subjects as opposed to the commissioner, his duty was to oppose the commissioner. This requirement forced on him the custom of opposition even when he might not himself be thus opposed: Opposition was the rule of the chieftainship. When cooperating groups of White and African Christians were split by the color-bar and independent Bantu churches emerged, they did not revert to simple paganism. They had to be Christian to oppose the mission churches. They drew on the customs of Christianity and exaggerated their true Christianity against the mission churches. For culture is not holistic or harmonious. The new churches selected parts of Christianity and emphasized certain Biblical passages. Out of these divisions among churches, schism after schism developed; and the closer groups approached one another through these schisms, the more they exaggerated the divisions between them. The Zionist-type churches, which were closest to paganism, insisted most strongly that they were not like the pagans: Their members were possessed by the Holy Spirit, and pagans were possessed by demons; their spirits were angels and saints, those of the pagans were devils.

Underlying these processes, as custom changes, is a large-scale set of processes by which individuals and small groups seek to gratify certain interests. In gratifying these interests they combine and struggle; and they have to mark their combinations and struggles by some means or other. This means is custom itself. Custom for this purpose may occasionally be newly created, but often it is taken from the customs already available to the interested parties. In short, whatever the interests that individuals and groups are trying to serve, they have to act according to the customs available to them; and thus they draw on existing customs. These customs in turn shape the way in which individuals and groups seek to gratify their interests. Here I want to stress that a social system—the system of regularities that we assume exists in a social field—does not consist only of human beings. It is a complex structure involving the natural world, material apparatus, human beings, and the differentiated roles of those beings in society and culture, as well as the elaborate network of institutions and customs. Ultimately, the observable reality from which we work is the acts of human beings in relation to one another and to the natural world, and we seek for relations between those acts. But acts are in the end actions by individuals. Why a particular individual acts as he does, i.e., the relations between his various actions, is the field of psychological research. As social scientists, we take the acts as given, without concerning ourselves with a whole set of complex interactions, such as those involved in the fact that a man can love and hate his chief at the same time.[22] But, as I say, individuals act, and they act to gratify certain purposes, some of which are organic needs, some psychical desires, and some culturally imposed. All are involved in a process of cultural shaping and of customary control. It is these interests set in individuals, and the mobility of individuals and their ability to make new choices, that work in repetitive processes of stationary systems, and, *a priori*, that set in motion new processes that develop their own customary standardization. Interests exist in individuals. Those individuals, and the roles into which culture breaks them, have to seek gratification within society and its customary structure. The structure of the field and the structure of its parts are too closely interdependent for other than theoretical separation.

Our primary unit of observation is the action of an individual, involving the use of land and other resources, of weapons, etc. Each action also occurs inside a particular community with a certain culture. The power within a social field comes from the energy of human desire, need, fear, etc.—which are themselves complicated events whose internal structure is studied by other sciences. But it is the energy of individuals, variously charged with internal power and armed with social resources, that sets processes in the field to work. The direction and path of these processes, as well as the interests of the individuals involved in them, are determined by the total structure of the field, which is set by culture; and culture can be broken into a mass of customs. Some of these customs are combined in institutions; many are inconsistent with one another and set in motion contrary processes. It is for these reasons that I do not consider it profitable to think of cultures as in contact. Individuals of different social fields come into relationship, and their relationships are influenced by the cultural endowment of their original relationships and, later, of the new, emerging relationships. The influence, in any subjugated African area, of the new field of interdependence with Whites steadily increased until it affected every action in the originally independent field. In this framework of analysis, we can consider how individuals are moved by custom, and how they exploit custom to serve their interests. It is more difficult to move from the studies

22. Nadel, *Foundations of Social Anthropology;* and Gluckman, *Closed Systems and Open Minds.*

of cultures alone as in contact to examine social process. Hence this is the less fruitful methodology. But to see social processes without their cultural load is to blind ourselves to important problems.

I have stressed throughout that two complexes of events determine the major structure of a social field. These are the events involved in the control of military force and those involved in the arrangements for making a living. That is, politico-military and economic institutions control the major structure of the field. The complex of events involved in the way men and women marry to found families and rear and feed their children is, of course, of equal importance in social life. But it is not the arrangement of this domestic system of relationships that establishes the major structure of the whole field. Military power and control of the main ways in which people make a living for their families, and the way in which these complexes are related to one another, produce order in the social field as a whole; and it is this order that enables the domestic system to function. After the British conquest of Zululand, individual Zulu and their families continued to work to maintain themselves, and in doing so, they began, in a series of isolated and short-term movements, to come to terms with the dominant British power. In addition, they began to seek for goods by earning money in the new economic system that had now embraced Zululand. In time, their interested investment in the new economic system increased until all Zulu were involved in it, from the chief who drew a stipend from the government to the laborer who went to the mines at the distant Witwatersrand to earn money to clothe his family. Earlier in Zululand history, Shaka's military power was sufficient to bring the new elements introduced by the English traders under systematic control, and they subserved the working of existing political processes. I shall not repeat this point throughout my analysis, but I ask you to bear it in mind as I discuss the manner in which individuals and groups have used customs in serving their interests.

In addition to economic relationships and military control, the social system contains an elaborate arrangement of customs pertaining to individuals and groups. Customs are modes of behavior and belief that mark the independence of different individuals and groups within a social system; in any society, ways of speech and dress, particular types of action, conventions, and etiquette all serve to demarcate and distinguish the specific roles of individuals and the relationships between those roles. This symbolic function of custom exists independently of, even though it is connected with, the differential distribution of economic and military power among those individuals. But the customs have an autonomy of their own, since (as Durkheim pointed out) the customs transcend any single individual and often any single generation. They are passed on from generation to generation, and the individual who does not conform to some degree with custom provokes a social reaction to make him conform. What pertains to an individual alone is a habit and not a custom. I do not need to belabor this point, because I think it is now commonplace that the individual is conditioned largely by the culture in which he is reared; and culture is made up of a variety of customs.

Although the individual is thus conditioned by his community's customs, these customs work on the physical endowment of the human organism. Thus, this complicated endowment forms a fourth constituent complex in the structure of the social field. It is the striving of individual human beings to gratify their various wants and to achieve their goals that gives purpose to social life. In this striving, they work within a public order imposed by those who control military force, both within a system of economic relationships, through which they satisfy certain elementary organic needs and culturally defined wants, and also within the complex of institutions composed of customs. Complicated problems arise from the manner in which these different events are involved in one another within the individual psyche; and these problems form the field of sciences like psychology. As a social anthropologist, I take the end result of these complicated psychical and organic processes as given. When I come to analyze the processes of social change, I am concerned with the manner in which these final actions of human beings operate as a result of, and affect, the organization of customs.

Sociological movements are changes in the systems of relationships in a social field. That is, we can speak of a sociological movement when we observe changes in the power, the interests, and the modes of cooperation and clash of groups and social personalities. Like culture, a sociological movement transcends any of the individuals who participate in it, but nevertheless these movements are composed of individuals who are seeking to gratify their varied purposes. In this pursuit, individuals may start a new movement, either by creating new customs and beliefs to mark it off from previous conditions, or by drawing on existing customs, but weighing and combining them differently, or both. My present concern is with the general processes by which this was done in the history of the colonization of Zululand. I shall try to formulate these processes in terms that will allow them to be applied in other social fields.

All societies are composed of groups and social personalities who have variant customs. That is, all societies, if we look at details of speech and dress and behavior, are composed of heterogeneous culture groups—be they classes, political bodies, religious sects, lineages, moieties, or others. Sometimes there are marked differences of culture between the groups and personalities within a largely repetitive social system—as in medieval England for long periods, or as in the total system of East Africa, where pastoral Masai were in close contact with agricultural Kikuyu. Modern (in the 1930s) Zululand was a changing—or evolving—social system, composed of groups with radically different cultures; and in this sort of system, development of culture, involving transfers of customs, dying out of customs, etc., are of very great significance. Every new social movement produced by changes in the actions of individuals tends to be expressed in new alignments of custom. When developing struggles and emerging collaboration produce different relationships between groups or personalities, or produce new groups and personalities, they have to be marked by their own characteristic culture. This new characteristic culture not only serves to demarcate them from others, but also becomes the center of their interests. That is, sociological movements, which are formed by changes in the interest-relationships of persons and groups, are expressed in some or other cultural forms already available to the bearers of the movement. For social units must act in terms of culture. Once a sociological movement has established a cultural form, this form becomes a tradition which in turn influences the actions of those who bear it.

If you wish for a perhaps clarifying analogy, I suggest that an individual can act only in terms of his own mental-behavioristic habits: Even the neurotic, moved by unconscious conflicts, shows his neuroticism by giving particular values to ideas and actions in his community and by combining these ideas and actions in radical patterns that diverge from the traditional pattern. This is true of social units in a period of change.

Often, like neurotics, people acting as social units are unaware of both the sociological and psychological forces that move them; they tend not to understand the movements of which they are part and often do not even appreciate that they are part of a social movement. This is, of course, a tendency—there are many exceptions to it—but whether people are conscious or unaware of these underlying forces, they must express the forces in behavior; and whatever the origin of a movement, it is formulated in terms of the culture at the disposal of its members. The causes of a social movement may be contained in unexamined complexities of the social structure, but the movements themselves appear in public view as new configurations of existing customs and beliefs. These beliefs constitute partly the values by which the bearers of the movement rationalize the forces and interests of which they may not be consciously aware. Therefore, new movements among Zulu, Whites, and Zululanders—I use Zululanders to cover groups of Zulu and Whites—all these new movements are expressed in terms of either Zulu or White customs, or in terms of some combination of the two.

Moreover, since Zululand is a territorial zone of the field of the world system, its developments were determined partly by relationships within that system. Relationships between national and racial groups, between capitalist employers and their employees, between skilled and unskilled laborers, between peasants and industrialized proletariat, which were common to the world system despite great cultural and structural diversity, produce similar movements in all parts of the system. These movements, with subsidiary variations, have occurred in Europe, China, Malaya, America, Zululand, etc. In each they have taken similar as well as very different cultural forms. In Zululand these movements were expressed in many cultures: world culture, as in cooperatives, trade unions, anti-Semitism; Black Africa, as in labor migration and Ethiopian churches; South Africa, as in ascription by the Zulu of more negrophilism to English than to Boers; and Zulu culture, as in a revival of Zulu ritual.

When they participate in movements of this kind, people are often unaware not only of what moves their participation, but also of how they are using the customs available to them, and of how the change in their customary behavior will affect the whole system. When a pagan Zulu became a Christian he did not know all the tenets of Christianity nor even all the pagan beliefs he was expected to abandon, and he attached certain very vague values to both sets of beliefs. His conversion was cultural change, an alteration in the standardized behavior of a social unit. The social anthropologist has to discuss this total change, as he observes it. He does so in terms of custom and beliefs—of culture. We can discuss the change in these terms. But people changing their actions do observe the customs of the group they are abandoning, and the customs of the other group they are adopting. I shall use the term *endoculture* to describe the customs of a group as perceived by its members, and *exoculture* to describe the customs of a group when observed by members of another group in the same social system. *Culture* is thus restricted to the customs as observed by the social anthropologist.

This long introduction constitutes the background within which operate processes of change in culture. Before I put them before you, I must still make two provisos. First, none of the processes I delineate itself, wholly and alone, explains anything that happened in Zululand history. At any one time, many of these processes have operated on specific customs, some in the same direction, others in different directions. Secondly, these processes may operate on a particular custom with different weight, and even in different directions, at various periods. Wider social developments affect not only the processes of change which operate, but also the extent to which various processes affect any particular custom. To explain how particular customs persist and others die out, how some are offered in exchange by the dominant group and others refused, how there is a blending and independent existence of customs of the two groups in one of them would require an analysis of the history of each custom set in the continually changing pattern of the social system. That is, the history of any custom should be related to the functioning of the total system from period to period. For, as the structure of the total system alters, different processes may affect each custom. I am not undertaking this description of real changes, of the actual history of particular customs. I am attempting to abstract the processes of change which have been operating and merely illustrate them with examples culled from this actual history. But before I conclude, I shall take briefly one problem and show how the processes that I formulated may be applied to illuminate the history of particular customs.

The social reality on which I was working was very complex; and almost everything that could happen to a custom was happening. Hence, I began by formulating a range of possibilities. In a changing system of heterogeneous culture-groups, there are four possible ways in which culture can be used to express new movements:

(1) If a movement in a group can be expressed in endoculture customs, those customs will tend to survive.

(2) If a movement in a group can be expressed in the exoculture of another group, the first group will tend to adopt those customs.

(3) Where a movement can be expressed in either endoculture

or exoculture customs, the final event will depend on the total situation. Strong opposition gives a bias for endoculture, cooperation a bias for exoculture.

(4) If a movement can be expressed only in a group's own endoculture customs and in the exoculture customs of another group, these customs will be combined accordingly.

These rules apply to the survival and adoption of customs; conversely, customs not covered by them will tend to be dropped or rejected.

As I have said, these formulations are very wide, but it is necessary for me to state them clearly, for by combining them with other principles we shall be able to reduce them to more illuminating propositions. The main principle of the cultural expression of sociological movements has two important subsidiary rules, to which I shall refer as the first and second principles of the social load. I use *load* here in the sense that the sediment carried by a river is its "load"; hence, the social load is the culture that is carried in existing social movements.

The first principle of the social load is that social movements tend to be expressed in as much of the endoculture and the exoculture as possible; e.g., White opposition to the Africans tended to be expressed in the whole of their endoculture: They justify their superior position religiously by reference to the myth of Noah's curse that the sons of Ham should be hewers of wood and drawers of water; in the scientific rationales of Western society by pseudo-genetics, pseudo-history, pseudo-psychology, pseudo-sociology, etc.; and in exoculture terms, there was a tendency, marked in social anthropology, to attach great inherent value to African culture, for Africans by tribes, even while this culture was denigrated under the processes described above. Apartheid negrophobes have written much more sympathetic analyses of the perfection of African culture than left-wing negrophiles.

The second principle of the social load is that all culture tends to survive. I do not deny that customs decay and die. I am asserting that every custom tends to continue being practiced even though it will take new forms and develop new values to accord with the new system of which it is a part.

Changing sociological relations thus find expression in changes of culture. But in a changing system of heterogeneous culture groups, culture differences demarcate groups and social personalities and contribute to produce changes. As these principles work out in reality, the survival of old, and the adoption of new, culture are interdependent with sociological movements. Changes of culture express the movements, but the relations between cultural facts also determine what movements occur. Beliefs in sorcery and magic not only provided one form in which Zulu-White opposition was expressed, but also, throughout, with growing Zulu opposition to White political and economic domination, they restricted Zulu acceptance of White knowledge. Further, this difference in knowledge was a form of the cleavage between the two groups. Had Whites and Zulu come to form one undifferentiated group, these beliefs would not have acted in the same way; and if the Zulu had had no beliefs in witchcraft, under the then present conditions, their opposition to the Whites would still have existed and would have had to be expressed in what culture was available. The interdependence of culture and sociological relations is two-sided: I am in this analysis looking mainly at one side of that interdependence.

Social Cleavage, Conflict, and Social Inertia

(1) In any social system a dominant cleavage into groups affects all relationships in the system. In Zululand, the dominant cleavage has been successively that into small tribes, then that into king and subjects, and then that into Whites and Blacks. (But earlier dominant cleavages tend to persist as subsidiary cleavages into later periods.)

In any part of the system there may be a subsidiary cleavage, operating similarly in that part of the system to the way in which the dominant cleavage acts in the whole system, but the subsidiary cleavage will be affected by the dominant cleavage. Thus, in the Transkei relationships between commissioners and chiefs and local councils formed by the government had developed into a situation similar to that found in Zululand; but within Transkei society there was the additional cleavage, between chiefs and local councils, influenced by the dominant cleavage. The dominant cleavage has now developed to divide chiefs into "pro-apartheid" and "anti-apartheid."[23]

It follows that the dominant cleavage of a changing system must produce similar structural developments in all similar parts of the system, even if the cultural form be different. Thus, wherever industrialism exists, we find similar relationships between management and workers (although in Zululand these relationships had specific effects on the position of chiefs vis-à-vis their people). I propose to refer to this principle as the principle of the developing dominant cleavage.

(2) A consequence of the developing dominant cleavage is that

23. P. Mayer, "The Tribal Elite and the Transkeion Elections of 1963," in P. C. Lloyd (ed.), *The New Elites of Tropical Africa* (London: Oxford University Press, for the International African Institute, 1966).

a changing social system tends to develop along the lines of its dominant cleavage until it is radically altered and the conflict causing the
cleavage is wholly resolved in the pattern of a new system. This is
the principle of social inertia—as *inertia* is "that property of matter
by which when at rest it tends to remain so, and when in motion
to continue in motion, and in the same line or direction, unless acted
on by some external force" *(Concise Oxford English Dictionary)*. Social
inertia is a process of continual development in a certain direction,
possibly with great social changes. A very radical developing cleavage
can persist for a long time, but considerable quantitative shifts occur
to maintain it: In South Africa both increased force and economic
development are constantly displayed.

One implication of the principle of social inertia is that, if the
dominant cleavage in a changing system be into two groups, for every
form of cooperation between members of both groups, there will
develop a corresponding cleavage. If the cleavage be between two
culture groups, whenever members of the two cooperate in a group
based on the culture of one group alone, some members of the new,
emergent cooperating group and some members of the excluded
group will form a new group based on the culture of one group
alone, and some members of the new, emergent cooperating group
and some members of the excluded group will, if possible, form a
new group based on the customs of the cooperating group and the.
customs of the excluded group. I have cited how the formation of
Mission-churches produced independent churches using customs of
Christians and customs of paganism. Then there will be opposition
between the two newly-emerged groups, and this opposition will be
expressed according to the dominant cleavage of the system. Opposition of Mission-church and independent church immediately becomes
White *versus* Zulu opposition. And, under the principles of the social
load, all forms of opposition between Whites and Zulu affected this
new cleavage, and all cultural differences tended to be drawn into
it: Independent churches become involved in educational, land, political, etc., problems, and more and more Zulu culture is drawn in,
through schisms, to express the basic opposition. Dr. H. J. Simons
has allowed me to quote another example from his present research
on the radical movement of opposition in South Africa. Every time
a united movement of members of different color groups was formed,
it fragmented through the pressure of the color-bar, which affected
even those opposed to the bar; and shortly afterwards a new movement
to unite the groups would be set up, with small groups of extreme
protagonists staying out.

(3) A further implication of the principle of social inertia is that, where the dominant cleavage in a changing system is into two culture-groups, if members of either major group form a minor group based on strong adherence to the whole or part of the major group's endoculture, then this minor group will be strengthened in its following by its emphasis on its major group's culture, for it emphasizes cleavage against the other major group.

Thus, many pagan Zulu joined independent sects because they practiced Zulu custom. Similarly, it has been pointed out for tribes in East Africa that the pagans performed certain rites to defy their Christian fellow-tribesmen, although this defiance also had an anti-White significance.

(4) In a changing social system all developments tend to accord with the developing dominant cleavage. All changes that occurred in Zululand were used to express the dominant cleavage into Whites *versus* Zulu. When Whites introduced cattle sales, which benefitted the Zulu by raising the selling price of their beasts, they became for some Zulu a way of tempting them to exterminate their herds. One way in which this process works is by what Evans-Pritchard (following Freud) has termed "secondary elaboration of belief," i.e., by developing beliefs centered in the dominant cleavage to cover every new development. Interest groups opposed to innovations thus defended themselves: Zulu doctors attacked the teachings of native malarial assistants on these grounds, and conservative Zulu said that irrigation projects, native agricultural demonstrators, etc., by improving Zulu gardens, would entice the Whites to covet and expropriate them.

(5) In any social system, every group sets a value on its own endoculture. This, in combination with the preceding principles, enables us to infer that, where in a changing system the dominant cleavage is into two culture groups, each of these groups will tend to set increasingly greater value on its own endoculture, because it expresses the dominant cleavage. Thus, opposition between White and Zulu groups resulted in each one's setting a group value on its own culture. Among Zulu they were chiefly national traditions and ceremonies, and many that had become obsolete with the destruction of the kingship were being revived. Under a principle stated before, this group valuation strengthens the isolation of the group, as members of the other group are not allowed to participate.

Thus, customs tend to become endoculture values by which the members of each culture group can express the independence of the group, which is part of the values of the culture differences. Zulu sorcery and divination functioned in one set of social relationships and continued to operate in similar relationships, but in addition they had a new social value as part of the creed of some anti-White sects. The family ancestral cult could not acquire similar values as it operated only in kinship groups, whereas magic worked outside kinship boundaries: The chief's ancestral cult, which attached to political groups, could acquire these values.

Obversely, when the dominant cleavage is into culture-groups, each group also tends to set a value on the other group's culture as distinguishing the other group from itself. Whites set this value on Zulu culture, even while they denigrated it. Zulu similarly began to say that White culture was good for Whites.

(6) Evans-Pritchard has pointed out that "in all ... groups the status of members, when acting as such to outsiders and to one another, is structurally undifferentiated."[24] In the situation I have been describing, this rule works so that when members of one culture group attempt to introduce their endoculture to members of the opposed group the attack on the endoculture of this group unites it; and its opposition to the other group leads to, and is expressed in, opposition to the innovation. Individual members of the receiving group react to the innovation as members of the group against their opponents. However, if a member of the group for other reasons accepts the innovation, his fellow members may accept it from him, since they react to him as a member of their group. Although Zulu pagans abused Christianity and Christians paganism, pagan and Christian relatives lived together fairly amicably, and pagans accepted many of the White's exocultural customs from their Christian relatives, but they opposed them when pushed by the Whites. (By contrast, in the Transkei where evangelization had worked much longer, Christians and pagans formed distinct groups.[25])

The Cultural Expression of Developing Conflicts and Cleavages

Here I try to relate the general principles of the cultural expression of sociological movements to the principle that in all social systems there is a tendency for individual quarrels, arising out of clashes, to be expressed in socially recognized forms.

(1) If new conflicts can be expressed and partially resolved in old customs, they tend to persist. For example, Zulu could explain

24. M. Fortes and E. E. Evans-Pritchard (eds.), *African Political Systems* (London: Oxford University Press, 1940).

25. Monica Wilson, "Effects on the Xhosa and Nyakyusa of Scarcity of Land."

their ill luck or failures in the struggle for work with Whites by saying
that they were bewitched, for this explanation related the misfortune
to their competing with unrelated people. Occasionally, the misfortune
might be explained by saying that they were not informed of a relative's
death or had incurred the ancestral spirits' wrath; but the ancestral
spirits operated chiefly in the kinship group. A second example with
the same customs is: The native commissioner's condemnation of
beliefs in sorcery and of divination, as contrasted with the chief's
belief in them, expressed the antithesis of commissioner and chief
(described briefly above and more fully in *African Political Systems*);
and this antithesis strengthened the belief that could appear in action.
In some instances the accused sorcerer went for protection to the
commissioner, and the accuser sought the chief; and one man in
different situations might play both roles. Because the commissioner
did not legally forbid the ancestral cult (at times even encouraged
it), this cult did not become involved in the same way in the opposition
between the commissioners and chief, although the cult of the chief's
ancestors was strengthened as it differentiated him from the commissioner. Finally, the new conflict between Mission church and independent Zulu sects at first could be expressed in sorcery-magic-divination
beliefs more fully than in ancestral cult beliefs, although later ancestral
spirits reappeared as saints and angels. Nevertheless, as the independent sects consisted of unrelated people, the cult could not unite
them, as they could unite to heal from the ills of sorcery. Hence,
sorcery and magic survived under this process, but ancestral cult did
not.

(2) If emerging new conflicts in a group can be expressed in
exoculture customs, they will tend to be accepted. This process
appeared in the feeling of Zulu Christians that they must build good
houses and wear European clothes to show their Christianity and
their distinction from pagans. The pagans came to value the skin
loinskirt as a badge of paganism (the redblanket in the Transkei);
and there was a special, somewhat opprobrious, term for pagans who
wore trousers. This process also covers the general rule, formulated
by Frazer, that a conquering group tends to ascribe mystical power
to the conquered group, since it does not fear its force (Gypsies,
Celts, Jews). Many Whites believed in Zulu magical powers and thus
accepted the beliefs. They had no reason to accept ancestral cult
beliefs, because these beliefs operated in kinship groups into which
Whites did not enter. Also, Zulu accepted certain patent medicines
which were claimed to deal with animosity in personal relationships

as the cause of illness, but they feared the hospital's medicines and certain Christian beliefs connected with spiritual healing.

(3) If old and continuing conflicts in a group can be expressed in old endoculture customs, they will tend to persist. For example, conflicts of interest between brothers over inheritance, which dominated and continued to dominate Zulu kinship groups, are expressed in secular forms and used to be expressed in charges of witchcraft against a brother's wife; now they are expressed against the brother in a charge of sorcery. These conflicts were not expressed in the ancestral cult because it stressed amity in the group.

(4) If old conflicts in a group can be expressed in exoculture customs, they will tend to be accepted. In old Zulu culture there were no luxuries, and chiefs had approximately the same standard of living as their followers. Better houses, cars, clothes, etc., come to be believed to be appropriate to chiefs and not to commoners, and for reasons of prestige chiefs had to strain to procure these goods. The same process induced a small number of Whites to adopt Zulu magical sorcery beliefs to explain their own misfortunes, which they ascribed to the use of these powers by their competitors.

(5) Old customs will tend to persist if they can express the overt emergence of old conflicts that were previously repressed by other customs or broke out in publicly reproved violence, as in quarrels between Zulu fathers and sons,[26] which could not be expressed under old conditions save by migration. Under the Whites, this conflict was sometimes expressed in terms of sorcery, for a Zulu father might be accused by his son of killing the son's children. These conflicts would not be expressed in the ancestral cult, dependent as it was on kinship hierarchies; so that again under this process beliefs in sorcery tended to persist while beliefs in the ancestral cult did not.

(6) Exoculture customs that can express the emergence of conflicts previously repressed tend to be accepted. Family conflicts were a patent cause (although not, of course, the only or even the main cause) of Zulu young men's going out to work. In fact, Fortes believed that, among the Tallensi, where labor migration was not the social norm as it was in Zululand, family "conflicts appeared to be the cause of emigration rather than its consequence."[27] Similarly, conversion

26. Max Gluckman, *Custom and Conflict in Africa*, Ch. III.

27. M. Fortes, "Culture Contact as a Dynamic Process: An Investigation in the Northern Territories of the Gold Coast," *Africa*, 1 (January, 1936), pp. 44–45. (Reprinted in L. Mair [ed.]. *Methods of Study of Culture Conflict in Africa*, Memorandum XV of the International Institute of African Languages and Cultures [1936].)

to Christianity was often accepted for this reason. By 1890, Zulu parents were complaining to the commissioner that their daughters had run away to a mission, and family quarrels seem to have been the cause of these flights. In general, Zulu women, who not only were inferior in legal status, but also were always under severe emotional pressure,[28] were converted more readily than men.

Social Cleavage and Social Cooperation

In any social system there tends to be cooperation across all lines of cleavage. Therefore, in a changing social system, until the dominant cleavage is radically resolved in a new pattern, there is cooperation across that cleavage and every new cleavage tends to be compensated for by a new form of cooperation.

The main economic cooperation of Zulu and Whites was away from Zululand, in the labor-centers; and I cannot analyze this economic cooperation in my present terms as I did not observe it. But I must note that old and continuing modes of cooperation among the Zulu were expressed in this vast field of cooperation. Economic cooperation between kinsmen was continued into the labor-centers, in that kinsmen went to the same type of employment and lived together. But most importantly, the extended family was held together in the new system, mainly because, if they were to continue to cultivate their lands and to go away to earn money, Zulu had to be associated in large groups.[29] This association led to the persistence of the extended family; and, with it, of many customs associated with specific roles in it. This extended family was the field of many of the processes I have been analyzing.

(1) As I have described when discussing social inertia, in a changing system where the dominant cleavage is into culture groups, various cooperating groups involving members of both groups tend to emerge. For each new schismatic group produced by the developing dominant cleavage there will tend to emerge a new cooperating group. Thus, independent sects ranged in beliefs, and in cooperation with and hostility to, Whites and Zulu. Some married pagan Zulu in semi-pagan ceremonies, others would not; some were dominantly anti-White, others favored cooperation with Whites; some concentrated on divina-

28. Max Gluckman, "Zulu Women in Hoe Culture Ritual," *Bantu Studies*, 9, 3 (1935); and Max Gluckman, *Law, Politics, and Ritual in Tribal Society* (Chicago: Aldine Publishing Company, 1965).

29. See W. Watson, on Mambwe: *Tribal Cohesion in a Money Economy*.

tion of sorcery in the Zulu pagan way, others on messianic beliefs drawn from the Bible.

(2) Differences in the culture of two groups cooperating in a single social field make essential the development of customs of communication between them.

(a) If modes of cooperation between old or new groups and social personalities can be expressed in old customs, they tend to survive. Zulu saluted White officials with traditional salutes to chiefs, and this practice survives; they did not ascribe to commissioners mystical powers, which ceased to be essential attributes of political office (but see, against this, survival value, above). Magic could be used to get the favor of White employers and sacrifices were made to ancestors for good luck in this work.

(b) If a group cannot rely on its own endoculture in a new mode of cooperation with another group, it must accept the exoculture of the other. The simplest example is the learning of the other's language and the institution of interpreters. If both groups take the other's exoculture, they may be combined, as in pidgin Zulu-English–Afrikaans, which uses European grammar and a mixture of words with mainly Zulu roots.

(c) Even where a group is rejecting another group's exoculture for internal relationships, it may adopt the exoculture for cooperative relationships. Zulu raise their hats to Whites and to chiefs, but not to their own women.

(3) If new modes of cooperation within a group can be expressed only in the exoculture of an opposed group, this exoculture will be adopted. As kinsmen dispersed over South Africa and yet the extended family had to run its economic affairs as a joint farming–wage-earning effort, the Zulu adopted letter writing to maintain contact.

(4) If new modes of cooperation are in conflict with an old endoculture, the endoculture will tend to be dropped in relevant relationships. Thus, the value that the modern White civilization placed on heavy production and on differential wealth was in marked conflict with Zulu beliefs in sorcery, by which a man producing more than his fellows was liable to be suspected of sorcery, and a man with too many goods feared that he would be attacked by sorcery. This process tended to destroy beliefs in sorcery, as far as they affected these particular relationships.

These are the sorts of processes that I formulate to cover how customs are affected by and influence social movements; they are related to the general conception of a social system as a field of equilibrium but under tension (as Kurt Lewin sees all fields).

The Individual and Social Change

Radical social change tends to be associated with increasing individual variation and psychical (emotional) conflict. Among the Zulu, it appeared, for example, in the increasing number and types of "possessed" diviners and the increasing proportion of men among them. It is worth noting here that this general tendency could be expressed in the magical system but not in the ancestral cult, which was linked to kinship groups that restricted the emergence of individuals.

Individual differences of temperament, themselves largely the product of social conditions, are undoubtedly important determining forces in the processes of social change. But clearly every personality is also the center of an alignment of social relationships and of a complex of stereotyped customs, which limit the range of influence of personal variability. Some writers on Africa stressed the importance of the individual, because a popular commissioner could induce a tribe to accept an innovation while an unpopular commissioner could not.[30] I would agree that, although this idea is important, it occurs within the basic relationship of tribe and government. For the popularity of a commissioner cannot overcome certain basic divisions in the color-bar situation. In Zululand, the balance of oscillation between chief and administrator varied with their personalities; but it was within the limits set by their opposition. Variations of personality might ease or exacerbate relationships.

Sometimes a pre-eminent individual can produce radical change; but in the end this change may not affect basic social relations. Thus, men like Kgama of the Bamangwato and Lentswe of the Bakgatla in Bechuanaland each made virtually the whole of his tribe become Christians. Hence, there we did not find the relationship of conservatives *versus* radicals tied to paganism *versus* Christianity (as in the Transkei); but it existed. And the conversion of Bechuana chiefs itself raises sociological problems; I think it was associated with the role of missionaries in giving the tribes protection against the Boers.

In this background, I have tried to formulate processes that cover how individual behavior causes social change.

30. G. G. Brown and A. McD. Bruce Hult, *Anthropology in Action: An Experiment in the Iringa Province of Tanganyika Territory* (London: Oxford University Press, for the International Institute of African Languages and Culture, 1936).

(1) It is a general rule that, in any system of opposed groups the membership of which can be changed, individuals use the opposition of the groups to their own advantage by transferring from one group to another. An extension of this rule is that, in a system of opposed culture groups, members of one group will use the culture of the other group when it is to their advantage. An individual Zulu, who as a Zulu believed in opposing the Christianity of the Whites, sent one or more of his children to become Christians and be educated in order that later they might earn money as teachers. The Zulu social ideal was to acquire more and more cattle, with which they associated their national strength; but individual Zulu who held this belief still sold their own cattle, while they upbraided other sellers as traitors.

(2) Where developments under conditions of social change leave surviving two alternative modes of behavior, an individual, to secure personal advantages, will switch from one mode to the other and, if necessary, will change his membership in groups with which the modes of behavior are associated. Sick Zulu switched from mission church to Zulu sect to paganism in seeking cures; Zulu sects combined divination of sorcery with praying to Christ for a patient's recovery.

(3) If a type of behavior associated with a social personality or group is no longer possible under old forms in new conditions, it tends to be expressed in new forms. If it can be expressed in the exoculture of another group, it will be adopted. The Zulu prince who could no longer acquire political power in Zululand could seek power as a policeman or other authoritative employee of Whites, and Whites deliberately used princes in these posts. Individualistic tendencies and strivings for power, which could no longer be effective in national politics, turned into the religious field, which thus acquired great importance.

(4) If the interests of a social personality (or group) are threatened by the continued practice of some endoculture customs under new conditions, that personality (or group) will tend to cooperate in the dropping of those customs, even if they had previously contributed to maintain his interests. Although many diviners had continued to divine in terms of the ancestral cult, the interests of the ancestral-cult priests themselves, who were the heads of kinship groups, became partly to let the cult weaken in order to keep the increasing number of their Christian kin attached to them. Old Zulu headmen therefore whispered the prayers over sacrificial animals so that Christian relatives could eat of the meat under the pretense that it was a mere killing, and in time it often became that.

(5) Conversely, if a new social personality can use old abandoned endoculture customs in his interest, he will tend to do so. The Zulu priests of White mission sects used the old Zulu cultural relationship of misfortune to personal quarrels, the essence of divination of sorcery, by promising Christ's protection against enemies.

(6) The able members of the inferior group tend, like all elites, to try to move into the upper group. In Zululand, this was impossible, and there developed a series of complex processes: For example, the able person adopted what of culture from the superior group he could. But as the ablest came against the stringency of the color-bar, they tended to do one of two things. Either they altered White customs to give them an anti-White bias, as in Zulu sects or political movements, or they reverted to a strong evaluation of the glory of Zulu culture and to the re-introduction of old Zulu customs and ceremonies that, despite the evidence to the contrary drawn from their education, they believed would solve old and new problems.

(7) A final example of the form of process I believe can be formulated here is: If two or more sets of group interests intersect in a single social personality, it partially resolves the conflicts of those interests, although this personality is involved in strong personal conflicts. This was the position of Zulu chiefs. Customs from both groups will be adopted by this personality and acted on situationally to solve the conflict. Generally, we may note that, under all these processes I have been considering, individuals are to some extent solving the conflicts in custom and belief with which they are confronted by processes of situational selection and secondary elaboration of belief, as in a repetitive system. But in a changing system, in behaving thus, they tend to produce new customs, beliefs, and forms of alignment.

Summary

The processes I have cited are by no means exhaustive, but I hope that they are sufficient to indicate how I would approach these problems. What I am aiming at are formulations by which we can relate what happens to customs to fundamental changes in a total field. I seek to explain, and even predict, the maintaining, the abandoning, and the adopting of culture by heterogeneous culture groups in a changing society, by striking a balance between the processes of persistence, obsolescence, revival, and adoption, as they apply to particular customs or institutions. I repeat, in the complicated web of actual events, no process appears alone. Many events and many laws of many types produce actual behavior. And, at different periods in the changes of the total system, different processes will act with varying weight on particular customs.

Finally, as cause and effect are interdependent, so are culture and sociological movement: Customs produce movements and movements are expressed in and produce custom. With these provisos, we should be able to study the history of important customs throughout our period. I am going to summarize for you what has happened to the ancestral cult and magical sorcery beliefs. Indeed, I partly worked out my system of processes to answer a question put to me by Evans-Pritchard when I went to Zululand in 1936. Why, he asked, in Africa had the ancestral cult tended to die out while beliefs in sorcery and magic had survived, flourished, and expanded? This was the more striking since the government has attempted by force to eliminate the magical sorcery beliefs, but not the others. Since I aimed to pull together my preceding anaylsis by considering this problem, I have frequently cited as examples of the processes of customary change what happened to these various beliefs.

The priest-heads of kinship groups at first opposed Christianity and attempted to maintain the ancestral cult, for they reacted to Christianity as, among other things, an attack on the cult in which their position was part of their authority. Once the number of Christians, converted for various reasons, in a particular group increased, the dying-out of ancestral cult practices was necessary to prevent the break-up of the resulting mixed group of pagans and Christians, and kinship group headmen cooperated here.

This statement applies less to the political ancestral cult than to the family ancestral cult. Like kinship groups, tribes are composed of both pagans and Christians. But there has been a greater tendency for the ancestral cult of chiefs to survive, as it marked Zulu opposition to Whites. The relationship of the chief to his ancestors and to tribal traditions is one of the bases of his antithesis to the commissioner; and only the chief's, but not the family's, ancestors could acquire this political value.

The ancestral cult had kinship boundaries, magical sorcery beliefs did not. Because of this difference, magical sorcery beliefs could be extended to the increasing range of relationships, both of competition and of cooperation, whether they were with other Zulu or with Whites. I have tried to show how new conflicts and new modes of cooperation could be expressed in one set of beliefs and not in the other.

Secondly, since the ancestral cult works within kinship boundaries, it also involves acceptance of kinship hierarchies and identities of interest in the kinship group. Hence, the cult could not cover the new interests, which arose within the group out of the new economy and policy. Magic could deal with these interests; and magical sorcery beliefs could accommodate the emergence of new conflicts and of previously repressed conflicts. The ancestral cult could not. Again, we saw that magic and not the ancestral cult could handle the emergence of individuals diverging markedly from kinship stereotypes.

But Western emphasis on heavy production and the acquisition of individual wealth were tending to destroy this kind of belief in sorcery, witchcraft, and magic, because the beliefs were related to an economic system with little variation in productiveness or wealth. When I did my research, increased competition for work with Whites and greater variations of wealth had strengthened the fear of sorcery, as they did at the beginning of our commercial and industrial revolution. Temporary relief from this major conflict was sought in the cult of the patent medicine, which carried the prestige of white culture but claimed to deal with personal animosities.

I believe that the formulation of processes, such as I have sketched above, explains to me why one set of practices has survived and the other has not. More than this, it explains to me how one set is adaptable, and the other not; and how this variation in adaptability is related to the general changing structure of the social field. Had I the time, I could indicate that the formulations are valuable in that I could apply them to other phenomena. And the processes form an interdependent, logically consistent set of propositions. They are formulated in abstract terms, capable of application to any field or reality. They try to state invariable relationships between social movements and cultural changes. They may aspire to begin to be equivalent to a chemical table for the analysis of salts.[31]

---

31. Eric Woolf has argued, as I do, that it is certain social relationships that differentiate societies similarly influenced by industrial developments: "Kinship, Friendship, and Patron-Client Relations in Complex Societies," in M. Banton (ed.), *Political Systems and Distribution of Power*, Association of Social Anthropologists of the Commonwealth, Monograph No. 2 (London: Tavistock Press, 1965).

A MODEL OF THE MODERN MAN
Theoretical and Methodological Issues

ALEX INKELES, *Stanford University*

The term "modern" has many associations and carries a heavy weight of connotations. It is applied not only to men, but to nations, to political systems, to economies, to cities, to institutions such as schools and hospitals, to housing, to clothes, and to manners. Taken literally, the term could mean anything current that has more or less recently replaced something that was, in the past, the accepted or standard. In this sense, the first sailing vessels to replace the galleys propelled by oars were once modern, as was the clipper ship before steam, and steam before atomic power. Approached in this way, the modern becomes a catalogue rather than an entity, a random list of things rather than a concept.

Numerous scholars have sought to give the idea a more distinctive and coherent form. One line of thought treats the modern as the concrete embodiment of certain ways of doing things, as in patterns of education, urbanization, industrialization, bureaucratization, rapid communications, and transportation. Of course, some of these man-ifestations, such as cities, go back in man's history to points long ante-dating anything we would ordinarily call modern, while other developments, such as industrialization, do not. In any event, when emphasis is placed on the more or less simultaneous development of a set, complex, or syndrome of these patterns of social organization, then there can be little doubt that they were observed as such a syn-drome in no nation before the nineteenth century and became really widespread in the world only in the twentieth. The modern, then, can be conceived of as a style or form of civilization characteristic of our current historical epoch, much as feudalism or the classical empires were characteristic of earlier historical eras. This form of civilization is not manifest everywhere in the world, just as feudalism was not present in all the world in the eleventh to the fifteenth centuries. Similarly, modernity in any given part of the world where it does appear is not exactly the same everywhere. It varies in accord with local conditions, the history of a given culture, and the time at which it was introduced.

Within these limits, there exists a syndrome of characteristics readily recognized at both the national and sub-institutional levels. The exploration of that syndrome is the focus of the activities of numerous scholars. Thus, Robert Ward[1] provides ten characteristics defining *economic* modernization; these characteristics include the intense application of scientific technology and inanimate sources of energy, high specialization of labor and interdependence of impersonal markets, large-scale financing and concentration of economic decision making, and rising levels of material well-being. Samuel Huntington[2] offers a more compact list of three processes that define *political* modernization: the replacement of a large number of traditional, religious, familial, and ethnic political authorities by a single, secular, national, political authority; the emergence of new political functions, legal, military, administrative, and scientific, which must be managed by new administrative hierarchies chosen on the basis of achievement rather than ascription; and increased participation in politics by social groups throughout the society along with the development of new institutions such as political parties and interest groups to organize this participation.

Whereas the first line of analysis in the study of modernization gives emphasis to patterns of social organization, there is a second line that more emphasizes the cultural and ideational. Whereas the first approach more stresses ways of *organizing* and *doing,* the second assigns primacy to ways of *thinking* and *feeling.* The one approach is concerned more with the *institution,* the other with the *individual.* The first is more narrowly sociological and political, the second more sociological and psychological.

The socio-psychological approach considers modernization mainly as a process of change in ways of perceiving, expressing, and

1. Robert Ward, *Political Modernization in Japan and Turkey* (Princeton: Princeton University Press, 1964).

2. Samuel Huntington, "Political Modernization: America vs. Europe," *World Politics,* XVIII (April, 1966), pp. 378–415.

valuing. The modern is defined as a mode of individual responding, a set of dispositions to act in certain ways. It is, in other words, an "ethos," or a "spirit," in the sense in which Max Weber spoke of "the spirit of capitalism." As Robert Bellah expressed it, the modern may be seen not "as a form of political or economic system, but as a spiritual phenomenon or a kind of mentality."[3] As such, it is much less tied to a particular time and place than is the definition of modernity in terms of institutional arrangements. If modernity is defined as a state of mind, the same state of mind might have existed in Elizabethan England or even in Periclean Greece.

Of the two main themes in modernization, the institutional has received far more attention than the individual. Indeed, a conservative estimate is that major studies of economic and political modernization at the institutional level outnumber those at the individual some twenty to one. Once fully aware of this fact, the group formed at Harvard's Center for International Affairs to study the social and cultural aspects of economic development decided to commit itself more or less exclusively to studying the impact of the modernization process on the individual.[4]

Our decision stemmed from two convictions: First, we wanted to examine the impact on men, the human costs, if you will, of their exposure to the complex of urbanism, industrialism, mobility, and mass communication. A widespread belief, almost a fundamental conviction, among many intellectuals is that the process of industrialization inevitably brings with it great, indeed excessive, social disorganization, the disruption of social ties, and the consequent disorientation of the individual. Although the assertions are many, the facts are few. We began with the conviction that many of these claims were exaggerated, others unsupported by evidence, still others simply wrong. We believed that work in industry not only could be, but in many parts of the world actually *was,* an educational and liberalizing influence on the men who experience it. We felt it had the capacity to increase their initiative, to widen their participation in society, even to increase their sense of personal worth and dignity.

3. Robert N. Bellah, "Meaning and Modernization," *Religious Studies,* 4 (1968), pp. 37–45.

4. The group was headed by Alex Inkeles, a member of the senior Center faculty, and included as principal members Edward Ryan, Howard Schuman, and David Smith. Support for the research came principally from a grant from the Rockefeller Foundation. Field work in India, Pakistan, and Israel was supported by the Office of Educational and Cultural Affairs, Department of State, through a grant of local currencies under Public Law 480. The National Science Foundation underwrote several major phases of the project, and the Air Force Office of Scientific Research provided funds for technical studies of translation and for computer time.

Our second conviction was that the effective functioning of a modern society requires that citizens have certain qualities, attitudes, values, habits, and dispositions, which can be inculcated in men by their experience at work in factories. Modern society has been characterized as a "participant" society. It requires of its citizens a readiness for new experience and an acceptance of innovation, a concern with public issues at the community and national levels, a sense of efficacy that encourages and supports programs of social change and the ability to move freely from place to place and to integrate one's self with new co-workers and new neighbors in new living arrangements. A nation can, up to a point, develop industrially and undergo large-scale urbanization without experiencing fundamental changes in the psychology of its population. It will then be a country with a developed sector, but it will not be a truly developed *nation,* much less a modern *society.* If many countries are to avoid the terrible national schizophrenia that affects those nations with a small, modernized sector and a vast hinterland of traditionalism, they must find some way of incorporating and integrating all of their citizens into the modern sector of society. Numerous students have stressed that development is not an automatic process. History is full of dramatic cases of interrupted and arrested development.[5] We believe that this condition is most likely to be produced when the modernization of industry or administration is not accompanied by changes in the mentality, in the attitudes and habits, of the population, which must, after all, operate the new industry and bureaucracy, consume its products, deal with its demands, respond to its appeals, and relate to its style of functioning.

What we wanted, then, was a study of modernization that focussed on the common man—the peasant and the worker newly entering industry. The study should deal with the experience of these men in their encounter with the new institutions of the emerging modern order—the factory, the city, mass media, political parties, large-scale, government bureaucracy. Our study should be conducted in developing countries, in which the process of modernization is most evident and in which the need for modern men is most pressing. To avoid the danger of premature generalizations based on a single combination of special attributes that might be quite fortuitous, we wanted a study conducted not in one but in several, quite different countries. To

5. See, especially, S. N. Eisenstadt, "Breakdown of Modernization," *Economic Development and Culture Change,* 12 (July, 1964), pp. 345–367.

permit us to disentangle the complex web of influences that have been claimed to generate modernity, we felt that our study should not deal with a single source of influence but should precisely control and measure a large set of variables. This type of analysis should be based on large samples purposefully drawn to permit us to give answers to the theoretical and descriptive questions to which our research is addressed. To avoid prejudging, we felt that our research should not be based on a single, simple, and narrow conception of the modern but on a complex, elaborate, and differentiated conception that would permit us to study separately the elements and components of modernity—which, indeed, would permit us to test empirically the very idea of whether or not there is such a thing as a "modern man."

With this set of specifications, we began a large-scale comparative research project in six developing countries—Argentina, Chile, India, Israel, Nigeria, and Pakistan. Of the numerous aspects of the Harvard Project on the Social and Cultural Aspects of Development, I have selected for discussion in this forum what is perhaps the most fundamental issue: How shall we conceive of and measure individual modernization?[6] The form that my answer takes is not so much a discussion of competing strategies as a detailed exposition of one effort to elaborate a complex and reasonably complete model of individual modernity. Even within the course of this single effort, however, three different strategies in fact did compete for our attention and allegiance, so that in discussing this one effort I have a passing opportunity to comment on a number of others. Beyond this, I will take this occasion to indicate some of the forces that we believe generate more modern attitudes and behavior in individuals and to suggest some of the vicissitudes that accompany this process.

Conceptual Model of Individual Modernity

The great danger in any definition of the "modern" is that some more powerful group may arbitrarily impose its own traditional *values* on a less powerful group as if it were bestowing the same benefit

6. The main outlines of the study and the principal findings will be reported in a book to be titled, *Becoming Modern*. Preliminary published reports on some phases of the project may be found in: Alex Inkeles, "The Modernization of Man," in Myron Weiner (ed.), *Modernization* (New York: Basic Books, 1966); and David Smith and Alex Inkeles, "The OM Scale: A Comparative Socio-Psychological Measure of Individual Modernity," *Sociometry*, XXIX (December, 1966), pp. 353–377. Documents describing the sample design and reproducing the questionnaire may be obtained by ordering Document No. 9133, American Documentation Institute.

it confers when it offers a railroad network, a television station, a well-equipped field hospital, or any one of a dozen other so-called miracles of modern technology. Do we not do something peculiar and distorting if we make the American businessman's grey flannel suit more modern than the Indian civil servant's high-necked coat or for that matter his *dhoti*? Isn't it potentially misleading, as well as arbitrary, to treat monogamy as more modern than polygamy? Indeed, are we not presuming a great deal when we consider an Arab chieftain more modern merely because he replaces his camel with a Cadillac or even a small jet plane? The tendency to equate the modern with foreign technology does not prevail only in the West. In the state of Bihar, in India, a man is considered more modern if he believes that food cooked on charcoal tastes better than food cooked on dried cow dung cakes and insists that factory cloth feels better on the skin than homespun cloth. He might be right on both counts, but should we consider him more modern merely because he uses charcoal and factory-spun cloth?

The issues are subtle, complicated, and difficult, and they could occupy us a long time, but if I pursued them all I would never get on to telling how we attempted to resolve the problem in our research. Indeed, I could argue that the position one really takes on these issues is manifested most clearly, not in what one says about them, but rather in the precise way in which one designs his measures of modernity.

In our questionnaire-guided interview, we touched on some thirty different themes and explored each in greater or lesser depth. All of the major themes were examined and tested to assess their relevance for our general research objectives. Some of the themes to which we assigned distinctive status we now view more as merely sub-themes. Other themes, which we earlier did not distinguish with the stamp of a key phrase and code letters, emerged either in our field experience or in the course of our analysis as important and worthy of the status we had assigned to other subjects. We take some pride, however, in the fact that no theme was used in our study unless a substantial theory linked it to modernization, a theory either accepted by us or affirmed by authorities whose standing in the field made testing their ideas important. As I tell our story and present our findings, I believe that it will be apparent that most of our decisions were justified by the outcome of the research.

The thirty-odd themes we explored are not a random list. They have a definite inner structure, a structure derived from the main research objectives of our project. They reflect the interests and ideas of the staff members who joined in this co-operative venture and the theories advanced by leading students of the modernization process. Although each theme could reasonably be explored in its own right, we originally conceived of some of them as holding together in a syndrome, or complex, of attitudes and values that for us constituted the core concept of modernity and the central focus of our research. This sub-set or syndrome of themes constitutes our *analytical model* of individual modernity.

This model did not, however, touch on all the themes that students of modernization have pointed to as major concomitants or effects of the modernization process. Many of these popular ideas were supported by some evidence but warranted further testing, others were virtually untested by empirical field research, and still others we believed were wrong and we wanted to prove them so. This second set of themes was selected on a more eclectic basis. They were not viewed as tied together in a distinctive pattern or syndrome. Each might stand or fall alone without affecting the validity of any other. We refer to them as the *topical themes* on modernization.

Both the analytical model and the topical themes dealt mainly with attitudes and values. We are cognizant of the possibility that a man might think and speak in the modern vein but still *act* in a more traditional way. It could be argued that the ultimate test of the modernization process lies not in its ability to teach a man how to give "modern" answers on a questionnaire, but rather in its ability to produce men who in their everyday lives perform like modern men. We could not assume that the connection between *thinking* modern and *acting* modern was automatic and perfect. Indeed, we had good reason to suppose that it might be tenuous and uncertain. We resolved, therefore, to collect materials that would permit us to judge the modernity of men by their actions rather than their words. This test of individual modernity we called our *behavioral measures*.

Let us now turn to a brief exposition of the theory and the content of each of these three approaches to modernization—the analytic model, the topical themes, and the behavioral measures—as they were actually elaborated in our research.

The Analytic Model

We began with the desire to develop a conception of individual modernity that did not blindly and arbitrarily impose Western customs and Western standards of value on the citizens of developing countries. Attaining a value-free measure of modernity is quite difficult, however. With the exception of Japan—and Russia if you wish to include it with the East—all the major nations we can consider modernized have a European tradition. Thus, it is extremely difficult to disentangle those elements of their social and cultural systems that are distinctive to, and necessary for, the maintenance of a modern society from those that are really "traditional" for these European societies but that have incidentally become associated with, in a sense "dragged along" into, the contemporary era along with the more modern institutions. For example, everyone has noted how the Japanese, and indeed the elites in most of the underdeveloped world, have adopted the Western businessman's suit and his shoes, even though, in fact, this attire is in no way necessary for the running of a modern society.

Our solution to the problem was to avoid an abstract list of values and instead to develop a list of modern qualities that met the demands or requirements of running a factory. We will encounter little argument, we trust, when we propose that the factory is one of the distinctive institutions of modern society. Indeed, industrialization is a very large part of the modernization process. Many would claim that it is the most essential element. Industrialization, in turn, depends on the factory—the large-scale, productive enterprise, bringing together large numbers of men in one work place, systematically ordering their relationship with one another on rational considerations expressed in formal rules, relying on concentrations of inanimate power and the systematic application of technology, and guided by a hierarchy of authority resting largely on technical skill and administrative competence.

The factory as an institution has no nationality; it is not English or French or Dutch or, for that matter, European. It does not violate the important taboos of any religious group, major or minor. There are no proscriptions against entering such a place, or working in such a place, in Islam, Hinduism, or Buddhism, and believers from all these religions have found it easy to take up work in factories. Because almost everyone wants the benefits of industry, taking the factory as the key to modernization minimizes the seeming imposition of alien institutions and their associated customs and values. We proposed, then, to classify as modern those qualities that are likely to be inculcated by participation in large-scale, modern, productive enterprises such as the factory and, perhaps more critical, that may be *required* in the staff if the factory is to operate efficiently and effectively.

There are, of course, many ways of looking at the factory as an institution. We do not claim that our list of qualities and requirements of factory life is exhaustive or even definitive. But each of the themes is important as an attribute of factory life and is, simultaneously, a quality of men that has more general relevance for life in a modern society. We further narrowed the range of themes by focussing particularly on those features of factory organization that we assumed would be notable to and would most influence a naïve worker from the countryside. We justified this approach by our special interest in the factory as a learning setting, as a school in ways of arranging things, of thinking, and of feeling, which contrasts markedly with the traditional village. Men who enter the factory after growing up in an urban setting will, of course, notice much less contrast between the environment in which they grew up and the one they encounter on entering the factory. In either instance, of course, we were assuming that the themes we selected were the most notable and influential. Only our research experience can indicate how accurate our assumption was.

Just how we derived these qualities from a study of factory organization may or may not be readily apparent. Unfortunately, in this report, I must restrict myself to a brief exposition of the qualities we defined as modern within the framework of our analytic model. Since I do not, at this point, offer any particular justification for our choice of themes, let me for present purposes assert that we simply defined the modern man as having these qualities.

Readiness for new experience and *openness to innovation and change* constitute the first elements in our definition of the modern man. We believe that the traditional man is less disposed to accept new ideas, new ways of feeling and acting. We are speaking, therefore, of something that is itself a state of mind, a psychological disposition, an inner readiness, rather than of the specific techniques or skills a man or group may possess because of the level of technology it has attained. Thus, in our sense, a man may be more modern in spirit, even though he works with a wooden plough, than someone who already drives a tractor. The readiness for new experience and ways of doing things, furthermore, may take a variety of different forms and contexts—in the willingness to adopt a new drug or sanitation method, to accept a new seed or adopt a different fertilizer, to ride on a new means of transportation or turn to a new source of information, to approve a new form of wedding ceremony or new type of schooling for young people. Individuals and groups may, of course, show more readiness for the new in one area of life than another, but we can also conceive of the readiness to accept innovations as a pervasive, general characteristic that makes itself felt across a wide variety of human situations. And we consider those who have this readiness to be more modern. Representative of the questions intended to tap readiness for new experience is the following:

> Suppose you could get along well enough where you are now, earning enough to provide food and other necessities for yourself and your family. Would you be willing to move to another place far from here where the language and other customs are different if *there* you could live twice as well as here?

Our assumption, of course, was that people open to new experience might more readily respond to the opportunity we described. In this example, the readiness to move might, naturally, be tempered both by the amount of economic pinch the man felt and by the importance to him of improving his standard of living. No question, however, is entirely unambiguous or uni-dimensional, and some of the most interesting problems in analysis come from disentangling the diverse motivational forces that may come to bear on an individual's answer to any one question.

The realm of the *growth of opinion* represents the second in our complex of themes. This area is itself divisible into a number of sub-themes or scale areas. We define a man as more modern if he has a *disposition to form or hold opinions* over a large number of the problems and issues that arise not only in his immediate environment but also outside it. Pioneering work on this dimension has been done by Daniel Lerner of the Massachusetts Institute of Technology and was reported in his book, *The Passing of Traditional Society.* Lerner showed that in the Middle East the individuals within any country, and the populations of different countries, varied greatly in their ability or readiness to imagine themselves as the prime minister or comparable government leader and thus to offer advice as to what should be done to resolve the problems facing the country. The more educated the individual and the more advanced the country, the greater was the readiness to offer opinions in response to this challenge. The more traditional man, we believe, takes an interest in fewer situations and events, mainly those that touch him immediately and intimately, and, even when he holds opinions on more distant matters, he is more circumspect in expressing such opinions.

We assessed the individual's readiness to hold opinions on a wide range of subjects and issues by a series of different measures. A crude indicator was the number of times he responded to our questions by saying, "I don't know," or "I never thought about that." More informative were our evaluations of the number and themes of his replies to questions about the most serious problems facing his nation, his local community, and his family.

We also consider a man to be more modern if his orientation to the opinion realm is more democratic. Here, we mean that he shows more *awareness of the diversity of attitude and opinion around him,* rather than closing himself off in the belief that everyone thinks alike and indeed just as he does. In our conception, a modern man is able to acknowledge differences of opinion; he has no need rigidly to deny differences out of the fear that they will upset his own view of the world. He is also less likely to approach opinion in a strictly autocratic or hierarchical way. He does not automatically accept the ideas of those above him in the power hierarchy or reject the opinions of those whose status is markedly lower than his. In other words, *he puts a positive value on variations in opinion.* We tested these values by asking people whether it is proper to think differently from the village headman or other traditional leader and, also, by asking whether the opinions of a man's wife or young son merit serious consideration when important public issues are being discussed. These questions proved to be a sensitive indicator in helping us to distinguish one man from another and, we believe, will be an important element in the final syndrome of modernity we will delineate.

Intimately related to our study of opinion but conceived as a separate dimension were our measures of *information.* We consider that being modern means not merely having opinions but being more energetic in acquiring facts and information on which to base those opinions. It is one thing to opine that capitalists are bad when you are explicitly asked your opinion, another to know actually what and where are Moscow and Washington.

Time is a third theme our measures deal with at some length. We view a man as more modern if he is oriented to the present or the future rather than to the past. We consider him more modern if he accepts fixed hours, that is to say, schedules, as something sensible and appropriate, or possibly even desirable, as against the men who think that fixed rules are something either bad or perhaps a necessity but unfortunately also a pity. We also define a man as more modern if he is punctual, regular, and orderly in organizing his affairs.

The relationship of this orientation to time to measures of modernity is a complex issue and presents me with an opportunity to point out that it is a mistake to assume that our measures of modernity differentiate between traditional and non-traditional people as they would ordinarily be defined. For example, we believe that the Maya Indians had a better sense of time than their Spanish rulers, and they preserve it to this day. The qualities we define as modern can, in fact, be manifested in a people who seem to be relatively unmodern when you consider the level of technology or the amount of power they have. We are talking about properties of the person, which, in turn, may be a reflection of the properties of a culture that could emerge in any time or place. That these qualities may be more widely diffused in industrially advanced countries does not make them a monopoly of those national groups.

Efficacy is a fourth theme, one that is especially important in our conception of the modern man. The modern individual believes that, to a substantial degree, man can learn to dominate his environment in order to advance his own purposes and goals, rather than being dominated entirely by that environment. For example, a man who feels efficacious is more likely to respond positively to the question, "Do you believe that some day men will fully understand what causes such things as floods, droughts, and epidemics?" The more efficacious man, even though in fact he has never seen a dam, would, we believe, say, "Yes, I think that some day man will do that."

The sense of efficacy is, of course, not limited to feelings concerning man's potential mastery over nature. It includes, as well, the belief that one can effectively do something if officials are proposing what one considers to be a bad law, that care will help prevent accidents, that human nature can be changed, and that men can arrange their affairs so that even nations can live in peace. His sense of efficacy, then, expresses the modern man's confidence in his ability, alone and in concert with other men, to organize his life to master the challenges it presents at the personal, the interpersonal, the communal, the national, and the international levels.

Planning is a theme closely related to efficacy, but we initially conceived of it as important in its own right. We consider a man more modern if he is oriented toward planning and organizing affairs and believes in planning as an approach both to public affairs and to his own personal life. We asked such questions about public affairs as: "What does the country need most: hard work by the people, the help of God, or a good plan on the part of the government?" And to assess thoughts about the more private, personal realm, we asked: "Some say that a boy should be taught to handle things as they come up without bothering much about thinking ahead. Others say that a boy must be taught to plan and arrange things in advance. What do you think?"

Calculability (or *trust*). By our definition, the modern man is one who has confidence that his world is calculable, that other people and institutions around him can be relied upon to fulfill or meet their obligations and responsibilities. He is more prepared to trust a stranger than is the traditional man. He does not agree that everything is determined either by fate or by the whims and particular qualities and characters of men. In other words, he believes in a reasonably lawful world under human control. This, therefore, is a theme we might also expect to find closely related to the sense of efficacy.

Distributive justice, especially with regard to technical skill, provides the seventh theme in our set. One of the central principles of modern organization is that rewards should be proportionate to skill and measured contribution to the purposes of the organization.

Exceptions to this rule are, of course, ubiquitous in modern society, but even so the principle is much more emphasized and practiced in such settings than in most traditional orders where rewards are more determined by power, by special status, or haphazardly, by the pleasure of those who control the distribution of benefits. The beliefs that rewards should be according to rule rather than whim and that the structure of rewards should, insofar as possible, be in accord with skill and relative contribution are what we call the sense of distributive justice. As thus formulated, the principle has its most obvious application to work in organizations such as factories or office bureaucracies. When applied to other roles such as that of a customer dealing with a merchant or a citizen dealing with an official the principle is often referred to as the principle of *universalistic,* as against *particularistic,* treatment.

Our chief measure of the sense of distributive justice is derived from a set of questions in which we first set the ordinary worker's pay as a standard (say, of 100 rupees per month) and then asked what should be the *relative* pay of a foreman, an engineer, a factory manager, and several professional workers such as a doctor and a school teacher. To assess attitudes about particularism we also added, in some countries, a few questions on special treatment; we asked, for example, whether our respondents thought it good or bad that people having business at a public office would first seek out a friend or acquaintance with connections before going to transact that business.

Aspirations, education, and the new learning. Each culture has a traditional wisdom, which is most widely diffused among and most strongly believed in by the peasantry and others who make up the common folk. In these settings, what formal schooling exists is often used for purposes of religious education and is devoted to inculcating and preserving traditional values. The secular school and the new learning, which we in the more developed countries take so much for granted, are radical innovations in many of the developing countries. The subjects taught and the values disseminated often compete with, may indeed challenge and contradict, the traditional wisdom. We defined the more modern man as having an interest in and placing higher value on formal education and schooling in skills such as reading and writing and arithmetic. He feels that modern learning and even science are not intrusions into a sacred realm, which should be left a mystery or approached only through religion, but rather that science and technology will benefit mankind by providing solutions to pressing human problems. We measured attitudes in this realm by asking how much schooling a man should try to get for his son if costs were no obstacle, whether schools should more teach morality and religion or the practical skills, and what the father prefers for his son's future occupation.

Awareness of, and respect for, the *dignity* of others is a quality many people feel has been lost in the modern world. If we wanted to make a judgment as to whether this quality was, in fact, more deeply instilled and more widely distributed in traditional societies, a great deal would clearly depend on which traditional society we used as a standard of comparison. Many intellectuals are firmly convinced that *all* men enjoyed greater personal dignity, even if they consumed fewer goods, when they lived in the pre-industrial, pre-urban age. We are not persuaded that this dictum is true. Indeed, in our study, we adopted the rather radical position that the factory may be a training ground that inculcates a greater sense of awareness of the dignity of subordinates and restraint in one's dealings with them. We feel that the manager in a factory is more obliged to respect the dignity of a worker than is the owner, boss, chief, or patron in his relationship to the peasant in the most traditional villages. Indeed, we expect that the modern man not only will be more protective of the dignity of weaker and subordinate persons in the work settings, but will extend the principle to other relationships and thus will manifest such behavior in his treatment of all those inferior in status and power, such as women and children. Thus, we asked:

"Which of the following is more correct, regarding a boy's dignity: Is it less important than a man's, as important, or more important?"

The Analytic Model and the Modern Man

Taken together, this set of ten to a dozen themes constitutes our analytic model of the modern man. In contrast to the common man of traditional society, a modern man accepts innovation and change, is open to new experience for himself and those around him. He expresses this openness, in part, by valuing formal schooling and believing in the potential benefit of scientific and technological experimentation and exploration. He also expresses his openness by taking an interest in external affairs, seeking new sources of information about all manner of things including public events that do not necessarily touch his immediate life. His involvement and participation in the wider world is reflected in his holding opinions over a wide range of issues, in his awareness of the diversity of opinion of those in his environment, in his tolerance for differing opinions, and in his respect for the right to an opinion by those weaker and less prestigious than he is. The more modern man has a greater sense of efficacy. He feels less dominated by fate and is more convinced that man, by his own efforts and by combining his efforts with others', can organize to master nature and arrange social affairs to assure mankind a reasonable degree of security from calamity, conflict, disease, and hunger. This sense of efficacy rests, in part, on a feeling of confidence or trust in his associates, a sense of the calculability of organizations, superiors, co-workers, and subordinates, and of the reasonable certainty that they will fulfill their obligations to him. The feeling assures him of the support he requires for performing his share of the common task. Planning is for him a highly valued way of attaining both his personal goals and the collective tasks in which he participates. Intimately associated with this value is a strict sense of time and an insistence on the importance of the careful scheduling of events. The modern man expects to receive rewards in accord with his skill and his relative contribution to the common effort. For his part, he acknowledges the value of education and technical skill and is prepared to see them rewarded proportionately. But he feels that these rewards should be part of a formal system, governed by rules universally applied and not restricted to particular individuals and special circumstances according to accident or the whims of the powerful. Correspondingly, in his treatment of others, especially those weaker or less important than he, he is aware of, and avoids diminishing, the sense of dignity and personal worth of those under his care or control.

Any such list of characteristics conceived to represent a social type raises a host of issues. In certain ways the whole of our research effort is meant to deal with those issues. But a few matters must perhaps be dealt with individually.

To begin, let me acknowledge that our formulation of the dimensions of modernity, in fact, the very dimensions we have selected, is, necessarily, somewhat arbitrary. Thus, we are quite ready to acknowledge that the theme of calculability might better be expressed as trust; indeed, the items by which we measure calculability suggest as much. Furthermore, the logical and empirical distinctiveness of some of the dimensions we have defined separately is certainly open to question. It is not at all obvious, for example, that openness to new experience and the ready acceptance of change should be treated as separate dimensions. Equally, it might be argued that the sense of efficacy and the belief in planning both are facets of one more general underlying dimension. To a certain extent we ourselves held this belief from the beginning, but it seemed wiser initially not to prejudge such questions. To an important degree our research is intended to test the extent to which these, and others, *are* really distinctive dimensions. To maintain them apart initially in no way impaired our ability to join them later. In making such combinations, wholly different themes might well be introduced. Ever since Weber wrote *The Protestant Ethic,* "rationality" has been popular in discussions of modernization, and some of our items might be approached in terms of this concept. Similarly, many of them could be re-combined under the general rubric of "changed orientations to authority," which Bellah sees as one of the key elements in attitudinal modernization. But one must begin somewhere, with some distinctions, with some selection of the elements one conceives as making up modernity. No harm is done so long as we all recognize that this is a definitional statement, an analytic model to be tested, and not a dogmatic assertion that the elements we have designated are absolute, exact, and the only elements that could reasonably enter into a definition of modernity of attitude.

However clear and appropriate our *conception* of any dimension of modernity, our effort to *measure* it may be inadequate. Thus, it may be quite sound to consider the readiness for new experience characteristic of modern men. But asking a man if he would move to a strange land may not be much of a test of his openness to new experience. Although we were quite confident that, for the example of new experience, we had found the key to effective question wording, in other instances, such as time orientation and dignity, we were much less confident. Unfortunately, if a given dimension proves unrelated to modernity, we have no absolute test to tell us whether it is really so, despite our assumption to the contrary, or whether the apparent lack of association is derived from the awkwardness or inappropriateness of the questions we asked. Where we fail to find an association we can only try as honestly as possible to assess the adequacy of our questions, as such, area by area.

Although we may be correct in our assumptions about some of the dimensions we have selected for study, we may still be wrong in our most fundamental assumption that all the dimensions relate to each other as a syndrome of characteristics we can sensibly label *"modern man."* The sense of efficacy may indeed be something that distinguishes one person from another, and we may have succeeded in measuring it with a fine degree of precision. The same may be true of openness to new experience and respect for the dignity of subordinates. But it does not automatically follow that men who have a high sense of efficacy also are ready for new experience, or, even if they are, that they also are careful not to humiliate those weaker than they are. One of the fundamental assumptions of our research is that these qualities do indeed cohere, that they are a syndrome, that people who have one trait will also manifest others. In other words, we believe that we may speak not only of men who have one or another modern *characteristic,* but of men who may meaningfully be described in their wholeness as *modern men.* But we must acknowledge that the existence of this type of man is only an assumption, to be tested against the evidence. Moreover, to follow our study with interest, one need not necessarily accept either the general idea of a composite "modern man," nor each element in our list of dimensions without exception. Even if there is no effective syndrome, it may be important to discover who are the men with higher educational aspirations or a stricter sense of time and to learn what are the forces that gave them *these* more limited characteristics.

Alternatively, one may quite properly accept the idea that there is indeed a syndrome of attitudes that holds together but reject the assumption that some particular dimension is really a distinctive part of it. We have, for example, already mentioned the widespread belief—not unshared among the staff of our project—that modern man has less rather than more sensitivity to and respect for the dignity of others than did the traditional villager. Similar doubts might be held about the sense of time and the interest in planning. After all, to run a family farm takes a rigorous sense of time, and the farmer who doesn't plan ahead is likely to find himself far behind at harvest time. By contrast, the factory worker is paced more by the factory whistle and the rhythm of the machine or assembly line, and he can leave most of the planning of his work to the foreman and the engineer. It might then be that openness to new experience and a sense of efficacy go together and are found more among urban industrial workers, whereas a strong sense of time and high value on planning also go together but are more commonly values strongly held by peasants.

Finally, we must consider the relationship of our analytic model of modernity to other conceptions. Of course we are proud of such originality as our conception may display, but many of the other models of modern man that have been proposed in the recent past seem to have many elements in common with ours. We have already noted Lerner's interest in the opinion realm, which he expressed in the concept of empathy, or the "ability to see oneself in the other fellow's situation." He also proposed that a mobile society "has to encourage rationality," and in it "people come to see the future as manipulable rather than ordained and their personal prospects in terms of achievement rather than heritage."[7] We can recognize here much the same emphasis as that contained in our concepts of efficacy and our theme of aspirations and technical skill. Further, Lerner speaks of the mobile person as "distinguished by a high capacity for identification with new aspects of his environment; he comes equipped with the mechanisms needed to incorporate new demands upon himself that arise outside of his habitual experience."[8] Again, the strong resemblance of this idea to our concept of openness to new experience and readiness for change is apparent.

Similar parallels can be observed between elements in our conception of modernity and those proposed by several others. Robert Ward, for example, in his *Political Modernization in Japan and Turkey*, presents a list of eight features of what he calls "intellectual modernization"; and among them are items very similar to our themes of aspirations for new learning, acceptance of change, dignity, and growth of opinion. Ithiel Pool also defines the modern not in terms of GNP nor

7. Daniel Lerner, *The Passing of Traditional Society* (Glencoe: The Free Press, 1958), p. 48.
8. *Ibid.*, p. 49.

the proportion of the labor force in industry, but "rather in terms of values and modes of behavior" shared by a population. Among the values and ways of acting he describes as modern are elements closely akin to our themes of efficacy, aspirations, and openness to new experience.[9] Wilbert Moore lists among the more "specific values and principles of conduct appropriate to modernization" rationality in problem solving, punctuality, recognition of individually limited but systematically linked interdependence, and achievement and mobility aspirations, each of which is easily translated into the language of our list of themes.[10] Indeed, we can find similar themes delineated in work as far afield and as far back as the classical economic writings of the late nineteenth century. Thus, Alfred Marshall asserted that there were qualities that make a great industrial people and are wanted not in any occupation, but in all, such as: "To have everything ready when wanted, to act promptly and show resource when anything goes wrong, [and] to accommodate oneself quickly to changes of detail in the work done. . . ."[11]

In the light of this evidence we can hardly argue that our analytic model of modernization is bizarre or even terribly unorthodox. Although derived by a different process and following its own path from an initial concern with the factory as an organization, our analytic model includes many elements in common with those of other students of modernization who began from other starting points and were guided by different theoretical concerns. Our list is certainly more ramified than most, and our research does, perhaps, give greater emphasis to certain themes, such as the sense of efficacy or the openness to new experience. Nevertheless, the lists are basically similar. We are perhaps somewhat different in our insistence that the elements of the model hold together as a coherent *syndrome* of modern attitudes, but this idea is also implicit in the approaches of many of the scholars who have thought extensively about individual modernization. The basic distinction, therefore, is that we have not been content only to define the qualities of modern man. We have gone beyond this idea to render our definition operational by converting it into a set

9. Ithiel De Sola Pool, "The Role of Communication in the Process of Modernization and Technological Change," in Bert F. Hoselitz and W. E. Moore (eds.), *Industrialization and Society* (Paris: UNESCO, 1963), pp. 275–293.

10. Wilbert E. Moore, "The Strategy of Fostering Performance and Responsibility," in Egbert de Vries and J. M. Echavarria (eds.), *Social Aspects of Economic Development in Latin America*, Vol. I (Medina: UNESCO, 1963).

11. Alfred Marshall, *Principles of Economics*, 8th ed. (London: Macmillan & Co., 1946). pp. 206–207.

of specific measures. And we have gone further still in subjecting our ideas to an empirical test in several different cultures simultaneously to ascertain how far men in nature do approximate our model of the modern man and to determine the forces that make men modern.

The Topical Model

The analytic model of the modern man was derived primarily from a theoretical consideration of the requirements of factory life. The components were selected because they were assumed to cohere as a psychological syndrome. While not arbitrary, such a conception is clearly limited and highly selective. Scholars studying the modernization process as it involves the individual often point to quite a few other problems as central issues. Some of these factors are identified as pre-conditions of modernization; that is, the assumption is made that, unless these issues can be resolved, a society's successful attainment of modernization will remain highly problematic. Others are identified as the accompaniments or consequences of modernization, the price, in a sense, that people pay for obtaining the benefits, such as they are, of entering the modern world. Each problem has its own sponsors, as it were, men who have particularly devoted their energies to its explication and investigation. In some instances their argument rests on a good deal of evidence; in others it is merely an assertion of opinion, however plausible.

Some of these problems were of special interest to one or more members of our research team, and to satisfy their interest we undertook to study them. Others, less interesting to us, still seemed issues of recognized importance sufficient to impose on us an obligation to include them in our research. We would thus provide further information, from *new* settings, that could be brought to bear on the standard issues of modernization research. Some of these problems had previously been studied in relative isolation, whereas our research provided an opportunity to relate them one to the other. There was finally a third set of issues about which we felt that either popular thought or expert opinion was in error, and we took the opportunity to see if evidence would support or disprove the opinion.

Because each of these problems was treated by itself, and because the set as a whole was not derived from any common conception or unified theory, we called the set our "topical model" of modernization. This part of our study dealt with about ten major areas, several of which were further divided into major sub-themes.

Kinship and Family

With the possible exception of religion, no institution of society is more often depicted as either an obstacle to or a victim of modernization than is the extended structure of kinship. Wilbert Moore sums up the prevailing opinion when he says: "In general, the traditional kinship structure provides a barrier to industrial development, since it encourages reliance of the individual upon its security rather than upon his own devices."[12] The image of these family ties as a *victim* of the modernization process is well presented in M. B. Deshmukh's report on the migrant communities in Delhi, where Deshmukh observed, "The absence of social belonging, the pressure of poverty, and the evil effects of the urban environment made . . . the family bonds, regarded to be so sacred in the villages, . . . of absolutely no importance" in the migrant colonies.[13]

After reviewing the question we concluded that there was certainly some truth to the frequent assertion that increasing urbanism and industrialism did tend to diminish the vigor of extended kinship relations. Examples of societies that emphasize extended kinship ties would be those with a strong clan system, as in China, or those in which life is organized around a kin-based compound community or a multi-generation, extended family such as the famous Zadruga of Yugoslavia, in which all the brothers, their wives, and their children occupied a common household, worked common land, and shared more or less equally in the benefits of their cooperative economy. We had little reason to doubt that, when urbanism increased the physical distance between kin and industrial employment decreased their economic dependence, the strength of kinship ties as manifested in common residence, frequent visiting, and mutual help in work would decline. A series of our questions inquiring about residence, visiting patterns, mutual help, and the like was designed to test whether these assumptions were true.

While ready to follow popular assumptions up to a point, we also came to the rather radical conclusion that in some ways industrial employment might actually *strengthen* family ties.[14] We felt that many of the common assertions about the family and modernization were

---

12. Wilbert E. Moore, *Industrialization and Labor* (Ithaca: Cornell University Press, 1951), p. 79.

13. M. B. Deshmukh, "Delhi: A Study of a Floating Migration," in *The Social Implication of Industrialization and Urbanization* (Calcutta: UNESCO Research Center on the Social Implication of Industrialization in Southern Asia, 1956).

14. The stability of the family, and even of more traditional family ties, under conditions of urbanization and industrialization has been noted, among others, by Lewis for Mexico, Lambert

much too sweeping and general, that they combined the extended and the immediate family, and that they failed to discriminate between degrees and types of kinship relatedness. It could well be, for example, that, while the experience of modernization weakened *extended* family ties, it would strengthen those to a man's family of *procreation* and would lead him to cling less to his mother and cleave more to his wife.[15] Again, it might be that, while a man gave less attention to his more extended kinship ties after moving to the city, the increased stability and improved well-being that characterize his life as an industrial worker might lead him to accept more fully some of his kinship obligations, at least as compared with his less secure and more impoverished brother still earning his living as a peasant in the village. We tested these relationships with a set of questions on kinship obligations, such as:

> Suppose a young man works in a factory. He has barely managed to save a very small amount of money. Now his relative [selected appropriately for each country, such as a distant cousin] comes to him and tells him he needs money badly since he has no work at all. How much obligation do you think the factory worker has to share his savings with this relative?

Women's Rights

Intimately related to the changing pattern of family relations, but broader than it, is the question of the status of women in society. Most of the traditional societies and communities of the world are, if not strictly patriarchal, at least vigorously male-dominated. The extreme example, perhaps, is found in the Islamic religion, in which a man each day says a prayer of thanks to God for not having made him a woman.

We predicted that the liberating influence of the forces making for modernization would act on men's attitudes and incline them to accord to women status and rights more nearly equal to those

for India, and Husain for Pakistan. See Oscar Lewis, "Urbanization without Breakdown: A Case Study," *Scientific Monthly*, LXXV, No. 1 (July, 1952), pp. 31–42; Richard D. Lambert, *Workers, Factories, and Social Changes in India* (Princeton: Princeton University Press, 1963); and A. F. A. Husain, "Dacca, Human and Social Impact of Technological Change in East Pakistan," in *The Social Implications of Industrialization and Urbanization* (Calcutta: UNESCO, 1963).

15. This idea is in line with the main conclusion of Goode's world-wide survey of changing family patterns. Goode notes that the ubiquitous accompaniment of industrialization appears to be the weakening of extended kinship ties, a dissolution of lineage patterns, and a strengthening of the nuclear family. See William J. Goode, *World Revolution and Family Patterns* (Glencoe: The Free Press, 1963).

enjoyed by men. We tested the men's orientation through questions on a woman's right to work and to equal pay, to hold public office, and to freely choose her marriage partner.

Birth Control

Few points about the contemporary world have been better documented than the fact that in many under-developed countries population is increasing so rapidly as to equal and sometimes exceed the rate at which the supply of food and other necessities increases. Despite an annual growth rate of some three percent per year in per capita gross national product, some of these countries are either standing still or even falling constantly behind in the standard of welfare they provide for the population and in the general development of their economy. One solution obvious to almost everyone is to reduce the number of children born to the average family. Although birth control depends in great measure on scientific technology and on particular practices guided by that technology, even the most spectacular advances in science, such as the new contraceptive pills, cannot have the desired effect except as they may be supported by the motive to use them and by patterns of interpersonal relations that make that motivation effective. To assess attitudes in this area, therefore, we inquired into our respondents' ideas of the ideal number of children and into their readiness to restrict that number under various conditions.

Religion

Religion ranks with the extended family as the institution most often identified as both an obstacle to economic development and a victim of the same process. The classic case of resistance is that of the Asian religions, and many studies going back to Max Weber's have noted that religion is a major obstacle to modernization because it is the bulwark of nationalism and a repository of beliefs and values incompatible with modern science, technology, and the idea of progress.[16]

Many students of the subject argue rather vigorously that the individual's adherence both to the fundamental doctrine of his tradi-

---

16. Milton Singer, "The Modernization of Religious Beliefs," in Myron Weiner (ed.), *Modernization*, pp. 55–67.

tional religion and to the religious ritual and practice it requires of him will be inevitably undermined by urban living, industrial experience, and scientific education. Thus, speaking about West Africa, Dr. Geoffrey Parrinder notes: "It is sometimes said that Africans are incurably religious. . . . But the ancient religious beliefs cannot stand the strain of modern urban and industrial life. . . . [They] have been attacked by what someone has called 'the acids of modernity'."[17]

Systematic evidence for this proposition is, however, much less ample than one might imagine. We thought it appropriate, therefore, to attempt to ascertain the facts by asking a series of questions designed to measure religiosity and secularism, and we inquired into such matters as the role of God in causing and curing sickness and accidents and the contribution of a holy man, as against a great industrialist, to the welfare of his people. We also took note of the regularity with which our subjects prayed or otherwise fulfilled the formal ritualistic prescriptions and proscriptions of their religion.

We were prepared to find that the influences assumed to make for attitudinal modernity in general would also lead to greater secularism, that is, rising education, urbanism, and industrial experience would all lead to greater secularism, more faith in science and other remedies, and less reliance on religion. Yet we also made the less conventional assumption that the fulfillment of religious obligations *in practice,* especially in ritual, might actually increase as peasants shifted from their life as farmers in the village to workers in urban industry. As with the fulfillment of kinship obligations, we reasoned that the poor, harassed peasant would often lack the funds to pay for special religious services and would have neither time nor energy to undertake many of his ritualistic obligations, especially as the lack of local facilities might increase the trouble to which he must go in order to do so. We concluded, therefore, that, in the city, with religious facilities often more numerous and easily accessible and income steadier and more substantial, the industrial worker might find it less a burden to pay for the services his religion might require.

The Aged

The special role of the aged is intimately linked to the strength of the family and the vigor of religion in most traditional settings. The respect, indeed the veneration, shown for the aged is often con-

17. Geoffrey Parrinder, "Religion in Village and Town," in [*Proceedings of the*] *Annual Conference, Sociology Section* (Ibadan, Nigeria: West African Institute of Social and Economic Research, University College, 1953).

sidered one of the most distinctive marks, as well as one of the outstanding virtues, of the traditional society. It is widely believed that two
of the most common, indeed almost inevitable, concomitants of industrialization, urbanization, and modernization in general are an eroding
of the respect for the aged and the fostering of a youth culture in
which old age is viewed not as a venerable state to which one looks
forward, but rather as a dreadful condition to be approached with
reluctance, even horror.

On this issue of age, as on the family and religion issues, we
were not inclined to follow automatically the dominant opinion. It
seemed clear that the structural changes accompanying modernization
must certainly undercut the special position of the aged. In an era
of technological revolutions, for example, it would be hard for the
village elder relying on his long personal experience to preserve his
authority indefinitely in competition with the agricultural expert relying on the latest scientific advances. As young people come to earn
their own living in factories and shops without dependence on their
father's land or animals, it seems inevitable that the father's authority
over them should be lessened. The mass media and other models
of new and competing styles of life should, in turn, make it difficult
for the elders authoritatively to enforce the old norms and ways of
doing things.

Yet we also felt that many analysts had perhaps exaggerated
the corrosive effects of industrialism on the treatment of the aged.
Nothing in urban living *per se* requires a person to show disrespect
for the aged, and nothing in industrial experience explicitly teaches
a man to abandon the aged. Many an old man and woman in the
villages have been abandoned by their children because the children
lacked the means to support them. Steadier wages and generally more
stable conditions of life for those gainfully employed in industry could
well enable those who enjoyed these benefits to be more exacting
in their fulfillment of obligations to old people. And they might well
be as respectful of the aged as their more traditional counterparts
farming in the villages.

Politics

Political modernization has been cited by many scholars as an
indispensable condition of the modernization of economy and
society.[18] To characterize the citizen of a modern polity the word

18. Lucian W. Pye, "Introduction," in L. W. Pye and S. Verba (eds.), *Political Culture and Political
Development* (Princeton: Princeton University Press, 1965).

"participant" is often used, as is the word "mobilized." There is an expectation that the citizen of a modern polity will take an active interest not only in those matters that touch his immediate life, but also in the larger issues facing his community. His allegiance is supposed to extend beyond his family and friends to the state and the nation and its leaders. He is expected to join political parties, to support candidates, and to vote in elections.

Our study was not designed to answer the question of whether or not a society could modernize its economy and still manage with a traditional political system. Nor is it appropriate for testing how far modern political institutions can operate effectively unless the citizens are also "participant" and "mobilized." But we were in a position to say how far men who were otherwise modern in their attitudes and values would also be modern in their orientation to politics. And the design of our study gave us an unusual opportunity to understand the social forces that generate in men those qualities the sociological studies of politics have identified as necessary or desirable in the citizens of a modern polity. We therefore added a large number of questions, in some countries as many as fifty, that permitted us to assess the politically specific and politically related attitudes of the subjects of our research. We included questions on political participation, attitudes toward politicians and the political process, evaluations of the effectiveness of the government, and levels of political knowledge and information.

Information Media

Just as the wearing of a watch is often the first dramatic sign of a man's commitment to the modern world, the acquisition of a radio may be the act that really incorporates him into that world. In his study of modernization in the Middle East, Daniel Lerner treats the way in which people accept the mass media as one of the key elements in his classification of them as traditional, transitional, or modern. Indeed, he holds that "no modern society functions efficiently without a developed system of mass communication."[19] The model of modernization, he claims:

> exhibits certain components and sequences whose relevance is global. Everywhere, rising literacy has tended to increase media exposure; increasing media exposure has "gone with" wider economic participation (per capita income) and political participation (voting).... That ... same

19. Daniel Lerner, *The Passing of Traditional Society*, p. 55.

basic model reappears in virtually all modernizing societies on all continents of the world. . . .[20]

Because other students of modernization, such as Ithiel Pool and Karl Deutsch, give heavy emphasis to mass communications as one of the key issues in the modernization process, we felt obliged to include it as one of the themes in the topical model. Our working assumption was that a modern man would more often expose himself to the media of mass communication—newspaper, radio, movies, and, where available, television. We considered it much more problematic that he would thereby shun the more traditional sources of information and advice such as village elders, traditional political leaders, or religious functionaries. Experience in research on communications behavior suggested that those who were very active in establishing contact with some sources of information tended to be outstanding in the frequency of their contact with *all* sources, modern and traditional. We were quite strongly convinced, however, that, when it came to *evaluating* the different sources of information, the more modern men would have greater confidence in and rely most heavily on the newer mass media, whereas the less modern would rely more on the more traditional sources. Indeed, we expected that the most traditional would look on the new-fangled mass media, such as the movies, as possibly dangerous and harmful to the morals of the young.

Consumption

His role as a consumer is one of the most problematic aspects of the life of a citizen in a developing country. On the one hand, we hear repeatedly that economic development is impossible unless the great bulk of the population enters the money economy and begins to demand and buy modern items of mass consumption. Otherwise, the argument runs, the market for goods is too small to support national industries that can operate profitably, the circulation of money is too weak to satisfy the requirements of a modern monetary system, the base of the tax system is too narrow, and so on. On the other hand, we so often encounter the phenomenon of an alleged run-away inflation, presumably created by an uncontrolled demand for consumer goods that far outstrips the capacity to produce and, much more serious, far exceeds the growth in wealth and productivity. The result is that national outlays exceed national income by excessive

20. *Ibid.*, p. 46.

amounts. To the extent that these outlays are for consumption rather than for investment in future production, deficit financing and mounting inflation follow each other in a vicious circle, economic stability is undermined, further investment is hindered, and economic stagnation or even retrogression must follow.

Economists can perhaps suggest some ways of resolving the apparent contradiction between these two models of development. For our part, we found ourselves reluctant to decide whether we should consider as more modern the man who believes mainly in savings or the man who believes that one should spend his newly-acquired income in obtaining beds, sewing machines, radios, bicycles, or whatever are, for his country, the most desired and reasonably accessible of the new goods of modern mass production. In the end, we came down on the side of spending. We predicted that the less modern man would be guided by his tradition and encouraged by his circumstance to consider frugality a virtue and the chasing after goods a frivolous and perhaps even slightly immoral preoccupation. By contrast, we expected the stimulus of the city and work in industry to persuade men that there was a plenitude of goods in the world for all to have. We also anticipated that his firmer financial position plus, perhaps, easier access to credit would stimulate the urban worker to affirm the rightness of a consumption ethic. Through various questions we solicited information about the goods a man owned and would like to own, and we sought his views on frugality and liberal spending.

Social Stratification

Traditional societies are generally defined as having closed class systems, in the extreme, possessed of a rigid caste structure. Mobility is minimal, men are born into the positions in which they will die, and sons succeed their fathers generation after generation. Status and prestige are assigned mainly on the basis of long-established, hereditary, family connections. Authority is feared and respected, often held in awe, and treated with an elaborate show of submission and deference. In an open, modern society, all of these features of stratification are supposed to be quite different. Along with the changed social structure, attitudes and values about stratification are expected to change significantly. Prestige comes to be assigned more on the basis of education and technical skill, and the belief that mobility is possible for one's self and especially for one's children becomes widespread. The move to industrial labor or white collar work is perceived by most who experience it as an improvement of their social standing. They come to feel more a part of society, citizens on an equal footing with others in the national polity. To test how far such patterns of change were being experienced in the countries we studied and to assess the relationship of changed attitudes about stratification and social classes to modernizing influences and to modern attitudes in other areas, we asked a series of questions dealing with the attitudes and experiences relating to social class and to social mobility.

Psychic Adjustment

No belief is more widespread among critics of industrialization than the conviction that industrialization disrupts basic social ties, breaks down social controls, and therefore produces a train of personal disorientation, confusion, and uncertainty, which ultimately leads to misery and even mental breakdown among those who are "uprooted" from the farm and "herded" into the great industrial cities. The anthropologist Slotkin has stated:

> No matter how compatible industrialism may seem to be, since industrialism is usually a fundamental innovation, it and its ramifications tend to produce cultural disorganization. . . . Is forced rapid industrialization worth the severe cultural disorganization it usually entails, and its attendant social and personal maladjustment? Or is it more important to maintain cultural organization, conserving social and personal adjustment?[21]

We could not accept the assumptions that underlie this statement. It was our impression that in many traditional villages the strains of making a living, indeed of merely staying alive, were often enormous, as they certainly are in many parts of India and Pakistan, and for the hired hands who do most of the agricultural work on the large and nearly feudal Chilean hacienda, or *fundo,* as they call it. A fresh reading of many field studies and literary accounts of village life revealed jealousies, betrayal, exploitation, conflict, and hatred, which we could hardly see as inevitably conducing to good adjustment and sound mental health. By contrast, we noted that the shift to industrial work often seemed to guarantee more income and greater security. Opportunities for self-expression and advancement, and increments of status and prestige, often accompanied the move to the cities, and we felt that they would actually conduce to greater

21. J. S. Slotkin, *From Field to Factory* (Glencoe: The Free Press, 1960), p. 31.

mental health among industrial workers, even in the sometimes chaotic setting of developing countries. We gained confidence in this rather radical position from the evidence of numerous studies on the relationship of mental health to occupation and status in the more advanced countries. These studies rather consistently showed an inverse relationship between mental illness and status in society as well as status *within* industrial organizations. In other words, those higher in skill and income generally had better mental health.

There seemed good reason to evaluate the move from farm to city work, and the move from new worker to experienced worker, as improvements in status. It was reasonable, therefore, to assume that in developing countries the experienced worker well integrated into the industrial system might be *better* adjusted than one still on the farm. This proposition could be entertained without denying the possibility that those newly arrived in the city, having lost the security of the place they knew well but not yet having found a secure place in the industrial order, might indeed manifest a high degree of psychic malaise.

To test these ideas we needed measures of personal adjustment. We therefore asked several fairly simple questions, about satisfaction with one's job, social status, and opportunities, like those that had served well as indicators of adjustment in studies of industrial social-psychology. We relied mainly, however, on a simple test of psychic adjustment, known as the Psychosomatic Symptoms Test, which had proven itself remarkably useful in culturally diverse situations as a quick and simple diagnostic assessment of individual mental health. We also administered the Sentence Completion Test, which is used mainly as a measure of personality traits in interpersonal relations, but which sometimes throws light on psychic adjustment as well.

This completes the list of special topics we undertook to study as a supplement to our investigation of the analytic model of individual modernity. As I noted earlier, our initial approach to these topics was to treat them as an unrelated assemblage of individual themes. For each we made a different assessment of its relationship to modernization. Nevertheless, examination of the full array of topics leads one inevitably to the supposition that all, or at least some sub-set, of these different themes may reflect one common underlying dimension of modernity. Men more independent of the extended family might also be more interested in practicing birth control, more accepting of scientific rather than religious explanations of natural events, and more ready to expose themselves to the media of mass communication.

The Behavioral Model

Sociology is often charged with being too abstract, divorced from the concrete reality of social life. Even when he leaves his study to go into the field, the sociologist almost invariably puts an instrument— his questionnaire—between himself and the direct observation of people in social action. Insofar as the sociologist wishes to study large numbers of individuals he does not have many alternatives. And many people are too quick to dismiss as unimportant those changes in men that are limited to changes in attitude. We are not persuaded of the justice of this point. What men do is much influenced by the climate of opinion in which they find themselves. If a man, especially a young man, hears all around him an opinion conducive to modern behavior he is likely to act in accord with his impulses in that direction even if the elders are expressing only *opinion* and are not themselves personally acting in a modern way. Yet we were aware that a question-naire need not restrict itself to questions concerning *attitudes*. The questionnaire may also be used to elicit information concerning the behavior of the man who answers it. We were acutely aware of the possibility that many of our subjects might espouse, might even have sincerely adopted, modern attitudes and opinions, while they still continued to act in their usual traditional way in the course of their daily human relations. We wished, therefore, to obtain as much infor-mation as we could about the actual behavior of our subjects. The materials we gathered for that purpose we called "behavioral measures," and, taken together, they constitute the third, or "behavioral," model of individual modernity.

The self-reported behavioral measures were those on which the subject rated himself, in effect, by stating that he did or did not do certain things. For example, he was asked to indicate whether he had voted, to report how many times a week he attended religious services, read a newspaper or listened to the radio, and whether and how often he talked with his wife about politics, his job, and raising the children. Such self-reported behavior is, of course, subject to many distortions. A man may not remember accurately, or he may remember very well but give you one or another answer according to the impres-sion he wishes to create. The same risks are run in inquiring into opinions, however, and we could not, therefore, accept the possibility of distortion as sufficient to rule out self-reported behavior as evidence relevant to our judgment of a man's modernity.

Nevertheless, we were sufficiently impressed by the potential limi-tations of measures of self-reported behavior to supplement them with such *objectively* ascertained measures as we could reasonably mobilize. Some of these measures were built into our interview procedure, and this device permitted us to rate all of our subjects. For example, to test how far a man might accurately be reporting that he read the newspaper or listened to the radio every day, we asked everyone to name several newspapers and radio programs, and we also tested them on the extent of their knowledge of political leaders who figured prominently in the news. We must acknowledge that a man might well really listen to the radio and not be able to tell us the names of any programs, but quite apart from judging his truthfulness we learn something important about him when we make this discovery.

Finally, the objective measures of behavior obtained through our questionnaire were supplemented by information from outside sources, notably the subject's factory. The problems inherent in collecting such information obliged us to restrict the investigation to a subsample of the factory workers in each country. For this sub-sample, however, we collected as much information about each worker's performance as the work situation and the factory records permitted. Each worker in the sub-sample was rated by his foreman or other supervisor on a series of scales as high or low in dependability, ambition, flexibility, competence, carefulness, and consideration for others. In addition, we went to the factory records and noted whatever information they contained on the man's productivity, his attendance record and punctuality, his participation in training courses, and the path of his promotions. Thus, we sought to deal with what many would define as the most critical aspect of the modernization process—its outcome in harder, more regular, more skillful work, in short, in that increased productivity that presumably leads to the economic progress believed to be the essential foundation for political and social modernization.

Summary

The three models of individual modernization—the analytic, topical, and behavioral—guided our thinking as our research took shape, and their mark is therefore clearly visible in the content of our questions and the general design of our questionnaire. The distinctions emphasized by the three models were useful in assuring reasonable thoroughness in the selection of themes within each area, yet they prevented us from taking too narrow a view of the process of modernization. The distinctions among the models viewed as dependent variables permitted us to be much more precise in deciding which influences to study among those generally assumed to generate modernity. Taken together, the three models served, therefore, as a convenient organizing principle within which to encompass the considerable diversity of the various themes and areas we explored in our research. Indeed, this seems an appropriate point to draw together the various elements touched on in the preceding pages, and I therefore present in Chart 1 the complete list of the major topics in our questionnaire, each identified by its code letters and grouped under the model to which it has greatest relevance.

Chart 1. Main Themes and Areas of the Questionnaire, by Key Letter and Model

Analytical Model		*Topical Model*		*Behavioral Model*	
Aspirations, occupational and educational	(AS)	Active public participation	(AC)	Political activity	(AC)
Calculability	(CA)	Citizenship	(CI)	Family behavior	(BD and WR)
Change orientation	(CH)	Consumption attitudes	(CO)	Consumption behavior	(CO)
Dignity	(DI)	Family size restrictions	(FS)	Information test	(IN)
Efficacy	(EF)	Identification with nation	(ID)	Media information test	(MM)
Growth of opinion	(GO)	Kinship obligations	(KO)	Opposites word test	(OT)
Information	(IN)	Mass Media	(MM)	Psychosomatic test	(PT)
New Experience	(NE)	Religion	(RE)	Sentence completion test	(ST)
Optimism	(OP)	Psychosomatics and adjustment	(PT)	Interviewer's ratings	
Particularism	(PA)	Work Commitment	(WC)	Supervisor's ratings	
Planning	(PL)	Women's rights	(WR)	Factory records	
Time	(TI)				
Technical skill and distributive justice	(TS)				

Useful as the models might be in organizing our thinking, they do introduce some artificial, or at least arbitrary, divisions not necessarily found in nature. The models lead us to separate into three parts some realms that might perfectly well be seen as more coherently joined in one. For example, in approaching the realm of opinion, the three-model arrangement induces us to treat general attitudes relevant to that realm as part of the analytic model, attitudes towards the mass media as one theme in the topical model, and the frequency with which a man listens to the radio as a theme in the behavioral model. Obviously, someone might want to ignore our distinction and treat all the questions as different aspects of a more general study of mass media and opinion in developing countries.

What applies to any one realm can indeed apply to all the dimensions taken together. Although each model was justified in its own terms as theoretically and empirically distinct, all could be conceived of as manifestations of a more general, unified, underlying dimension of modernity that could encompass elements of all three of the measures. It might well be that a man strong in the qualities of the analytic model, such as efficacy and readiness for new experience, would also be interested in politics, be inclined to grant women more rights, and so on through various themes of the topical model. This same man might, on our behavioral measures, prove to be well informed about the content of the mass media and be shown by the factory records as rarely missing work, as most punctual, and as having a high production record. Clearly, then, our materials permitted us to develop still a fourth model of modernity, one much more general, in that it includes elements of the analytic, topical, and behavioral models. We designated this model by the letters OM, which stand for "over-all modernity" measure, but we felt the choice particularly apt because, in Hinduism, OM is a mantra representing the triple constitution of the universe. Of course, we should keep in mind that OM, like the analytic model, is a theoretical construct. Until we have empirically tested the facts, it remains an assumption, a hypothesis only, that the elements of the other three models might indeed combine to yield a relatively unified measure of modernity. In fact, empirical testing of these ideas by analysis of our data shows that the relations between the different elements that may be considered alternative measures of individual modernity are quite complex and by no means obvious.

II. Modernization and Convergence in Developing Areas

The theme of this symposium, held on May 9–10, 1968, was the extent to which the modernization process produces convergence toward a uniform industrial culture in developing areas of the world. Theories of modernization and convergence are rooted in over two centuries of social theory, but the recent burgeoning of interest in cross-cultural, comparative research has again brought this issue to the forefront of social scientific concern. The interplay between processes such as industrialization and urbanization that may produce similarities between societies and the processes through which traditional societies maintain their integrity and, consequently, their differences from each other are the theoretical problems to which this symposium was addressed.

Wilbert E. Moore received his Ph.D. from Harvard University in 1940 and is now Professor of Sociology and Law at the University of Denver. He was for many years on the faculty of Princeton University and was also Sociologist on the staff of the Russell Sage Foundation in New York City. In 1966, he served as president of the American Sociological Association. Professor Moore has long been interested in the specific issues to which this symposium is addressed. A recent statement of his position appears in a paper entitled, "Industrialization and Industrialism: Convergence and Differentiation," which was prepared with Arnold S. Feldman and presented at the Fifth World Congress of Sociology in 1962. Among his books are *Industrialization and Labor*, 1951; *Labor Commitment and Social Change in Developing Areas* (with Arnold S. Feldman), 1960; *Industrialization and Society* (with Bert F. Hoselitz), 1963; *Man, Time, and Society*, 1963; *Social Change*, 1963; *The Impact of Industry*, 1965, and *Order and Change*, 1967.

Karl Deutsch received doctoral degrees from Charles University, Prague, in 1938 and from Harvard University in 1951. He is Professor of Government at Harvard and has taught at Oxford, Yale, and Princeton Universities, The University of Chicago, and Massachusetts Institute of Technology. His publications include *Nationalism and Social Communication* (rev. ed., 1966), in which he elaborates a general theory of social communication and integration; *The Nerves of Government* (rev. ed., 1966), in which he continues his search for empirical methods to measure communication processes; and *Politics and Government: How People Decide Their Fate*, an introduction to comparative political analysis (1970). Professor Deutsch also is the author of *The Analysis of International Relations* (1968), and *Nationalism and Its Alternatives* (1969), and is co-author of *Political Community and the North Atlantic Area* (1947), and the *World Handbook of Political and Social Indicators* (1964). He is a Vice-President of the International Political Science Association and was President of the American Political Science Association in 1969–70.

Manning Nash, Professor of Anthropology at the University of Chicago, received his B.S. from Temple University and his M.A. and Ph.D. degrees in anthropology from the University of Chicago. He is a Fellow of the Royal Anthropological Association of Great Britain and Ireland, the American Anthropological Association, and the American Association for the Advancement of Science. Among his many publications are *Machine Age Maya: The Industrialization of a Guatemalan Community, The Golden Road to Modernity, Primitive and Peasant Economic Systems*, and *Anthropological Studies in Theravada Buddhism*. He has done extensive field work in Burma and Malaya.

SOCIAL AND POLITICAL CONVERGENCE IN INDUSTRIALIZING COUNTRIES—
Some Concepts and the Evidence

Karl W. Deutsch, *Harvard University*

In discussing some aspects of modernization it might be most useful to use a four-step model. All such divisions are rough, of course, and fit very imperfectly, but they may suggest some insights, if we use them with caution. The zero state, or non-modernization, would be the first level. It is characterized by a subsistence economy, rural residence, a tradition-dominated culture and technology, intense localism, low mobility in space and among social groups and classes, the predominance of face-to-face relationships, few meetings with strangers, and little change.

We should then go to monetization, as it is called by today's economic advisors, or the "commercial revolution," as it has been called by the historians of Western Europe. Monetization is the first stage of the modernization process and is frequently associated with considerable social change in a particular direction. Anthropologists probably could find some examples of cultures where money has been introduced and used fairly widely, and where, on the whole, the rest of the culture has not been profoundly changed nor made dynamic; but whether such societies exist or not, for perhaps eighty or ninety percent of mankind, cumulative processes of change follow from monetization.

Then comes the introduction of more elaborate tools, in particular the use of inanimate power. We may accept this key to change as the test for the second stage of this process of modernization, the stage of industrial revolution.

From this stage, many societies have gone on to the stage of high mass consumption, which involves the heavy use of electricity. We may use the per capita consumption of electric energy, in contrast to other forms of energy, as one of the indicators of this stage. Another indicator would be the per capita consumption of steel; a third would be the spread of durable goods to consumers; and a fourth checkpoint would be the beginning of partial, but not full, automation in the handling of materials.

Finally we may begin to look at the fourth stage, the stage of high technology, which does not yet exist fully in any country but which can now be foreseen.

Let us look at some data to see what we can learn about each of these stages. For the zero stage, the non-modernizing societies, we find among 122 countries listed in the first *World Handbook of Political and Social Indicators* ten societies that still are predominantly non-modern. The gross national product per capita for these countries, including Ethiopia, Afghanistan, Laos, Togo, and Nepal, ran in 1957 from $45 to about $57. The estimate for 1970 for such largely pre-modern societies might still be under $80 per capita, since real incomes have grown somewhat and the value of the United States dollar has shrunk.

The use of money is pervasive in the first-stage countries to the extent perhaps of more than one-half of their gross national product. Of the thirty-seven early modernizing societies I found (and remember, of course, that in one and the same country, some regions might be greatly advanced and some might be much less developed)—for example, Burma, Ceylon, Ghana, Indonesia, Haiti, or Nigeria—the 1957 per capita GNP figures ran from $60 to $140; they would be perhaps 50 per cent more for the early 1970's. In this category I should also place what the authors of the first *World Handbook* called "traditional civilizations," such as India, Pakistan, and mainland China. Their average per capita incomes are low, but their cultural resources and modern sector are larger—indeed they may now be shifting to industrialization.

The third set of countries, those passing through the stage of an industrial revolution, I would subdivide into two stages, early and late industrialization. The early industrial revolution category comprises forty-seven countries in the world, and they range from Egypt and Morocco to Cuba and Cyprus. All have some industry; Cuba, in fact, is moving to the boundary of the early type, where mass consumption becomes a problem—such as in regard to television—but they are not there yet. Here, the 1957 dollar figures for GNP per capita run from $142 to $467, or, in round figures, approximately $200 to $700 in 1970 dollars.

The high level, late industrial revolution stage includes a range of countries from Poland to Israel and Finland. Their 1957 per capita incomes ranged from $475 to $794, or, again in very round figures for today, from about $700 to around $1200 per capita income. Fifteen countries are in this category, so that the whole class of industrial revolution countries in the world totals sixty-two. And with the early modernizing—or merely monetized—countries, the total is ninety-nine transitional countries altogether.

Then you have the countries of high mass consumption, and what sometimes are loosely called "post-industrial" societies (but I have great reservations about calling them that). These fifteen countries in the world range from The Netherlands to the United States, and their per capita incomes ranged from $836 to $2577 in those innocent days of 1957; for us in 1970 these figures may run from $1200 to about $4000.

Finally we have the high technology society. Although no country in the world as we know it today has reached this stage of high technology, regions in the United States, and possibly in some other parts of the world, are beginning to move toward this level. Therefore, although the number of national cases in 1970 is still zero, the approximate per capita income for this stage, once it is attained, would probably begin at $5000 in 1970 dollars.

What is the meaning of the higher per capita GNP figures for the more modern countries? They mean a wider range of choices. They mean more power and more opportunity, for good or evil. They may mean more cleanliness or more pollution, more education or more advertising, more peaceful growth or more warlike destruction, more life or more death.

The great bulk of the world's countries is now going through the transitional process toward higher levels of power. We may compare this designation to Daniel Lerner's distinction between "traditionals," "transitionals," and "moderns," but Lerner's "moderns" would probably already be in the late industrial revolution; therefore, Lerner's scheme would include the late industrial revolution countries with the societies of high mass consumption. We can argue, of course, about where to put our cutting points for statistical analysis, but I suggest that we can collect data on groups of countries with somewhat known characteristics of behavior, and we can see immediately whether there is really a startlingly greater similarity between, shall we say, two late industrial revolution countries, such as Finland and Japan, or between two pre-modern countries such as Nepal and Ethiopia. (To some extent our conclusion might depend on which particular dimensions we pick before we make a quick statement about differences or similarities.)

The Concept of Convergence

But this leads us to the next question—namely, what do we mean by convergence? And how do we recognize it when we see it? Let us again begin with a puzzling case from history. Japan acquired steam engines and textile manufacturing techniques in the 1890's and early 1900's, while England did so more than 90 years earlier. Since 1900, Japan and England have been moving toward the modern industrial stage, and they have shared modern industrial technology for 70 years. Have they become more similar or not? Is there in any particular sense a continuing convergence, or increasing similarity, between England and Japan? In 1860 or 1870, England and Japan were different enough to excite the imagination of Gilbert and Sullivan, but by 1900 England and Japan had become fairly similar in some respects; indeed Japanese naval officers were being trained at the British Naval Academy in Portsmouth, and the Japanese Navy was being equipped with British-built ships and guns. This was a fairly high degree of convergence; indeed, the Japanese standardized some British ammunitions at the time. But by 1936 in some ways Japan was more different from England than it had been in 1910. In 1942, when Japan made war on Britain and her colonies, she was still more different in some important ways. Today Japan has some similarities with England, but also some very striking differences. For all its complications, such as the student unrest at the London School of Economics, British university life is not quite like life at the university in Tokyo. Convergence, from the Anglo-Japanese experience, implies an original reduction of great differences; but then two or more societies proceed within hailing distance of each other along a somewhat wavy path into the future, so that, from then on, the similarities or differences between them may increase or decrease over a time span of any two or three or four decades. But there is no further move toward identity, or toward the disappearence of the residual differences.

Something similar holds for the differences between the United States and Japan, or the differences between Germany and France, or the differences between China and India in the modernization process. The same principle seems to apply to the United States and the Soviet Union according to my colleagues Zbigniew Brzezinski and Samuel Huntington.[1] We find again some reduction of the original great differences between the two societies, until they arrive within hailing distances of each other. Nonetheless, the ideological differences remain large; communication between the two societies most often is a shouting across the remaining gap; and then each follows its own wavy progress into the future, where sometimes the two societies zig and zag in unison, but, more often than not, when one of them zigs the other one zags. From time to time, therefore, the differences seem to be increasing, then again decreasing, but the trend behind the fluctuations remains at a reasonably constant distance between the two. Yet, as the results of change accumulate, both societies may become increasingly more different from their own past than they are each from one another.

This cumulative estrangement from their own past is an important point. Nevertheless, even though these differences are large and growing, other elements of each society's past remain, and they continue to be internalized as key aspects of its national culture; the practices of the rival country are not internalized to any such degree as are one's own traditions.

Convergence may be defined operationally by several tests. First, there is a social and political similarity of the structures and processes in the two countries; second, the relative amounts and importance of reciprocal transactions increase. Third, there is a reciprocal internalization of memories, traditions, symbols, and values: will the culture of country A internalize, accept as its own, and practice the traditions, symbols, or patterns of country B. Two countries, just as two people, could be very different from each other and still internalize some of each other's memories or values or patterns of behavior.

A fourth definition would be the expectations of peace, which is not the same as similarity at all. In the 16th century Charles V wrote a letter to King Francis of France in which he said, "I desire exactly as my royal brother of France desires: the City of Milan." From the days when two heads of state had a similar desire for the

1. Zbigniew Brzezinski and Samuel P. Huntington, *Political Power: USA-USSR* (New York: Viking Press, 1964).

same city, to the early twentieth century when two sovereign states desired the same oil fields, and to our own days when two opposing ideologies might desire control of the same supposedly strategic small country somewhere else in the world, similarity by no means has been a guarantee of peace.

If we look more closely at the aspect of similarity, we must again ask for dimensions within the concept of similarity: in what ways are the societies to be considered more similar? Which dimensions are to be selected? And on what grounds? Clearly, many economic and industrial practices are similar in many countries, East and West, but in certain other respects they are different. In the 1930's the cut of the shirts of various political movements became increasingly identical, but the colors in which they were dyed—brown, black, blue, and so on—were strikingly different.

Some Possibilities of Measurement

We could get beyond this problem by making a statement analogous to the physicist's concept of the mean free path of a particle. A physicist can say, "I cannot possibly predict into which particle a gas molecule will bounce, but I can make a general statement as to approximately how far in a container on the average a gas molecule can move before it bounces into another one." Similarly, we could make a statement about the probable similarity of the average comparison.

Let us, for example, select a considerable number of societal aspects that are important to political scientists or to sociologists or to anthropologists. Let us, for the sake of interdisciplinary peace, rate all of them equally; and for the sake of peace within the professions, let us rate equally the aspects preferred by different eminent theorists within each, so that we can give Durkheim, Parsons, and Sorokin all their due. Then let us assign all these aspects to a society (or nation) A, and write them so as to generate the rows of a matrix. Then let us assign the same aspects to society B, and write them across the top of a piece of paper—it will be a large piece of paper, I fear—and generate columns of a matrix. We then can say that the rows refer to the traits of Society A, and columns to the traits or aspects or dimensions of Society B, and the entries in each cell could be the degree of cross-national similarity—the correlation of some data, for instance—of each pair of traits in A and B. Later on we may also ask whether the intra-national correlations among different traits are the same for the two societies or not, but for the moment we shall just compare the cross-national correlations of the measures for each trait. We can then look for the most likely degree of similarity in every cell in this matrix. The bigger the matrix, of course, the more numerous the entries.

We can use samples from this matrix for some general definition of similarity. On the average, if we pick out at random a number of relevant dimensions—that is, dimensions meeting some minimum criterion of relevance—what are the chances that we will get a statistically significant level of similarity? What are the chances of getting one that accounts for more than 50 per cent of the variance (if that should be the cutting point we pick) in more than 50 per cent of the cases? That is, if more than half of the traits selected will be found, in successive samples, to resemble each other to more than half of their variance, we will say they are "similar." If we then repeat this procedure for two societies, at two different stages in time, we can say whether on the whole this average amount of similarity has increased or decreased.

To be sure, this method is crude, and statisticians obviously could think of a considerable number of refinements of it. Nevertheless, we could begin to develop statistical profiles of the relevant aspects of societies, and we could get statistical measures of similarity not only between any two traits but also between the distribution of high degrees of resemblance among traits. Thus, we could see whether, over time, they increase or decrease.

A somewhat better way would be to weight the different dimensions by their importance in each country. We could try to get panels of experts who could tell us that in country A collective idiosyncrasies are more weighty in their influence upon social or political outcomes than are individual ones. A possibly better way would be to say: Let us weight dimensions in proportion to their probable effect on other dimensions. We could estimate this effect insofar as we have causal knowledge or social science knowledge of the extent to which, for example, economic practices tend to have an effect on other kinds of behavior, or to what extent basic childhood training practices are more consequential than recent practices in advertising. Thus, supposing two countries are similar in advertisements but dissimilar in childhood training, we might get a fairly wide consensus that, according to Drs. Sigmund Freud, Erik Erikson, and others, the prevailing pattern of childhood training is more important than the prevailing kinds of advertisements, and therefore we ought to give more weight to rearing patterns as the more basic aspect. Various of these tests would overlap in their results. We could probably measure the similarity dimension between two countries or two cultures in several ways, imperfect and unsatisfactory to be sure, but still they would give us some significant and reproducible information. We could measure the degree of reciprocal internalization of values through depth interviews and survey methods and through projective tests. We might be able to learn from the evidence collected by anthropologists about the degree to which a certain aspect or trait or a certain value has been internalized by the people of one country, to the extent that this evidence will allow us to make predictions about what these people are likely to do, how they will act, and what kinds of artifacts they will produce. Thus, our evidence from other sources could be confirmed or could at least be judged compatible with the field notes that anthropologists bring back. It would not be a sharp or conclusive proof or disproof, but it could move us some distance away from unsubstantial guessing and closer to knowledge backed by evidence.

Convergence and the Likelihood of Conflict

We could then determine the expectations of conflict, or the probabilities of conflict, between two societies. Even though two such societies are similar, they might be given to conflicts. The "mirror image" hypothesis advanced by Urie Bronfenbrenner and others has to some extent been corroborated by the partial evidence for mirror image phenomena that Robert Angell and David Singer found in their content analysis of American and Soviet elite periodicals: The mass media and elite media of each country portrayed the supposed motivations of the elite leaders of the other country such that the pictures were mirror images of each other, not in all respects, but in a number of important ways. This state of affairs between the U.S. and the U.S.S.R. could be treated as convergence, but here again the probability of conflict is conceptually distinct from the degree of similarity.

Let us approach this problem from another point of view. We could measure similarity by the amount of information two patterns have in common, measured in bits of some sort of another. In this case, if two patterns begin to resemble each other in the ways a photographic negative represents a photographic positive, we should get convergence. Very many patterns become alike, but some critical patterns remain different, so that where A says black, B says white. To this extent, black racists and white racists can "converge" by beginning to share many patterns about the excellence and superiority of their respective racial groups. Or, to take another case, certain propaganda methods used by the late Joseph Stalin and those of the late Senator Joseph McCarthy showed some alarming signs of potential convergence. Still, conflict would not be minimized among the adherents of similarly intolerant leaders or creeds. It turns out, in short, that the probability of similarity is probably not well related—in part, perhaps even inversely related—to the probability of peace. Indeed, if I had to make the briefest and crudest guess I could make, I would suggest that the relationship, like so many others, might be curvilinear. If we plotted horizontally the probability of similarity, and vertically the probability of conflicts, then two completely identical objects, A and B, would have a conflict probability near zero, for they would be certain to be identical, and two completely dissimilar ones—with a correlation close to zero between the traits of A and B—also would have a conflict probability of near zero. If the two countries or systems, A and B, should be complete opposites, however, the correlation between them would be minus one. We could then plot on the horizontal axis the average correlations between A and B, which would range from plus one on the right to minus one on the left, with zero in the middle. The probability of conflict plotted on the y-axis would be highest at correlation minus one: complete similarity but opposite signs or values. Conflict would be less likely at correlation zero, but there might be a secondary maximum at about $+0.5$ where enough positive resemblance between the two societies would permit them to quarrel about something and enough uncoordinated traits would disturb or spoil coordination. Some possible distributions of conflict probabilities, derived from such a model, are shown in Figure 1.

Such a two-dimensional diagram, as shown in curves I or II in Figure 1, would apply only those uni-modal cases where the correlations within pairs of traits for the two countries would be only positive and random, or negative and random. If we wanted to include cases where some trait pairs showed strong positive correlations while others were strongly negatively correlated—even though their average might work out to zero—then we should need another diagram, as shown in curve III in Figure 1. For such an average correlation of zero, derived from the bi-modal concentration of positively and negatively

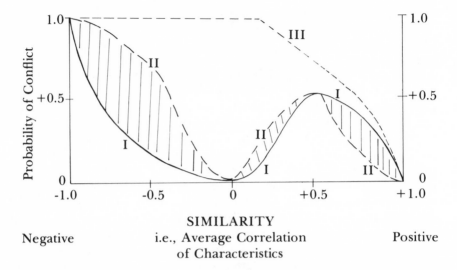

SIMILARITY
Negative   i.e., Average Correlation   Positive
of Characteristics

Figure 1. A crude model of the probability of conflict
between two interacting countries or societies, as a function of
the average similarity among their relevant characteristics

correlated trait pairs, the probability of conflict again would be high,
and it would decline only when even such a mixed average would
be strongly positive.

The quantitative relation connecting curves I and II could be
shown in a three-dimensional diagram. Here we add a Z-axis on which
we could plot the algebraic product of the sum of all positive correlations (ΣPC) times the sum of all negative correlations (ΣNC). The
smaller this algebraic product—that is, a product computed without
further regard for plus or minus signs—the rarer will be the coex-
istence of both positive and negative pair correlations between the
two countries, and the nearer will be the probability of conflicts
between them for the situations described in curve I, which has two
minima, whose average correlations are zero and plus one. The larger
the algebraic product (ΣPC) x (ΣNC), on the contrary, the nearer
will be the distribution of conflict probabilities to that shown in curve
II, which has a single minimum at the average correlation of plus
one.

Another variable is, of course, the frequency of transactions or
contact between the two societies. Generally, the frequency of recip-

rocal contacts or transactions increases the relevance of both sets of actors. The frequency of rewarding contacts increases the likelihood of integration, while the frequency of frustrating or penalizing contacts—more precisely, of contacts with the negative covariance of rewards for the two systems—increases the frequency of conflict. These ideas follow from the classic theory of reinforcement learning. We may now add that, under certain assumptions, a very high degree of structural or behavioral similarity, or both, between two interacting systems or nations may tend to promote harmony and integration, while a high degree of negative structural similarity (with average trait correlations close to minus one), or a frustrating mixture of strongly and positively correlated traits with entirely uncorrelated, or strongly but negatively correlated, ones would tend to increase the probability of conflicts.

Much of this description accords with common sense. Whales and elephants do not fight because they cannot get at each other. Creatures that share more bodily characteristics are more likely to share similar environments, and thus their opportunities for conflict multiply. As two unrelated and dissimilar societies become more similar, therefore, the probabilities of conflict between them may increase. Only later when they go toward becoming indistinguishable from each other, even in their values, might they become so assimilated to each other that the probability of conflict declines again. I would expect, therefore, that partial convergence in the policies of industrialization will be accompanied by an increase in conflict.

Convergence of Basic Values

Let us go from here to the search for at least some aspects of a minimum skeleton model of the process. I have been particularly intrigued with Professor Moore's question,[2] "Why do we have modernization?" As he was careful to point out, what happens when countries mobilize is not the same as why do they do it. As we look for an answer, I propose the following considerations.

We begin with certain cross-cultural values people have in common, and in most cultures in the world, regardless of what the cultures are, young people tend, luckily, to fall in love, and most often they do it with the opposite sex. The result, of course, is in time the founding

2. See Wilbert E. Moore, "The Singular and the Plural: The Social Significance of Industrialism Reconsidered," Chapter 5.

of families, the birth of children, and a birth rate. This result is now combined with a second cross-cultural trait: most cultures—though not all of them—put a high value on the survival of all children. All cultures that survive value the survival of some or most of their children. (Remember that, in fact, it is far easier to compute loving all one's babies than to internalize the notion the ancient Spartans held whereby one likes and loves only the 1-A babies and throws the 4-F babies off the top of a cliff.) It follows that cross-culturally most cultures in the world are predisposed to accept or do many things that will promote life.

The third cross-cultural effect or trait is one that Pavlov found in animals—curiosity, or the investigatory instinct. If you combine it with the world-wide availability of information—the demonstration effects about modernity—you will find that health habits and resources are likely to be diffused.

To be sure, many cultures are ingenious in fending off change, in teaching their people how not to learn. Many cultures have contrived to keep small handfuls of people at the Stone Age level for hundreds of generations. But the cultures that prevent their people from learning must do so largely by keeping populations stable, by keeping their net reproduction rates close to exactly one. The other ones grow, and as a result, of course, only a tiny minority of mankind still lives in Stone Age cultures. On the whole, the overwhelming majority of the world's population is all in societies that share the ability and propensity to learn and to change their behavior.

The first breakthrough, of course, comes at the death barrier: mortality rates are decreased. The annual death rates that stood as a barrier to population growth are lowered drastically from, let us say, four or five per cent of the population to one per cent of the population. The natural population increase, then, goes up from no change over the years to a two per cent increase per annum, an increase that will double the population every 35 years. In some islands and some small countries, of course, population growth rates of three and one-half per cent and even four per cent for short periods will double populations in about 18 years.

The basic value orientations then are the preference for life over death, the attachment to the survival of children, the curiosity to seek out demonstration effects of new ways of insuring food and life, and the propensity to respond to them, at least to some extent. These human traits seem to be universal, and they produce then a shift from stable populations to populations doubling every few decades. This increase produces a basic and pressing dynamic situation. It accelerates the demands for more food and for goods or politics to pay for them. If you can't export sisal or hemp or coconuts, you could export a threat by an internal Communist menace. In either case, the result might be that some big shipments come in. A demand for health and housing will lead to a demand for some urban patterns of settlement. Largely this demand also means a demand for higher inputs of information. People go to cities because more is going on there, and as soon as people do move to cities they will demand public amenities. Simultaneously, in the more advanced countries, come economic demands from abroad for minerals and materials of various kinds, strategic demands for basic resources, and ideological demands for converts.

Convergence and Cognitive Consistency

Here an aspect of Leon Festinger's work becomes relevant to our problem. Festinger observed that, if people make flat statements about the future of the world according to an ideology or religion they hold and in which they have made deep psychic investments, and if then these prophecies fail, they respond with redoubled efforts to secure new converts. If our outlook on the world has been left spectacularly unfulfilled by facts, we experience a painful dissonance between what we expected and what we see. Most often, particularly if we receive social support from our environment, we will not give up what we expected, because it is based on what we remember. Our expectations of the future are based on our memories from the past, and our memories from the past are part of our self-system, our integrity, our personality, and we don't like to give them up. As a result, we will redouble our efforts to find, discover, or, if need be, manufacture evidence to repair and restore our expectations— such as by gaining new proselytes.

If this be true, then it was predictable that the great outpouring of missionaries from the Western world in the nineteenth century would occur during the decades of mounting religious skepticism and agnosticism. In the century between Voltaire and Darwin, there was more missionary activity, as Christians from the Western world went to Asia and Africa, than in any other period since the late Roman Empire. The more threatened by secular and skeptical moods the traditional churches of Christianity in the advanced countries became, the more diligently they sent out missionaries. To be sure, there were other reasons, too. Missionaries telling naked natives to put on cotton could expect to get at least some subsidies in Manchester for their pious activities. But Oscar Wilde's notion that when an Englishman said "God" he meant cotton, and only cotton, was an over-simplification. The psychological mechanism pointed out by Festinger probably also made a contribution.

If, however, such a Festinger-type process exists, it presumably also works among Communists; and we may expect that as Communist doctrines and dogmas lead to puzzling clashes with reality, we may witness a sincere increase in Communist missionary zeal in the world, in order, again, to reduce cognitive dissonance in their own minds. This activity will by no means determine the policies of the major Communist powers completely, but it may at least insure a reasonable allocation of individuals and resources for propaganda for the next several decades, in order to keep the ideological propaganda contest going. The same psychological mechanism is also likely to make its contribution to the policies of the United States as the gain or loss of foreign allies or converts varies.

The world is now split between two major industrial civilizations, the Communist type and the Western, neither of which fully understands the industrial civilization by which they live; and in this contest between two powerful organizations, both at least partially ignorant of themselves and of each other, propaganda efforts to increase certainty and self-assurance will continue for some decades to come. As a result, a greater, autonomous, native readiness to accept innovations and to modernize will meet with a great autonomous foreign initiative and a great autonomous foreign impact that prods societies to make them modernize in some preferred direction.

Modernization and the Renaissance of National Cultures

We are dealing, therefore, not with a monocausal effect but, if there is anything to this skeletal model, with two autonomous processes. Each of them would work and would produce some substantial changes in the world, even if the other did not exist. The preference for life over death, the attachment to children, the curiosity for knowledge, the diffusion of better ways of promoting health and food will occur in any event and set going the population dynamic that has begun to double populations every few decades and thus to undermine previous arrangements based upon lower population densities. On the other hand, the search for materials, for the industrial civilizations, for the strategic reassurance through military bases, and for psychological reassurance through converts will be going on, even if the natives did not care whether their babies lived or died. In fact, however, we get both processes coming together and reinforcing one another.

Let us call one of these processes the native reaching out for more survival, more health, more food, and, therefore, whether we know it or not, for actively growing populations. Let us call this N—native dynamics, so to speak—and by native I mean here an ethnocentric slur, since native Californians and native Americans are very proud of their status. Let us call the foreign dynamic—and by foreign I mean the advanced countries—the dynamic of F. The effects of the native process may be larger than those of the foreign process in a particular time or place, so that the native outreaching is the most important part of the total process of development and the foreign impact is less. Or else F may be larger than N at some other time and place; and it may actually happen that at different times in the same country these processes alternate in their relative predominance.

In the nineteenth century in Japan for a short time, the push of the foreign initiative, for one or two years at least, seemed more serious than the native reaching out. Actually, as we know now from the historians, the Japanese themselves were groping for modernization, and the shift to urbanization, monetization, and many other things was also autonomous. The story of Japanese modernization is, to a large extent, a relatively temporary F input with a very strong N process that produced a striking development: if you take the whole time span of the first hundred years after the Meiji Restoration—or even the first fifty years—the result was overwhelmingly native-directed. After 1945 there was a strong foreign input, such that some Japanese intellectuals consider General MacArthur's administration of Japan as one of the great times of reform. Here again a large foreign input was officially fixed for a short time, but the native dynamic has once more taken over rather fully.

Nineteenth century Europe was almost entirely a case of native modernization processes, to the embarrassment of, let us say, Austrian or Russian imperial administrations, who often were quite unhappy about the rapid change among their subjects. Turkey, to some extent, began with foreign pressures but then shifted to native modernization in the days of the Young Turks and of Kemal Ataturk. In Africa and Asia, on the other hand, and in Central America, foreign impacts in the nineteenth and early twentieth centuries usually were much stronger than the native reaching out.

A good deal of research available can tell us something about the current development, as well as about the future, of these two processes, the native and the foreign. For most countries—and particularly for such giants as the United States and the Soviet Union—the native, autonomous reaching out for identity and a better life will likely become consistently stronger in the next several decades than any foreign impacts.

But in addition to asking which of the two impact elements is stronger, we have to ask, "What is the feedback process between the two?" Foreign impacts, in their effects, almost always reinforce native efforts at modernization, even though at times foreign administrators would like to keep the natives picturesque and traditional. The native movements in turn quite frequently reinforce the foreign impact, particularly when there is no foreign, direct, political control in that country. This has been the Japanese, Turkish, or Thailandic experience. Or else the native movements may discourage the foreign impact. In this event, very frequently the foreign observer will predict a complete stop of modernization. A second and more subtle look at modernization might show, however, that the native movement most often emphasizes tradition and the past mainly in its communication, its languages and symbols, while it accepts modernization concerning technology, man's dealings with nature, and social change—including shifts away from strict religious observances or from landowner privileges or extreme caste barriers.

With modernization one carries much more elaborate communications equipment—communications equipment that combines a great deal of differentiation and subtlety with a great deal of power to generalize in the readjustment to numerous interests and new types of inputs. To this degree, it is a sign of modernization that the predominant culture talks to its children in its mother tongue. It is a sign of a pre-modern culture that the only two communication codes available to children are either the familiar one from childhood, which is parochial and limited to the dialect of a small village or region, or the supra-regional, but relatively alien both geographically and usually also sociologically, being tied to a special upper caste of mandarins, priests, clerks, bureaucrats, or others. The modern society internalizes a communications code that is as familiar and meaningful to the users as their own childhood memories, but is widely applicable, through translation and language development, to information from a large part of the world. To this extent, the shift to the native tongue, to mother-tongue education, looks like nativism and traditionalism, like a return to the past, but it is, in fact, a commitment to the future. The native culture and its resources, together with the world environment, may jointly reinforce the native-directed effort at modernization. As a result, many countries may become more similar in technology but more different in language and in important aspects of culture.

THE PROBABILITY OF FUTURE OUTCOMES

Some Quantitative Estimates

Let us ask a question here about quantitative probabilities. Once again, for a skeleton model we shall have to use highly schematic figures. The native probability of reaching out for modernization is high, since it is promoted not only by the life-preserving values, but also by a desire for getting many other values, such as the basic values listed by Harold Lasswell—well-being, power, wealth, rectitude, enlightenment, deference, skill, and affection. At least five of these eight—that is, all except deference, rectitude, and affection—can be increased if we increase human power over nature. Indeed, if we increase technology and science, even affection values tend to increase, because the survival of a beloved person is closely related to affection values. Thus, at least six of the basic eight values will drive people to reach out for modernization. We may estimate, therefore, that the probability of modernization, and the probability of a native reaching out for it, could be approximately nine-tenths of the case histories in a world in which modernization becomes widely available. And this estimate implies, of course, that the probability of natives who do not so reach out will be no more than approximately one-tenth.

Let us assume, then, that one country out of ten, or roughly 14 out of 140 countries, would refuse to modernize. (To make this simplifying assumption, we must abstract from the fact that the country that does modernize will grow faster than the country that does not.)

What about the probability of foreign impact? It is high, since the economic, strategic, and ideological missionary motives of advanced foreign countries all are pushing them in this direction. In each case, some values may substitute for the other values or motives. The Dutch in the 1950s tried to retain or even increase their influence in Western Irian—the old Dutch New Guinea—even though it had no economic value and even though the local Papuas made unimpressive Christian converts after the Dutch had been there for some decades. Any one motive may suffice to produce foreign efforts and a foreign impact, and, since there are several good motives, the probability of the foreign impact could again be about 90 per cent. It follows, then, that about 90 per cent of the countries in the world are likely to be visited by traders or missionaries or colonels or by naval captains or air force officers in search of strategic facilities. The probability, therefore, that any country will be completely left alone by the world is one in ten or less. In actual fact, in the world today not even the isolated countries, Tibet or Nepal or Butan or Yemen, are being left very much alone. Furthermore, since each of the two processes, the native and the foreign, is good enough to produce modernization, the probability that a country will not be modernized by native efforts or by foreign impact is one-tenth of one-tenth, or only one chance in one hundred.

The probabilities, therefore, for modernization in our time are enormous, particularly if we substitute for the 141 countries for which data are given in the revised edition of my book, *Nationalism and Social Communication,* the 3000 dialects and languages or the several thousands of cultures known to anthropologists. Remember, too, that the modernizing cultures and language groups have higher survival rates and reproduction rates than the really successfully non-modernizing ones, which stick to the death barrier and keep their populations largely constant. As a result of these different reproduction rates over time, we probably get not one percent of mankind, which would still be 32 million people, but probably one-tenth of that or less that actually does escape modernization. The probability that any individual in the world will be born in the society that has successfully escaped modernization up to now, and will continue to escape modernization during his lifetime, might very well be less than one in one hundred, or even less than one in one thousand.

From here on we could develop questions of further key data on similarity or conflict probabilities, with some implications for research directions and for policy. Let us try to spell out at least one implication for policy by way of conclusion.

Let us assume that the policy maker would do well to be interested in our original problem of convergence, and let us call it, again, the probability of similarity. How probable is it that two societies will show a given degree of similarity as their degree of industrialization increases? Let us say that this degree of similarity could either be "high" or "low." Convergence theory says that similarity is gradually increasing in the world, and up to a point the theory may have some truth to it. But also interesting to a policy maker is the probability of peace between the societies that are more or less similar. (We cannot go here into the question of internal peace or stability, but we must limit this first discussion to peace between societies.) The probability of peace, too, could be high or low. This generates, of course, a fourfold table of possibilities, or, better, a six-fold table, if we distinguish the probability of peace between independent societies and between societies where one is politically dependent upon the other, as shown in Figure 2.

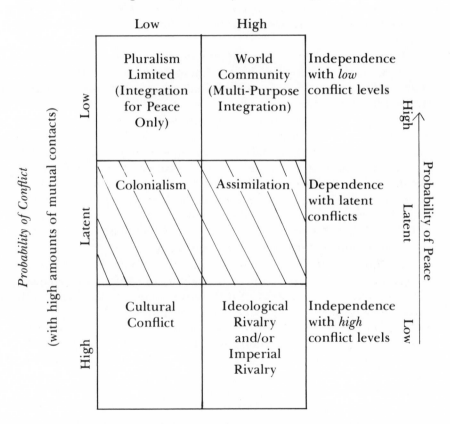

Convergence (Probability of Similarity)

Figure 2. A simple scheme of degrees of convergence and probabilities of peace.

If we have a high probability of peace and low similarity, we are dealing with pluralism. I have not put into the table the assumption that all these societies have a relatively high level of communication with each other. Air travel has made a good deal of the world accessible to us all, and the mass media have offered vicarious access to different societies. If two dissimilar societies are at high peace but one is dependent on another, we speak of colonialism, and if two societies are very dissimilar but are not likely to be at peace, we are dealing, of course, with cultural conflict. A typical example from history would be the barbarian invasions of Europe in the fifth century A.D., when highly dissimilar peoples came in and overran, or came into contact with, another culture. Cultural conflict usually implies political and social conflicts: either the barbarians take over an old civilized area, or people from the civilized area invade the area of some primitive peoples.

If the societies become very similar and the probabilities of conflict are high, we get ideological rivalry. Among countries with low probabilities of peace and high degrees of similarity, we often get ideological rivalry with mirror image effects. Or else we could get imperial rivalry, where again the different reigning imperial powers are forced to act similarly and to project upon the other side the images of their own dreams and nightmares. In cases of dependency and high similarity we could get assimilation as, for example, the way Cornwall assimilated to England, or the way in which French speakers in Louisiana assimilated, in part at least, to the American pattern. Finally, high similarity with mutual independence and a high probability of peace would give us the world community, which many people hope for, as I do, but it should be a long way away.

The question is, How do we go from the left-hand bottom corner of Figure 2, where there is a high probability of conflict, low chances of peace, and a low similarity of different societies, to the high level, particularly, as it turns out, when the two middle cells probably are no longer available. Colonialism is no longer practical on any large scale, and assimilation takes too long. The pathway through the dependency that was preferred during much of the nineteenth century is no longer available to us. Assimilation through dependency works at rates of one-fourth of one per cent per year or less. That is to say, to assimilate large settled populations culturally to the language and culture of alien rulers tends to take about four hundred years. In modern politics, we do not have time spans of four hundred years to wait for linguistic assimilation.

We really have only four options. We could try to go from conflict among highly different societies through forced assimilation and on to the world community, which means that we would have to traverse as a pathway to the world community a period of ideological or imperial rivalries or both. This is the cold war perspective, the perspective of building ever more massive blocs, trying to keep them monolithic. It was the vision of Joseph Stalin, who conceived of the rapid assimilation of local languages to regional languages and finally to a world language. It is implied in Stalin's article on linguistics, and though he doubtlessly had some trained linguists to help him write it, the basic perspective has the stamp of the old dictator's mind. Stalin did see the world that way; so did Churchill in his own way and so did others. All these men believed in the idea, again, of building a worldwide community with one culture, one process of assimilation, passing through an age of fairly forceful and explosive rivalry.

The opposite pathway would be to go through a stage of pluralism, through a stage, therefore, of carefully respecting the autonomy of different peoples and nations. It would mean to respect not only the growing similarity but also the remaining residual diversity of the world's culture, to expect some convergence, to know that some of this convergence may be convergence to mutual threat and danger, but not expecting it to go too far. It would mean managing convergence, rather than pushing it. This process might eventually get us to the world community. In my own view, and from a policy point of view, this pathway seems the more promising.

But these are speculations, based now on very limited knowledge. Since they are speculations on topics that are relevant to our survival, it might be worth replacing them with knowledge. To do so we shall have to replace many of the partial data and surmises we have now with better and more thorough data. It will cost us a great deal of work, but it may well prove worth doing.

The great industrial nations of the world may well be converging to greater but still partial similarity, to a greater salience of their remaining differences, to greater risks of deadly conflict, and perhaps to greater understanding of themselves and of each other. Whether they shall converge in ignorance or knowledge, toward war or peace, suicide or life, may depend in significant part on our own efforts.

THE SINGULAR AND THE PLURAL:
The Social Significance
of Industrialism Reconsidered

WILBERT E. MOORE, *University of Denver*

The observable world of social experience can prove embarrassing to social scientists, whose announced mission is the precise observation of social phenomena and the formulation of predictive propositions and generalizations that will lend a reliable order to mere facts. The contemporary world is, I believe, especially challenging to the fairly standard presuppositions and conceptual frameworks of most anthropologists and many sociologists, and it is not without difficulties for political scientists. Economists have been spared most of the embarrassment that I am about to explore by being remarkably parochial in the kind of political and institutional order within which their economic principles can be formulated. Psychologists, too, have been exempt from the challenge of social diversity among the world's population: they simply ignore it. No such safe refuges now exist for the social scientists who specifically attend to comparisons among the world's cultures, societies, or polities.

The chief basis for comparison and generalization across time and space has been a *culture* (used by anthropologists) or a *society* (used by sociologists), each seen as an integral, largely independent, and self-sustaining system of elements. Functionalism or the "holistic approach" taught us to see social facts, *and explain them,* in terms of other social facts, derived from the same system of patterns or beliefs. We were dissuaded from historical or etiological interpretations, although we were not barred from noting apparently extraneous or borrowed elements that could be traced to other cultures or systems.

This approach did not encourage the examination of these social or cultural systems for intrinsic sources of change. And it was scarcely equipped to deal with external intrusions that were extensive, diverse, and disruptive, yet emanated from a sufficiently common and cohesive source as to create forms of social organization and types of aspiration that reduced many of the visible differences in systems formerly differentiated through a relatively autonomous evolution.

The growing interdependence of the modern world, which implies the extensive breaching of the boundaries of formerly more or less independent systems, results from processes variously identified as industrialization, Westernization, or, the broader term, modernization. The conceptual differences among those terms will not detain us, for they are sufficiently interchangeable to let us gloss over the differences in meaning and attend rather to consequences.

The consequences of the massive and world-wide revolution of our time led me a number of years ago to write an article under the title, "The Creation of a Common Culture"[1]; much more recently I wrote a more conceptual, and conservative, article with the subtitle, "The World as a Singular System."[2] In the second article, and in various other writings to which subsequent references will be made, I paid considerable attention to persistent diversity. In the pages that follow I intend to review the theoretical and observational bases for the increased unity, or at least structural similarity, of mankind and his social patterns and the principal bases for expecting limits to homogeneity.

Essentials of Convergence Theory

It seems fair to say that the central notion of convergence theory, that is, the increasing homogeneity of social patterns through space, can be summarized succinctly: The common functional requisites of urban-industrial society lead to a narrow range of structural alternatives in their solution. Thus, a minimum statement of the theory is that industrial ("relatively modernized")[3] societies have more in common with one another than any does with a traditional ("relatively non-modernized") society, including its own historic state.

1. Wilbert E. Moore, "Creation of a Common Culture," *Confluence*, 4 (July, 1955), pp. 229–238.

2. Wilbert E. Moore, "Global Sociology: The World as a Singular System," *American Journal of Sociology*, 71 (March, 1966), pp. 475–482.

3. Marion J. Levy, Jr., *Modernization and the Structure of Society: A Setting for International Affairs*, 2 vols. (Princeton: Princeton University Press, 1966).

For this proposition there is a considerable body of evidence, most extensively marshalled by Marion J. Levy, Jr., in his two-volume work, *Modernization and the Structure of Societies*.[4] (Professor Levy's position is not precisely the one I have stated. He argues that, at the highest level of sociological generalization, *all* societies have more in common than they have differences. If, however, one attends to differences, the argument as stated here would apply.) Stated in this way, however, the implications of the theory are few. The theory says that generalizations about social structure are more tenable within dichotomous classes of societies than between them.

A somewhat stronger claim can be made by asserting, as a corollary, not only that the foregoing proposition is true, but also that observed differences are (a) anachronistic (a characteristic implying that they will narrow or disappear), or (b) relatively unimportant (because they are at a somewhat lower, descriptive level than the commonalities).

One may also infer that if a society moves from the non-modernized to the modernized category by some minimum criterion—Levy used a technological one—then appropriate changes in social structure are to be expected. The initial proposition argues for convergence among *industrial* societies—and we shall return to that—but is not directly responsive to the question of convergence among *all* societies.

In order to extend convergence theory to all contemporary societies and cultures, one needs a theory of modernization as such. Despite the extensive literature, to which I have contributed my share, on this subject, I think it proper to say that a succinct and comprehensive *causal* theory does not exist. Attention has been given to conditions, concomitants, and consequences,[5] and they are clearly relevant to convergence. Indeed, convergence theory is the principal source of their derivation. But these alleged generalizations are commonly, if implicitly, in the classical "If (modernization takes place) then . . . (certain other social changes must be met or later follow)" form. The likelihood that the if-clause will occur is not thereby directly examined.

I shall not here, because I can not, formulate the necessary and sufficient conditions for modernization. Yet I think some points need to be underscored, for they are relevant to our central concern with increasing homogeneity.

4. *Ibid.*
5. Wilbert E. Moore, *The Impact of Industry* (Englewood Cliffs, N. J.: Prentice-Hall, 1965).

Item: The autonomous integrity of tribal cultures or traditional agrarian and handicraft civilizations is subject to increasing breaches from external sources, even though colonialism is a relatively old phenomenon and some intersystem contacts have thus been present for considerable periods.

Item: Modern communication has added to older political, economic, and even religious influences in the non-modern world to accentuate awareness of differences, particularly in levels of material well-being.

Item: These influences have uncovered important *common* aspirations of mankind. The universal quest for meaning and order could be satisfied by very diverse values and modes of social control. The quest for material comfort, health, and longevity can best be met by rational improvements in technology, which is an essential ingredient of "modernism." Incidentally, this common if somewhat elementary sub-stratum of social values was rather systematically obscured by comparative sociologists and anthropologists whose emphasis was on cultural differences.

Item: The doctrine of modernization is almost universally subscribed to by political leaders and spokesmen in "new nations" as well as in older polities that have not hitherto shared in the conspicuous material benefits of economic rationalization. Extremely rapid urbanization (a vote with the feet) gives evidence that dissatisfaction is not narrowly confined, and widespread unrest that manifests itself in political disorder adds further confirmation. Whatever the first sources may have been, modernization is now an indigenous social force virtually everywhere.

It is this final, and culminating, point that justifies attention to the question of congruence, on a global scale and not just among fully qualified members of the club of industrial countries.

Uses of the Theory

The theory of convergence among modernized societies serves as an informative basis for cross-societal (or cross-national) comparisons and generalizations. If restricted to industrialized or highly modernized societies, it provides a richer (though patently more temporally and spatially limited) basis for generalization than that provided by the common features of all societies, minimally defined, that permit statements beginning, "Any society...."[6]

6. Marion J. Levy, Jr., *The Structure of Society* (Princeton: Princeton University Press, 1952).

A few examples of generalizations about the common features of modernized societies may serve to highlight the utility of attending precisely to commonalities. Some of these examples are widely noted in the standard literature; others are not.

Certain common structural features of industrial societies—that is, forms of social organization or patterns of social relationships—are clearly discernible amid conspicuous variations.

Item: Industrial societies are characterized by a physical and social separation between adult generations and among adult siblings and other kinsmen. This separation is often expressed as the destruction of extended kinship systems as corporate groups and the predominance of the nuclear family. All kinship reciprocities outside the immediate family will not, as a consequence, necessarily disappear, but they become relatively weak and somewhat discretionary.

Japan is an often-cited exception to this generalization, for the kinship system actually served for a considerable period as an agency of social transformation. Even though we can not deny the importance of that unusual and possible unique circumstance, later developments, particularly since World War II, are more nearly in line with experience elsewhere and would seem to justify calling the earlier situation anachronistic. Similarly, strong, intergenerational links in the French family system have persisted, but they are decreasingly common precisely among urban and industrial populations. This example too may qualify as anachronistic.

Item: Industrial societies are characterized by the bureaucratization of work, not only in various governmental services and public administration but also in the production and distribution of goods and services. Therefore, the extensive job specialization is coordinated through an administrative organization. The independent producer, whether of goods or services, represents a declining proportion of the economically active population. (Note that in communist states he nominally disappears.)

Item: In industrial societies most goods and services are monetized. Capital goods, credits and debts, and consumer goods and services are evaluated and recorded in monetary terms, and at least part of the transfers of goods and services take place in essentially impersonal markets. Because of the extensive occupational specialization and diversification of products and services, money becomes a kind of universal solvent, a necessary mechanism for permitting the specialized producer to become a generalized consumer for himself and his dependents.

Item: In industrial societies, formal education is used to produce a virtually universal adult literacy, which then becomes an assumed qualification, both for most occupational roles, but also for many others as well—such as the housewife in her shopping or the voter on political issues. Additionally, and more importantly, a graded system of formal education, with higher levels, is a principal mechanism of allocation to occupational position. Thus, educational level becomes an important variable and determinant of relative social status.

We may also attend to some less commonly observed convergences among industrial societies: the normative principles of wide applicability in economically advanced societies that are of lesser or virtually no importance in a traditional social order.

Item: Despite the persistent evidence of the human potential for irrational conduct, the normative expectation of rationality is firmly established in many contexts of social behavior in industrial societies. In determining how a task is to be done, deciding among alternative courses of administrative action, or choosing consumer goods, the actor is expected to use the best available information and logical inferences. However irrational or non-rational the actor's deep-seated motivational state may be, his overt acts are expected to conform to the norm of rationality. So extensive is this principle that it may be used to challenge traditional precedent, and thus it is an important element in the organization and institutionalization of change, which is another important characteristic of industrial societies.

Item: Time is always scarce in view of man's mortality.[7] Yet the precise division, allocation, and coordination of time are not common in most human societies. Outside of the medieval monastery, where a precise temporal order was an important ingredient of discipline, the most extensive temporal coordination is that of modern industrial societies. The normative principle here may be summarized as the norm of punctuality, although timed rhythms, sequences, and synchronization are important. Indeed, since timing is an essential element in the coordination of specialized activities, punctuality may also be viewed as an important aspect of work discipline in industrial societies.

Item: Industrial societies provide both a different and a far more diversified set of occupational roles than that characteristic of non-modern economies. A diversification of relative skill and rewards as well as merely lateral diversification are present. And positions are,

7. Wilbert E. Moore, *Man, Time, and Society* (New York: John Wiley & Sons, 1963).

at least ideally, filled on the basis of qualification and performance, not by ascription. Thus, occupational mobility between generations, and to some degree within careers, is a further characteristic of industrial societies. Several normative principles are relevant in this context: status achievement and universalistic criteria of selection are commonly noted. I suggest that we should also add, as a further commonality among industrial societies, the norm of achievement orientations. The individual is expected to compete for social placement, according to relevant criteria of competence and performance, and to be dissatisfied if his talents are not fully utilized (and, of course, rewarded).

We have been attending to the uses of convergence theory in orienting the comparative social analyst toward common features of a class of societies. Such an orientation rescues the observer from the banalities of cultural relativism: we do it this way, they do it that way. At least some of the visible differences are thus to be seen as superficial, as relatively minor variations on underlying common themes.

Yet we are also concerned with the modernization process, and thus with the potential spread of convergence in social systems. Accordingly, a second principal use of convergence theory is in temporal prediction: the direction in which societies must move if they are to be relatively successful in attempts at modernization. The notion of a "model industrial society" has been used by various scholars, including myself, as a predictive scheme for identifying the social consequences of industrialization where it has not yet occurred, or is at relatively low levels of advancement.[8]

Once more, I shall give illustrations rather than an exhaustive and orderly compendium of the consequences of modernization.

Item: There is no instance of relatively successful modernization (say, in terms of income per capita) within a strictly agricultural context. Thus, a common process of economic development and a common feature of developed economies is the shift from agricultural to non-agricultural production and distribution of the labor force. A growing proportion of the labor force outside agriculture may eventually lead to an actual reduction in the absolute number of agricultural workers as farming becomes mechanized and in other ways rationalized.

Item: A closely associated social transformation is the process of

8. Wilbert E. Moore, *The Impact of Industry.*

urbanization. Now, of course cities existed in the ancient world and in the ancient agrarian civilizations in Asia. Yet the pace of urbanization is certainly more rapid now than at any time in history, and it is nearly universal. There is thus little hazard in predicting that the urban character of social life will increase in the developing as well as in the developed countries. And cities of a given size class have strong resemblances to one another wherever they are found. Yet here we must enter a first cautionary note, in anticipation of other serious cautions to be noted later. The historic connection between industrialization and urbanization in the West has been exaggerated, but it was certainly closer than that which now prevails in much of the underdeveloped world. Much of the urbanization in Asia, Africa, and Latin America is taking place at a rate far more rapid than the expansion rate in manufacturing, and it often occurs in the virtual absence of industry. The failure of genuinely productive employment to expand as rapidly as available urban labor supplies leads to two *distinctive* characteristics of cities in the underdeveloped world: (1) in ecological structure, they are characterized by the peripheral or suburban slum, in contrast to the well-to-do suburbias of Europe and America; (2) the occupational structure is strongly weighted toward "services," mostly at very low skill levels and mostly characterized by extreme underemployment. Our caution, however, is not meant to deny that these cities are likely to move toward the Western pattern if indeed they become more prosperous.[9]

Item: The formality and impersonality of social relations at work or in the market place, so untypical of traditional societies, also appears in the maintenance of order and social control. In the process of modernization strangers are brought together in novel settings, kinship units are often geographically as well as socially divided, and other sources of informal controls by significant others are either weakened or destroyed. The problem of order, including congruence in expectations between parents and children, has scarcely been solved in any industrial society, and indeed it would be a mistake to assume an absence of conflict in more traditional regimes. Yet the problem is likely to be greater in degree in newly developing areas, precisely because the forms and rules are novel and, often, just in the process of formulation. Thus, to the lack of internalization of normative princi-

---

9. See Gino Germani, *Política y Sociedad en una Época de Transición* (Buenos Aires: Editorial Paidos [1962]).

ples in childhood must be added some measure of ignorance and uncertainty. If this is a problem for which time is no absolute cure, it may in time be at least alleviated.

Major Limitations, and Some Minor Ones

Convergence theory, though wrong in particulars, has been remarkably productive of verifiable generalizations and inferential hypotheses relating to the course of change (or rather its direction) in countries seeking to join the modern world. I have attempted so far to give the theory its due. I hope in the process to have put another shovel of earth over the coffin of the silly notion that modern sociology is rich with concepts and bereft of genuine theory. Overly equipped with concepts, with distinctions without a difference, my field may be. But poor in generalized theory it is not.

This is scarcely the occasion for reiterating my previous complaints that modernization theory depends too much on comparative statics and on before-and-after comparisons, and that it lacks both a systematic, causal analysis and rates, routes, and time-tables. Yet this failure is not altogether a theoretical one; it is partly such, since the questions have not uniformly been put succinctly and insistently. Also lacking has been the observational base, without which theory properly deserves the contempt with which it is viewed by some of my disciplinary colleagues.

Due deference having been given to a rather major theoretical development, we must now attend to some important limitations and to some qualms, quibbles, and exceptions of varying degrees of severity.

Let me state some elementary observations, with due apology for being elemental.

Item: What we used to call societies or cultures have some approximation to political entities, organized as national states.

Item: The contemporary national state is, in fact, multicommunal (racially, ethnically, linguistically, religiously) more often than not.

Item: Virtually no one of those states has a clear correspondence, along territorial boundaries, among the several major elements of what would qualify as a distinctive culture. The source and extent of political authority may, in fact, be the principal distinctive element from one area to another. Of course we may ignore political boundaries in the identification of distinctive cultures, but the role of the polity in institutional integration and in centralized decision-making should caution us against its neglect.

It is precisely the political order of national states that is a major limitation on convergence theory; for I find no persuasive evidence that the polities of industrial societies are becoming more alike. I do not deny that the administrative structure of the state is likely to take on standard bureaucratic forms, some a little more decentralized than others, some a little more inefficient or corrupt than others, but all with an unmistakable resemblance. Nor do I intend to deny that any modern polity and any state attempting to enter upon the modern world of affairs will count on a considerable degree of political participation. Everything from manipulated street mobs to Marxist study groups can be expected, including sham and possibly even genuine elections. A regime that does not provide for, and somehow contain, opportunities for political participation, for popular mobilization, can expect to encounter them anyway in the form of dissident, hostile, and disruptive activities.

Yet none of this activity leads to the expectation of a stable democracy as the proper form of the power distribution of an industrial state or one seeking to become an economically developed country. If a considerable measure of political stability is a requisite for economic modernization—and it clearly is—that stability is by no means assured in the new nations or the old and backward ones, and if it is achieved it may be in radically diverse forms.

Feldman and I have explored this persistent structural dissimilarity among industrial and also industrializing societies by using the notion of society as a tension-management system.[10] First, we think that for many practical and therefore theoretical purposes the term society had best be understood as a national state. That state is quite unlikely to be self-sustaining in an interdependent world political order. Yet the state is the principal source of order and centralized planning in a territory, a territory having some problems of historical course and current situation that are in significant degree peculiarly its own.

Thus, second, we think that polities have different characteristic tensions and modes for their solution. These tensions arise from different histories and historic paths to the present. Part of any current political structure (which may be reflected in differing weights attached

---

10. Arnold S. Feldman and Wilbert E. Moore, "Industrialization and Industrialism: Convergence and Differentiation," *Transactions of the Fifth World Congress of Sociology*, Vol. II, International Sociological Association, Washington, 1962, pp. 151–169.

to the several administrative organs of the state) will include the residues of procedures previously adopted in surmounting obstacles in the way of either order or planned, developmental change. Perfect and debt-free resolutions of such problems as talent shortages, conspicuous inequities in placement and income distribution, or massive migrations to new sources of economic opportunities do not even exist in responsible textbooks, to say nothing of the real world of experience. The partial resolution of such problems leaves political, administrative, and even unofficial remnants that are by no means trivial. Moreover, the partially independent evolution—or at least change—in different areas leads to substantial differences in institutional weight and balance. Here one economic class or segment was especially strong and seeks to maintain some semblance of its advantage; there a religious structure retains significant influence; somewhere else a linguistic or tribal group is especially influential or disenchanted. The state, as the ultimate arbiter of such organizational and institutional balances, must either persistently reflect the social setting in which it operates, or act ineffectively.

It is at least faintly painful to a dedicated generalist about social behavior to enter upon a discussion of persistent and important differences, but, once attended to, they are theoretically instructive. Ironically, the commonalities that convergence theory would lead us to expect could not occur without the differences in political structure that we have just been exploring. For only by partially resolving problems that are in some degree unusual, by maintaining an always precarious balance of interests that differ in time and space, can any social system maintain the essential and interdependent conditions for a modern economic order.

However, a further point of commonality warrants attention: the growing importance of the polity in economic affairs, everywhere. For late-comers, for economies now called, optimistically, newly developing, the state is the principal agency for the mobilization of resources for modernization. We should not, therefore, expect to witness even an approximate replication of the predominance of private entrepreneurship in the historic development of the Western world. (The historic role of the state was, of course, much more substantial than "liberal" economic dogma would lead us to believe; and, generally speaking, we have been badly served by historians on this point.) Yet it turns out that the post-industrial society is by no means trouble-free. Whether to maintain stability, to foster continued growth, or to achieve more equitable distribution of economic and other benefits, the state in industrial society, it turns out, intervenes not only as arbiter but also as producer and distributor of goods and services. Even in avowedly pluralistic societies, the preservation of a private sector is neither automatic nor easy.

The late-comer in the modernization process has some serious disadvantages. Catching up may prove impossible under current and foreseeable international political arrangements. Absolute standards may improve under a program of modernization, but prosperous countries continue to grow more rapidly in economic production than do poor ones. The bitter, inequitable Biblical phrase, "To him that hath shall be given ... ," remains a kind of truism.

Yet the late-comer has some small advantages. The new nation does not have to replicate technological history by painful and costly trial and error. Here the singular system of the world operates. And in political arrangements and announced ideologies, a kind of selective eclecticism from among available models is possible. (Clearly the systemic qualities of social patterns will not permit a kind of random assembly of structural elements to be viable, but previously untried combinations are not necessarily lethal, as we can now see widely demonstrated.)

The central theme to which we are now attending is political variability, and it is to that theme that the discussion of political eclecticism and novelty is addressed. For the international political setting, and world history, add reasons for *not* expecting a precise replication of political structures and legal institutions. The fact of existing diversity makes further diversity possible and virtually assures it, particularly as one or another element or ideological orientation must be adapted to genuinely different social contexts.

Some diversity of political organization is derived from the very fact that new nations are formed as nominally independent units. If Calvinistic Protestantism was important to the development of capitalism—a thesis I see no reason to reject—it is clearly neither a necessary nor a sufficient condition for current developmental efforts. Yet a fairly strong case can be made—and here I agree with Smelser[11]—that nationalism is a kind of contemporary (and more collectively-oriented) equivalent to Protestantism as an essentially religious ideology appropriate to achievement and the expectation of beneficent change.

Nationalism—to which, note, no old industrial state is immune,

11. Neil J. Smelser, "Mechanisms of Change and Adjustment to Change," in Bert F. Hoselitz and Wilbert E. Moore (eds.), *Industrialization and Society* (Paris and the Hague: UNESCO and Mouton, 1963), Chap. 2.

and few wear it lightly—becomes a kind of secular religion, justifying current suffering or relative deprivation for the greater, and the future, good. Especially in new nations, it becomes a collective identity quest, the search for a historic, contemporary, and future *difference* from all other states.[12] (The circumstance that the past, at least, is likely to be expressed in ethnic or otherwise cultural terms should neither surprise nor delude us. Only old states can afford a genuine, national, political identity, and it is precarious, even so.)

We are thus provided with a further reason not to expect political homogeneity or convergence, and that reason is simply that national leaders will that it not be so. We do not, as social scientists, have to take public protestations at face value, and we are silly if we fail to observe that some of those protestations make a genuine difference. Indeed, the failure of some of us adequately to take account of purpose, including collective purpose, in human affairs may lead us into an overly rigid and overly mechanical view of inevitability. Silliness may abound among political spokesmen who promise the impossible, but it can not excuse the dispassionate observer if he fails to note that spoken dreams have an effect on reality. Those effects may be profound.

There are other social patterns in which convergence is not to be expected, though they are clearly not at the same level of importance as the form and distribution of official power.

Item: Linguistic differences persist, and their persistence multiplies the problems of communication that an interdependent world requires. It is true that languages are subject to some interpenetration, particularly in technical vocabularies, and various *linguae francae* have developed, but language systems and even regional idioms remain remarkably intact.

Item: Theological systems and aesthetic forms and canons have a relatively weak linkage with social patterns and appear to persist or change relatively autonomously from ambient social settings.[13] This view has been challenged by Sorokin,[14] mainly in his massive attempt to gather everything into his cultural typology,[15] but I simply do not find the evidence persuasive.

Item: Even everyday and commonplace customs may persist in

12. See Wendell Bell and James H. Mau (eds.), *The Sociology of the Future* (New York: Russell Sage Foundation, 1971).

13. See Wilbert E. Moore, *Social Change* (Englewood Cliffs, N.J.: Prentice-Hall, 1963), pp. 75–76.

14. Pitirim A. Sorokin, *Sociological Theories of Today* (New York: Harper & Row, 1966), pp. 609–611.

15. Pitirim A. Sorokin, *Social and Cultural Dynamics*, 4 vols. (New York: American Book Company, 1937–40).

their differences, their significance being perhaps relatively superficial in the main shape of the social order. Thus, preferences in cuisine, in styles of greeting and forms of address, and even in manner of attire may become standardized only for a limited international and cosmopolitan set, but the old customs persist for the bulk of the population.

Item: Traditional recreational and expressive forms may not only survive, but even be refurbished. The appeal of the exotic as a tourist attraction would be endangered by complete homogeneity in social patterns. Moreover, local custom, particularly if it has some claim to being both indigenous and old, may serve as a symbol of cultural identity, an identity that even a revolutionary state may see fit to preserve or partially restore.

A Partial Summary

It is true that factories of a given size, product, and technology are going to look much alike, with some differences attributable to variations in the educational or skill levels of the labor force. The same is true of administrative agencies with comparable functions. It is also true that the social structure of cities will differ more from income levels and distributions than from "culture."

Convergence theory has served to identify very important commonalities among industrial societies and the predictable direction of change in newly developing areas. And, partly because some of the areas seeking modernization will succeed, the amount of structural homogeneity in the world will increase.

Yet world homogeneity is neither at hand nor predictable. On most measurable scales, "advanced" societies are changing more rapidly than "newly developing" ones, though it might be argued that qualitative change is greater in the latter—that is, that more discontinuity is experienced.

One does not want to engage in arguments that are likely to be more ideological than objective over what is fundamental and what is superficial. Surely the ways of making a living, the size and type of place in which one lives, the relations between parents and children, and the degree of education can scarcely be dismissed as superficial, and they are clearly headed for greater cross-national homogeneity. Beliefs, customs, language, and the way order is kept can also scarcely be dismissed as superficial, and they will certainly remain different for the foreseeable future.

INDUSTRIALIZATION:
The Ecumenical and Parochial
Aspects of the Process

MANNING NASH, *University of Chicago*

The time is past in social science when the spread of industrialization around the globe meant the turning of the world's cultural variety into "a single gray mass of industrialized workers" in a bureaucratic state. Equally, the vision that each newly industrializing society would make its distinctive adaptation has lost its romantic appeal. Instead, the significant and theoretically interesting questions about industrialization have grown from a considerable body of research literature. One of the most compelling problems in the analysis of the process of industrialization is accounting for the empirical unities and varieties in the path of industrialization and for the modes of social and cultural integration of industrialized societies.

It is clear that social and cultural uniformity among industrialized societies is precluded by the following features of the process:

1. *The time at which industrialization is undertaken.* Since a recapitulation of the experience of the industrialized nations is both unnecessary and impossible, the actual technology adapted at a given moment is unlikely to be a duplicate of the existing set of skills, knowledge, machines, and productive organization of any other society.

2. *The lead segment in the drive to industrialization.* A fairly cohesive group spurs the process of industrialization and consciously seeks to transform production. The organization, values, and membership of this lead segment have always varied and will continue to do so. The variance of this group will affect the path, pace, and products of the industrialization process.

131

3. *The process of diffusion and acculturation itself.* In the spread of social and cultural patterns and traits among societies, characteristics of the process result in novelty in the incorporating society. Recombination of elements, resynthesis of old and new traits, reinterpretation and stimulation of new patterns are ineluctable aspects of acculturation.

4. *The differential evolution of aspects of industrial society.* Industrial society is necessarily an unfinished business and continues to evolve. As in all evolutionary processes radiation and diversification are inherent. Cultural drift, innovation, and adaptation all make for variety in the forms of industrial and modern societies.

5. *The exogenous event-structure of history.* All societies are embedded in time, place, and interactions with at least some other societies. The stream of climactic events like wars, revolutions, assassinations, famines, economic crises, etc., are generated in other social systems, in nature, and in time. They differentially affect industrial societies, and the societies' modes of coping with them increase the scale of variety among such societies.

At the same time the range of social and cultural variety open to industrial societies, and the temporal routes toward an industrial society, are constrained. What keeps the social universe contained are the following features of industrialization:

1. There are generic, systemic features to industrial and modern societies. Some sets of social choices have nearly inevitable structural consequences, so that modern industrial society is a singular class of societies, despite the plurality of the members of the class.

2. Existing, modern, industrial societies are in part models for the industrializing societies. Modern societies have solved some of the problems of organizing complex and differentiated industrial societies. Some of these solutions will be incorporated by the industrializing nations. Furthermore, modernity is partly symbolic and emblematic, and some of the display and façade features of modern societies will be emulated as well as the technical ones.

3. No society can industrialize in isolation, and interaction with industrialized societies will shape the temporal path. Also, international monetary and other agencies will help structure similar time parabolas for industrializing societies.

4. Increased international communication and the nascent, emergent, supra-national communities of scientists, technicians, and other professionals will generate similarities among industrial nations.

5. Industrial society is part cultural projection and part competition for symbolic leadership and excellence and will mean concentration on similar cultural and social elaborations across social systems.

Industrialization

The ten assertions above are offered from the perspective of social anthropology and imply a cross-cultural and comparative view; but here they are concerned chiefly with the newly-developing nations of Asia and Africa, and some of the little industrialized societies of Latin America. The problems of European late-comers, including the Soviets, to industrialization can, in this paper, be ignored because of the work of Gerschenkron and others. What follows is an explication of the ten propositions, some theoretical rationale for them, and some empirical underpinning to them.

The time a society enters into the process of industrialization is in part fortuitous. In all of human history three great and unanticipated social transformations have occurred. These basic structural changes have so shaped the human career that they merit the title Revolution. The first revolution transformed an insignificant group of primates into tool and symbol users and formed the basis for human society. With cultural and symbolic adaptations, these first men spread all over the world and came to live in and dominate endless varieties of ecological niches. About 7,000 years ago, somewhere in the hilly, grassy flanks of the Fertile Crescent in the Near East, the next unforeseen revolution occurred like a mutation in genetics. This food-producing revolution, the Neolithic, laid the foundation for a settled human life based on a fairly secure, regular food supply. It was also the basis for the monumental civilizations of East and West Asia; and a similar Neolithic age in the New World initiated the processes that culminated in the civilizations of the Maya, Nahuatl, and Inca. This food-producing revolution, unlike the symbol and tool revolution, did not become the common property of all mankind. Some of the band of organized hunters and gatherers lived in environments unsuited for any cultivation, and others of them were pushed to peripheries of the expanding Neolithic civilization where some still exist.

The third revolution, occurring in the mid-1700s in Northwest Europe, is the industrial revolution, the harnessing of machine energy and the aggregating of workers at power-driven machines in a complex division of labor, the products of which enter into a wide, impersonal network of exchange relationships. Just as the tool and symbol revolution had its internal logic and dynamic, culminating in the fancy lithic industries of Europe, or the Neolithic had its culmination in theocratic civilizations with monumental expressions of the world view, so the industrial revolution has its own. The drive of the industrial revolution is the continual search for the application of tested knowledge to all aspects of production and the continual adaptation of the social structure and value system to facilitate this process. Apparently, its culmination or historical climax has not yet been attained.

The historical moment in which a given society enters into the stream of industrialization helps to shape its adjustment. The first industrial nations moved through a fairly standard pattern of textile and processing industries to giant complexes and steel mills and assembly plants. No newly-industrializing nation is likely to follow this pattern, and hence the nature of the labor force, the kind of management, and the structure of employee relations are not likely to be those of the older industrial societies. In fact, the older complex of textile and processing industries can not now generate enough economic momentum to industrialize a relatively non-industrial economy. The older spread of textiles and light industries to Asia in the mid-1800's did result in an ever-expanding industrialization, partly because of the colonial and semi-colonial economic status of Asia, but also because textiles and light processing industries were, even then, not the leading edge of industrialization.

Now that many Asian nations are seriously entering the worldwide stream of industrialism, their already dense populations, their relations with the already industrialized societies, and the new tools and skills from which they will make selections preclude a close similarity among one another, and between them as a class and the already industrialized. This is so even at the level of the social organization of production, and more so as one moves from the technological and economic sub-systems to those less intimately connected with production—i.e., religion and expressive systems. The way Japan has structured its labor force in a highly successful industrial adaptation is the outstanding example of how much variability there can be in the process and how crucial is the historical moment when industrialization is feasible for an aspiring nation.

Industrialization, again in the context of the new nations of Asia and Africa, is too important a feature of modernization to be left to historical chance or to the vagaries of cultural diffusion. The policy-making segment of the new nation, its governing class or its elite, seeks deliberate and rapid industrialization. The five ideal types of spearhead groups for industrialization suggested by Kerr, *et al.*[1] hardly capture or even make manageable the phenomenal variety of actually existing elites. The ruling Congress coalition in India, long committed to industrialization as a matter of economic policy, is a mixed group of politicians, intellectuals, scientists, bureaucrats, and some army officers. The major component of this elite on the national level is the close contact with Western civilization. The Nehru biography is an apt comment on how Westernized this elite was and is. Membership in this elite depends on a command of English, Western education, and a commitment to the major lineaments of parliamentary democracy. The elite is organized through the control of the Congress party and is willing to deal with both the Soviet area and the United States: a huge industrial complex is being built with the aid of Eastern European technicians and financing, while other industries are built with West European and United States technicians and funds. At the same time indigenous, private entrepreneurs, such as those from Tata Steel, continue to expand their industrial capacity. This capsule description of the elite shows that they have more diversity, more lines of enterprise, and more political and social commitments than those of earlier industrializing nations. This diversity was not possible before the industrial revolution transformed parts of India and left it chiefly a non-modern enclave in the metropolitan system of the British Empire.

To underlie the diversity of the elite and the base cultures and societies from which they begin the drive to modernity, one need only look at some other ex-colonial new nations. The military regime of Ne Win's Burma shares almost nothing with the military regime of Ayoub Khan of Pakistan except the common name. And farther afield, Suharto's junta is radically different from the Nigerian junta. All this is not merely to point to empirical diversity and to say that because the drive to modernity begins from disparate foundations its paths and final products must be equally as diverse. There is a systematic, built-in difference in the way a Westernized, parliamentary elite can mobilize and direct the people toward modernity and the way a charismatic, military regime can or would perform the same tasks. The values, organization, and modes of communication between

---

1. C. Kerr, *et al.*, *Industrialism and Industrial Man* (New York: Oxford University Press, 1964), p. 50.

elite segments and the human material from which a modern society must be fashioned set the parameters for social and cultural variation in defining the permissible paths toward industrialization and the modes of viable integration of a modernizing society. More research is needed to say with any confidence what the trade-offs between consensus and coercion, between consumer incentive and state accumulation, between pragmatic and passionate ideological appeals, between equalitarian income distributions and badly skewed ones, and between other options sets are for any particular elite mobilizing a given sort of society.

Variations in Industrial Societies

The largest source of variability in the process of industrialization stems from how the ineluctable modalities of that social change must be initiated. Newly modernizing nations must select technology from the world store of knowledge and tools and adapt and incorporate them in their own social systems. This process of acculturation, whether involved or not with industrialization, has a structure of its own that inhibits cultural identity among inter-communicating societies, irrespective of the number, frequency, or kind of behavior and symbol diffused from one society to another. In acculturation, minimal recombination, reinterpretation, resynthesis, and stimulation of new patterns occur. Examples abound in the literature, and they confirm the necessary diversity in industrial societies. Two action patterns separate in the donor culture may be recombined in the receiving culture so that new elements and new behavior ensue. The diffusion of the bath tub to the peasants of Upper Burma results in its use in the making of condensed milk. Or the introduction of a textile mill in Guatemala results in a work schedule that accommodates nursing mothers and, at the same time, inhibits the emergence of a career factory girl.[2] Descriptions of Japanese factories, the administrative structure of a Chinese factory, or the way the Santal move into steel mills[3] all provide examples of the numerous aspects of recombination in the diffusion of an industrial technology to the less industrialized.

Reinterpretation comes about because meanings attached to behavior and even to artifacts are typically more difficult to diffuse than the overt, observable act and artifact. What may be in the indus-

2. Manning Nash, *Machine Age Maya* (Chicago: University of Chicago Press, Phoenix Books, 1967).

3. Martin Orans, *The Santal; A Tribe in Search of a Great Tradition* (Detroit: Wayne State University Press, 1965).

trialized nations an impersonal organization for the prosecution of strictly-defined economic ends may, on transfer, become a more or less familial organization, even one with rituals of adoption into the firm for employees and commitments to lifetime bonds. What in the industrialized nations are taken as self-evident meanings attached to the productive organization are not self-evident to either the elites or the non-elites of developing nations.

Notions about machine maintenance or the possibility that a machine may be abused, pride in handling tools, or the tinkering inventiveness common to the already-industrialized nations may be meanings difficult to spread. They may in fact be an idiosyncratic elaboration verging on industrial sacred or cult behavior.[4] The industrial performance can be symbolized and given meaning by a wide set of codes, and the conventional understanding of the already-industrialized about the rest of society to the symbolic and technical imperatives of the industrial complex are bound to be reinterpreted to fit the deeper meanings of the industrializing nations.

Borrowing will set off new behaviors in the receiving society because the context into which the elements from an industrial society are injected is so initially different. A textile mill in Guatemala results in the workers' forming a *cofradia,* a religious brotherhood for the upkeep of a saint's festival, while the owners of the mill cooperate with the local union in the laying of a tile floor in the community church. The introduction of something as simple as matches in an African society results in an increased rate of adultery, since fires can be lit only when a woman has slept with her husband.

Some of the core meanings may never get diffused at all, or, if diffused, they may be socially encapsulated in ways not known in the already-industrialized societies. The rational, pragmatic approach of a factory worker to his job and machine need not leak out into other areas of his life, just as the magical or religious associations from his non-factory life need not contaminate his performance within the world of work. Individual persons, social groups, and cultural patterns certainly need not be seamless balls of consistency.

Combining the three sources of variation already noted in itself makes for a multiplier effect of increasing differentiation among industrial societies. And if we move, again, from the productive organization and technology where the constraints toward similarity seem systematically greatest toward family, polity, law, religion, and expressive system and style and ethos, the range of possible free variance

---

4. J. S. Slotkin, *From Field to Factory: New Industrial Employees* (Glencoe: The Free Press, 1960).

is measurably expanded. What sort of government must an industrialized society have? What sort of family and household organization? What sort of salvation idiom? etc., are questions that on inspection turn out to be rather without meaning, or answerable on such a high level of abstraction that they are theoretically and empirically uninteresting.

Industrial societies are not closed, completed social systems. Modernity is everywhere an unfinished business. No society has fully adapted to the requirements of modernity and for good, theoretical reasons. Not all human behavior can be scaled along a cost versus benefit axis and choices made in terms of some principle such as mini-max. In human cultures, goals, objectives, or benefits are not given but are themselves objects of the social process; and there are varying degrees of consensus and dissension about the relative ordering of social and individual goals. Because a good part of the behavior, perhaps most of that intimate, primary, and meaningful interaction, that provides the empathetic basis for social interaction takes place outside of the sphere of market exchange, effective rationality is a value-governed choice, not a cost–benefit calculation.

The more limited productive organization and economy of industrialized societies are continually under stresses to change and adapt. The processes of continued differentiation and of integration, in more and more complex forms, appear as almost a defining characteristic of modern societies. Perhaps the most dramatic instance of technological change in production in the mature industrial societies is the advent of automated systems of production and information processing. The effects on the structure of the labor force were, as few as ten years ago, unanticipated. Nor would the role of labor unions as defenders of the vested interests of the unionized, rather than as leaders of social protest, have been predicted twenty-five years ago. What the productive organization and technology of the already-industrialized will look like twenty-five years from now is largely beyond the realm of prophecy.

What is clear is that, while the industrial societies, the homelands of innovation for the foreseeable future, are adapting to a steady stream of innovation, the industrializing societies are likely to lag and adapt to an earlier form of technology and productive organization. The gap need not always exist and a permanent form of international stratification need not be posited, but continual divergences in evolution, among the industrialized societies and between the industrialized and the industrializing, seem assured at least until the end of the century. Even the phenomenon of leap-frogging—that is, a newly industrial society's making innovations whose productive efficiency is greater than that of an already-industrialized society—is possible, but, again, it produces divergence rather than parallelism.

Beyond the technological and productive spheres, even more divergence among industrial societies and industrializing ones may confidently be expected. Most forms of social organization in an industrial society are remarkably labile. Even basic, primary groups of family, kinship, neighborhood, and friendship cliques are structurally protean and in content subject to continual replacement. The transition, in the United States, for example, from child-centered, duty-governed, near life-time families to companionate, mate-centered, fulfillment-oriented, serially monogamous families is still underway. The old cliche, "the family, its function and destiny," no longer has social meaning when the experimental attitude toward familial life is so on the increase in the United States.

Similar structural differentiation and cultural redefinition are apparent in most domains of most industrialized societies, and the likelihood of ubiquitous social and cultural change is high. In the industrializing countries the divergences in aspects of society continue. The industrialization of India does not make the range of Indian family forms like the range of Japanese forms, and one could run that sort of permutation through every industrializing society and through all of the sub-systems of those societies.

Social systems are set, of course, in time and space, and the flow of exogenous events frequently has major social and cultural repercussions. Wars, epidemics, revolutions, famines, gold rushes, and collective social movements will probably continue in the world, will differentially affect societies, and will add to the kaleidoscopic arrangements of industrially-organized social systems.

Generically Modern Societies

This stress on the sources of variety among industrial societies does not mean that as a genus of social systems they are not easily, empirically, and categorically distinguishable from other genera of, say, primitive and peasant. The use of the phrase "generically" modern societies is premised on two different sources, both in essence comparative. Modern societies as a class are compared with non-modern and less modernized societies to see in what ways they differ. And modern societies can be contrasted against their pre-modern structure to see how they have changed. The sum of these two comparisons lays the basis for speaking of the generically modern.

In generically modern societies the economy is fully differentiated from other sub-systems and tends to be the lead sector in continuing social and cultural change. The empirical indices underlying the modernity of the economy are fairly easy to obtain. The occupational diversity in bureaucratic organizations with high human and factor mobility is the most salient of social facts about the modern economy. The substitution of the farmer for the peasant in the countryside of modern societies is but an aspect of the spread of monetization for most goods and services, a sort of effective drive toward rationality when money measures can be used and when performance is the core of the economy. These systemic constraints on what the economy can be like socially and culturally in a modern society are visible on even casual inspection in the United States, the Soviet Union, Japan, and Western Europe. A comparison of the Europe of pre-1500 with the Europe of 1750, or pre- and post-Meiji Japan, is also tied to an understanding of the peculiar institutional setting of modern economies and the built-in drive for the application of science and knowledge to all aspects of production.

If in generically modern societies the means of production are set in a socially differentiated economy with system drives to efficiency, the means of reproduction, the family, and kinship also have typically modern features. The corporate kin groups (the clans, the phratries, and the lineages) are weakened and finally disappear. Their disappearance takes and orders the social path in the wake of modernization and is one of the best documented sequences of social change in the storehouse of social anthropology. But kinship, of course, continues as long as society does. In modern societies the family is the only kin grouping, and it tends to be small and nuclear and to pay attention to two chief tasks: the socialization of the young and satisfaction of the progenitors. Beyond the family are kinship networks and affective ties among kinsmen, but the optionality of kinship ties seems a part of modern familial life. Without a stake in familial property, without skill transfer within the family, and with the other agencies of socialization (school, job, peer, etc.) that provide the major means of social location, the family cannot be the central locus of attachment.

To move from the economy and family, those sub-systems most intimately tied to the technological and scientific bases for modernity, to religion and world view is to move to spheres of action less closely tied to systemic constraint. In religion three major (but at rather high levels of abstraction) characteristics can be posited. Religion in a modern society becomes separated from direct sanction and direct guidance in daily life. The modes of reasoning in religion approximate those in any other sphere of modern culture—autonomous rationality becomes the standard against which a religious assertion is judged. Thirdly, there is more concern with private fate and individual salvation than with a vision of the ideal society or the kingdom of heaven on earth. This rationalized, individualized, and modernized religion does not stand alone in a modern society and culture but competes with strong fundamentalist drives among persons to whom the loss of a cosmic meaning to the social order is a deprivation. In my view religion must, and does, accommodate to living with science, with fundamentalism, with hostility, and with indifference in a modern society.

Two other social sub-systems seem to have narrow parameters in the generically modern society. The system of social stratification, at least, cannot be of the estate or caste variety if modernization progresses very far. A class system, of some sort, is generically the legitimate system of social inequality in a modern society. The class system fits with the expanding economy, with the application of science to daily life, and with the decreasing role of the family as placing agent in the social system. It fits because of the decrease in ascribed status and the increase of allocation based on economic performance. The openness of class systems in modern societies is one of the major problems of integration. But that the culture of deference stresses that the performer and goal attainer and the major goals are in the economy and science is patent.

Related to the system of stratification is the way the polity and the legal system of the generically modern society are structured. The rule of law is related to the property rights and performance capacities in the economic sphere, on the one hand, and to conflict modulation, on the other. Justice and equity compete in modern societies, and law is much more of a procedural system resting on specialized consensus than a nearly sacral body of precedents or a code of justice. The proliferation of administrative bodies, of quasi-judicial committees, of arbitration and mediation agencies moves the law from tradition and religion toward procedure and management. The law is the expression, more and more in modern societies, of the achieved and precarious political consensus, not the unveiling of the modes of justice.

The political organization of modern societies rests, inevitably, on a participant polity. A participant polity implies a political structure based on the consent of the governed, and all modern governments claim to represent the interests of their citizenries. The ideological enshrining of the participant polity appears a prime requirement of political life in a modern society. Special action structures, not so closely tied to the government, are also part of the political structure of a modern society. The political integration of any modern society is in some sense "fragile," resting as it does on consensus, procedure, and participation and cross-cutting special action structures. But the fragility is lessened by the sense of the legitimacy of performance and by the ever-increasing inclusion of persons in the participant polity.

The generic features of a modern society just listed are systemically linked, and the internal logic of their linkage is apparent. When men make some institutional choices in the economy and in applied science there are inevitable (or as nearly inevitable as that word is socially meaningful) consequences. The first set of choices is more or less open, but, once *some* modernity is launched and some parts of the economy are modernized and industrialized, then the process of modernization is akin to an infection: it will spread throughout the social structure and cultural pattern; or there will be continual social upheaval and the bearers of the modern and the non-modern will struggle for the positions of command over strategic political and economic resources; or, conceivably, the slow or rapid onset of social and cultural recession will leave the society in chronic difficulties, seemingly insurmountable by its elites. Just how much modernity in what institutional loci and among how many modern men is needed to make the transition to viable modernity is an open research topic.

Similarities in Industrial Societies

But even as the systemic, generically modern aspect of a society leaves much room for variation, so are industrialized, modernized societies alike in many ways beyond the systemic linkages to the economy and application of science. One source of the similarity is that modernizing societies see that already modern societies have solved some of the problems in the social and cultural organization of modernity. In part, then, selective borrowing and incorporation of some of the non-systemic aspects of already-modern industrial societies will probably take place. For example, market allocation in an industrial society is one of the most efficient means of combining factors of production, but a modern society does not need, as the Soviet experience has shown, to rely chiefly on the market. But as modern societies value efficiency and as they engage in trade activities, some market mechanisms are bound to come into play. Furthermore, modernity is partly symbolic and emblematic, and much of what is modern is mere façade and sheer display. But modernizing societies will borrow some of this, too, and to use the medieval distinction some of the accidents of industrial society as well as the substance will create similarities among societies. It is not accidental that when Attaturk began the modernization of his country he forbade the wearing of the fez, nor that the *obi* and *kimono* are rare garb on the Ginza. The fads, fashions, and youth culture of already modern societies appear irresistible to the modernizing and industrializing, for the symbolic and expressive participation in what appears to be the human species' most dynamic form of social organization is, in itself, a form of satisfaction.

Since the now industrializing societies of the world undertake their transformation in a world where industrialized societies exist, they will get help, advice, technology, and personnel to participate in the enterprise of social change. The technicians will bring with them not relativistic notions, nor sets of options, but ideas of *how* it is proper to run industrial enterprises, *what* modern men should know, and *which* forms of social organizations are proper. Since the industrializing society is somewhat dependent, some of these notions from the industrial cult will be incorporated into the modernizing society, although systemically they need not be. When the armies of the modernizing countries are inspected, for example, the rigidities of the particular army depend on which modern nation was its mentor as much as on the generic and systemic rigidities built into the military mode of organization. In addition to the nation-to-nation exchange, there are international agencies who will supply capital, credits, or foreign exchange, or arrange terms of trade. And these international agencies have their particular standards of worthy projects, of supportable plans, and they must conduce, at least in the short run, to a non-systemic increase in structural similarity among developing and modern social arrangements.

As a society industrializes and modernizes, international and supra-national communications increase. There also begin to emerge groups and kinds of men who are cosmopolitan and supra-national. An association of scientists has as a professional body an international understanding. The bonds between scientists in two different nations or societies may be, and often are, stronger than the bond between a scientist and his non-scientific fellow citizen. The growth of the supra-national professional community, the international agency man, the technicians of modernization, the peripatetic economic advisors, or even the professional revolutionaries and the professional counter-revolutionaries will add to the structural similarities among modern societies.

Finally, every society is in great part a cultural projection, an emotionally charged and symbolically defined way of life. Industrial modern societies, no less than their predecessors, must provide symbols, condensations whereby the members can graphically and economically grasp the essential meaning of their lived-in social reality. Industrial societies appear to have two major symbolic modes of elaboration, which their members value highly and apparently use to measure the successes of collective effort. Industrial societies have the drive to make their claims of scientific innovation eponymous. Who invented it first? is a question industrial man finds interesting and, if the answer favors his culture, he is proud. Modern societies also pride themselves on scientific leadership and accomplishment, not only for the military and economic advantages that leadership bestows, but also for the ethnic and symbolic meaning of that leadership. The race to make the first landing on the moon, in our time, is an exemplar of the symbolic elaboration that industrial societies are committed to.

If the five sources of variability were permutated with the five sources of similarity, perhaps some sort of nodal points would emerge and give a more specific set of parameters for industrial and modern societies. But in view of all the research that awaits in the world and all the hypotheses that need sorting into those confirmed, disconfirmed, and unconfirmable, this indoor sport is wasteful scientific effort. From what we now know about the processes of industrialization, the path of research is fairly clear and consensually defined. But if the ultimate aim of all science, social included, is the conscious, knowledgeable intervention of man in his own affairs, what do we know about speeding, guiding, directing, or reducing the human tolls in modernization?

Conclusions

This is not the place to write even partial recipes for a historical process of the magnitude of industrialization or modernization, but only to draw three major conclusions that might affect policy decisions, both in our own society's involvement with modernizing societies and for the newly developing nations themselves. First, and now I move into areas where opinion and judgment play an equal role with fact and finding, the natural process whereby the first industrial nations made that transformation is not socially and historically open to the new nations of Asia and Africa. The government or the rulers are, in this world, at this time, the custodians of the economy and responsible for its levels of performance. As such they must plan, and plan successfully. What sort of planning depends on what sort of state they have, but certainly the major planning problem is to restructure incentives so that modernity becomes a goal sought by most people. An alternative to poor planning and poor performance will, I believe, be a call for the revolutionary reconstruction of the social order.

Secondly, it appears that the minimal time span for modernization is at least a generation and more likely two. Consequently, planners, elites, and peasants and workers can save themselves the anguish they feel when they fail to modernize in the five- or seven-year arbitrary time spans that societies set as targets for themselves.

Finally, in order to increase the probability that governments or planners or spearhead groups are doing better than a policy of just "hands off" would do, mass social experimentation, a plan or program tried in one area and controlled against a matching area, is necessary. To make this simple but powerful device for increasing knowledge socially feasible, the government or elite must be consensually formed, and the experimenters must be dedicated to the general welfare and the public interest of those they govern. So, in the end, it is a value position that governs the governed who would modernize and industrialize.

III: Revolutionary Ideology and Nation Building

This symposium focused on one of the issues most relevant for a comprehensive understanding of contemporary turbulent politics. It is also an issue that has been relatively neglected by social scientists. Westerners, accustomed to a political process in which ideological cleavages are small and where the majority agrees about basic values, tend to view the culture-building aspects of revolutions with disdain, as irrational and wasteful.

Prior to the twentieth century, successful social revolutions were rare. Since 1900, however, at least four major revolutionary upheavals have dramatically changed the political and economic geography of the world. These revolutions have not satiated whatever spirit or force that gave rise to them; indeed, the revolutionary impulse continues and is more infectious than ever.

Traditionally, the study of revolutions has focused on factors in the social structure, e.g., the quest for and struggle over power, the nature of leadership, the recruitment of followers, the nature of the opposing forces, and the social and economic changes accomplished by successful revolutionary movements. Revolutionary movements as "culture-building" agents, however, have been neglected. Yet one cannot understand phenomena like the Mexican revolution, the victory of communism in China, Fidel Castro's Cuba, the "cultural revolution" in China, or black nationalism without looking on the movements as attempts to create new "world views" or total ideologies. This ideological reconstruction, or culture building, is seen as a more important task, in the short run, than economic achievement; it is also a step necessary to achieve substantial economic and structural changes in the long run.

Peter M. Worsley, Professor of Sociology at the University of Manchester, is a graduate of the University of Cambridge. He received his graduate education at Manchester and completed his doctoral work in social anthropology at Australian National University. In 1970, he was Jacob Liskind Visiting Professor at Brandeis University. His essay re-evaluating Tallensi kinship studies was awarded the Royal Anthropological Institute's Curl Bequest Prize. He is best known for *The Trumpet Shall Sound,* a book on Melanesian cargo cults, and *The Third World.* He also edited *Introducing Sociology* (1970).

Erik Allardt was appointed Professor of Sociology at the University of Helsinki in 1958, and is presently Research Professor appointed by the Finnish National Science Council. He has been Visiting Professor at the University of California at Berkeley, the University of Illinois, and the University of Wisconsin, and he has done field studies in Australian New Guinea. Editor of *Acta Sociologica* since 1968, Professor Allardt's published works include *Drinking Norms and Drinking Habits* and (with Urjo Littunen) *Sociologi* (5th edition, published in Swedish and Finnish). Together with Stein Rokkan he also edited *Mass Politics,* published in 1970.

Robert C. North received his Ph.D. in political science from Stanford University, where he is now professor of Political Science and director of studies in international conflict and integration. His publications include *Kuomintang and Chinese Communist Elites* (1952), *Moscow and Chinese Communists* (1952), *Possible Trends in Sino-Soviet International Relations* (1962), *Chinese Communism* (1966), and *The Foreign Relations of China* (1969); he has co-authored *M. N. Roy's Mission to China* (1963), *Content Analysis* (1963), and *Chinese People's Republic* (1966). In addition, Professor North has published about 25 articles on international politics.

REVOLUTIONARY IDEOLOGIES AS AGENTS OF CULTURAL AND STRUCTURAL CHANGE*

ERIK ALLARDT, *University of Helsinki*

By definition, the concept of "revolution" indicates changes in the human environment. One may ask, however, what kind of changes revolutions actually bring about. There are, of course, major and minor changes, just as there are great and small revolutions. However, differences other than those that can be described by the magnitude of revolutionary change also seem to exist. Revolutions are regarded not only as influencing social structure but also as causing cultural change. The relationship between revolutions and cultural change is, however, an intricate one. The problem is not entirely empirical, but has many difficult conceptual aspects, as we can see most readily by focussing on revolutions in the making, specifically, revolutionary ideologies. Ideology can be regarded as a system of evaluative principles about the ends of human action, about the means of attaining those ends, and about the nature of social and physical reality. To say that an ideology is revolutionary implies a redefinition of ends, means, and the nature of reality. It follows that a revolutionary ideology, by definition, is to a certain extent building and creating culture as it is usually defined.

Do Ideas Influence or Constitute Reality?

The problem of whether and how men's ideas or beliefs influence their actions is almost an eternal companion of sociological discourse. All major classical writers of sociology have taken a stand on this problem, and it has both an empirical and a conceptual aspect. One

* An earlier, and shorter, version of this paper, entitled "Culture, Structure, and Revolutionary Ideologies," appeared in the *International Journal of Comparative Sociology*, Vol. XII, No. 1 (1971), pp. 24-40.

can argue that at least in a certain sense reality is defined or constituted through the ideas men have of this reality. In the realm of philosophy this is of course a highly controversial question. While my intention here is not to advocate this view, this notion can be used to arrive at some useful distinctions.

Some of Wittgenstein's followers, and in social science particularly Peter Winch,[1] have argued that the world or reality is given for us in the language that we use. There is thus a clear correlation between our reality and the concepts we use. In order to understand the world, we have to have concepts telling what belongs to its reality. On the other hand, the meaning of the concepts can be understood only in the context of the forms of activity within which these concepts are used. In this fashion, the relationship between reality and our ideas or concepts about this reality is symbolic. The relationship between social reality and our ideas, according to this view, is not causal; it is not a question of two phenomena observable independently of each other. Observing the world necessarily implies a study of our ideas and concepts, and vice versa. Both reality and our concepts may change; but, when one of them changes, the other changes, too.

If this argument is correct, it implies that revolutionary ideologies and social reality are conceptually related. This already follows from the definition of a revolutionary ideology as something redefining reality. When one adopts a revolutionary ideology one gets a new reality. It seems clear, however, that this argument can not be carried too far. A revolutionary ideology in itself does not bring about a change in the existing power relations or in the exisiting institutions. On the other hand, it seems reasonable to say that a revolutionary ideology certainly implies a reinterpretation of existing power relations and existing institutions.

Many critics of Winch's notions have pointed out that many aspects of what social scientists would consider social reality can not be regarded as constituted by the ideas or concepts one has about reality. As Gellner put it in his review of Winch's book, "To understand the class structure of societies one must not only know what rank, etc., means in it, but also how many people occupy each grade, and this is a matter of counting, not understanding."[2] Winch himself makes

1. Peter Winch, *The Idea of a Social Science* (London: Routledge & Kegan Paul, 1958), pp. 14–15 and 51–57.

2. Ernest Gellner, Review of "The Idea of a Social Science," by Peter Winch, *The British Journal of Sociology*, 11 (1960), pp. 170–172.

a distinction between physical reality and social reality. When finding regularities in physical reality the criteria for regularity and similarity are the observer's, but when finding regularities in human behavior the criteria for similarity are those of the acting individuals. The ideas and concepts acting individuals have of their actions in a social context are what counts in defining something as the "same" social action. Thus, for instance, in defining the behavior of different individuals as religious action, the criteria for sameness are the religious ideas and concepts held by the acting individuals. If this be so, it seems reasonable to say that a great deal of what social scientists study is like physical reality. Phenomena such as the number of people in different classes, many kinds of suffering, the fact that only men and not women in some cultures inherit property, etc., may be observed irrespective of the meaning of the concepts and ideas of the acting individuals.

The discussion so far may appear as an unnecessary philosophical prelude to the problem of the cultural and structural effects of revolutionary ideologies, but it seems important to stress that the problem of revolutionary ideologies as culture—and institution-building—agents can be understood in several ways. The first problem is the conceptual relationship that exists between a revolutionary ideology and at least some aspects of what social scientists would define as social reality. Studying the results of a revolutionary ideology implies in this instance a logical and conceptual analysis of the content of this revolutionary ideology. By describing its content in detail, we will know what reality is like for the adherents of this revolutionary ideology. Parts of social reality, however, are hardly conceptually related to the revolutionary ideology. Therefore, the second problem is that reality may be affected by the revolutionary ideology, but this relationship is empirical. The problem for study is in this instance quite different: it amounts to a search for empirical regularities that would explain the effects of revolutionary ideologies on reality.

In looking for some distinctions that would help to separate these two problems, we might first ask whether any terms or labels already exist that would help us distinguish these two aspects of reality. Some aspects of the reality are permeated by the ideas the actors have about it, while some other aspects can be observed independent of the ideas of the actors. The suggestion here is that the terms "culture" and "structure" can be used for distinguishing these two aspects. The distinction implies that studying the relationship between a revolutionary movement and culture is entirely different methodologically from studying the relationship between a revolutionary movement and social structure.

The point of departure was Peter Winch, and, although his ideas are not very well known in the United States, they have created intensive discussions in Europe. Not only Gellner but others too have criticized him severely. Jürgen Habermas, who is very influential on the Continent, tried to refute Winch's idea of the identity between language (concepts) and practice (action).[3] My position is that both may be right, but they speak about different things. Nevertheless, their philosophical quarrel about the nature of social science might be translated into a useful sociological distinction.

Culture and Structure as Two Aspects of Reality

Culture has been defined in many ways, but most definitions imply that culture is a kind of a cognitive and evaluational structure. This formulation is explicitly used by Anthony Wallace and Bo Anderson.[4] The central terms in Wallace's description of revitalization movements are "mazeway" and "culture." An individual's mazeway is his total cognitive and evaluational structure, while the culture of a group or a society is the shared parts of the mazeways of its members. All definitions of culture stress the symbolic character of culture. Edmund Leach gives the following telling description:

> Culture provides the form, the "dress" of the social situation. As far as I am concerned, the cultural situation is a given factor, it is a product and an accident of history. I do not know *why* Kachin women go hatless with bobbed hair before they are married, but assume a turban afterwards, any more than I know *why* English women put a ring on a particular finger to denote the same change in social status; all I am interested in is that in this Kachin context the assumption of a turban by a woman does have this symbolic significance.[5]

American anthropologists often have a broader notion of culture than their British colleagues. As Krober put it in his famous definitional description, culture is "that which the human species has and other social species lack ... speech, knowledge, belief, customs, arts

3. Jürgen Habermas, "Knowledge and Interest," *Inquiry*, 9 (1966), pp. 285–300.

4. Anthony F. C. Wallace, "Revitalization Movements," *American Anthropologist*, 58 (1958), pp. 264–281; Bo Anderson, "Revitalization Movements. An Essay on Structure and Ideology in a Class of Exclusive Underdog Systems," *Acta Universitatetis Uppsaliensis*, 17 (1968), pp. 347–375.

5. Edmund Leach, *Political Systems of Highland Burma* (Boston: Beacon Press, 1964), p. 16.

and technologies, ideals, and rules . . . , what we learn from other men, from our elders and the past, plus what we may add to it."[6] Also in this omnibus definition the learned and the symbolic elements are pointed out. We may well adopt Wallace's definition of culture as the shared elements of the cognitive and evaluational structures of the individuals.

The point is that not only culture but also an ideology is a shared cognitive and evaluational structure. Conceptually, ideology and culture overlap. It follows from the definition of a revolutionary ideology and culture that the former by definition is culture-building. Of course, the total effect of a revolutionary ideology depends on its adherents and strength, but the general statement that ideology is culture-building does not need any empirical proof.

The same, however, can not be said about social structure. Of the many definitions of social structure, all somehow imply that stable patterns of interaction between the members of a society constitute its social structure. Stable patterns of interaction occur in a society through the existence of social groups and institutions. It is common and it also appears convenient to use our terminology in such a fashion that the structure of a society is, at least in its major aspects, independent of its culture. The same kind of structure may exist in different cultures, and it is accordingly symbolized and evaluated in different ways. We may again refer to Edmund Leach, who states that marriage is a structural relationship common to both English and Kachin society. It is, however, symbolized by a ring in the one and a turban in the other.[7] Facts such as the distribution of property, the power structure, the existence of marriages, etc., are all parts of the social structure and are also largely independent of culture. A change in the culture, for example by diffusion processes, may not necessarily influence the power relations in any substantial way. On the other hand, changes in the power structure of a society do not necessarily imply a cultural change.

What Types of Revolutions Have Culture-Building Effects?

While there is a conceptual relationship between ideology and culture, the relationship between ideology and structure is empirical. Revolutionary ideologies are not *per se* or by definition successful

6. A. L. Krober, *Anthropology* (New York: Harcourt, Brace & Co., 1948), p. 253.
7. Edmund Leach, *Political Systems of Highland Burma*, pp. 16–17.

in creating structural changes or in building institutions. Culture can be changed by changing the cognitive and evaluational models of people, but a structural change presupposes some use of power and power-based activity. An existing structure can erode because the powerholders lose some of their power, but new institutions have to be worked out. Institutions are built through work, and institution-building always depends on some form of leadership.

Whether an actual revolution is empirically related to culture-building or not seems to depend very much on the manner in which the revolution is brought about. Revolutions instigated from the top or through internal quarrels among the elite, as were most Latin-American revolutions, for example, do not as a rule create a new culture that would be shared by most people in the society. The culture-building effects of revolutions seem to presuppose mass participation and revolutionary ideological activities among the masses. By contrast, the Cuban revolution aimed at and also to a certain extent succeeded in constructing a new culture.

By and large, revolutions that succeed in reconstructing culture are instigated by under-dog movements in which there has been ideological activity. The transition to a Socialist society has sometimes, but not always, been correlated with a major cultural change. It seems reasonable to say that the Russian revolution brought about major cultural changes. One may, of course, ask whether some latent tendencies or depth structures in the present Soviet society are inherited from the historical Russian society, but on the manifest level the Russian revolution certainly created a major change in the conceptual and evaluational modes of the Russian people. It does not appear warranted, however, to say the same about many of the other Socialist countries in Eastern Europe, for, as we know, the Eastern European countries that underwent large-scale structural changes after 1945 preserved much of their traditional culture. The strength of the Roman Catholic faith in Poland provides a good illustration. The social and economic changes in Polish society certainly contributed to some cultural changes but available evidence indicates also that the structural changes did not create an entirely new culture that was shared by most Polish citizens.[8] The point is that the changes in Eastern Europe were not preceeded by revolutionary ideologizing aimed at redefinitions of culture. The crucial agent in the transformation of the Eastern European societies to Socialist societies was the

8. See, e.g., Zygmunt Bauman, "Values and Standards of Success of the Warsaw Youth," *Polish Sociological Bulletin*, No. 1–2 (3–4) (1962), pp. 77–90; and Antonina Kloskowska, "Mass Culture in Poland," *Polish Sociological Bulletin*, No. 2 (10) (1964), pp. 106–115.

Red Army,[9] and the transformation was a result of the general European situation. It was executed by a military-bureaucratic machine, and there was actually very little time for ideologizing beforehand.

These simple conclusions can be summarized in the following typology describing the relationships between types of revolutions and the reconstruction of culture. The typology is extremely crude, and there are revolutions or revolution-like incidents that are hard to place in the cells. The main point, however, is that the creation of a new culture that could serve as a cognitive and evaluational model for most members in a society clearly presupposes revolutions instigated by mass movements.

Revolutions instigated

	through an underdog mass movement	from the top or from the outside
Accomplished structural change including building of new institutions	1. Major structural revolutions Cases: The Russian Revolution / The Castroist Cuban Revolution / The Maoist Chinese Revolution Effects: Considerable: both culture-destruction and culture-building effects	3. Structural transformations Cases: The transformations of the Eastern European societies after 1945 Results: Some cultural reformation but small likelihood of creating a shared new culture
Minor changes, no institution-building	2. Unsuccessful underdog revolts Cases: The European uprising in 1848 / The Spartakus revolt in Berlin 1919 / The Hungarian uprising in 1956 / Numerous revolts in colonial countries Effects: Great variations in the culture-building effects	4. Elite revolutions or revolutionary attempts Cases: Most Latin-American revolutions Effects: No culture-building effects

9. Peter Worsley, "Bureaucracy and Decolonization. Democracy from the Top." in I. L. Horowitz (ed.), *The New Sociology* (New York: Oxford University Press, 1965), pp. 370–377.

Mass-supported but successful revolutions also may have strong culture-building effects. In fact, evidence about native movements aimed at the creation of a new culture shows that they often have grown particularly strong and even emerged after military defeats. Thus, military defeats preceeded the rise of the Grass Dance, the Hand Game, the Ghost Dance, and later Peyotism among the American Indians.[10]

It goes without saying that culture is changed and created mostly by slow evolutionary processes, and the discussion here concerns fast changes only. That is, the discussion about the existence or absence of culture-building is restricted to cultural reconstruction occurring in the time-span loosely defined as the aftermath or reconstruction period of a revolution.[11]

Empirical Relationships Between Culture and Structure

The typology about the kind of revolutions and culture-building does not tell us anything about the conditions under which the need for cultural reconstruction is apt to emerge. It follows from our definitions that no cultural reconstruction will occur as long as a highly developed and shared culture exists. There are of course always individuals who for different reasons do not share the general cultural heritage, but in a situation of generally shared culture their attempts at cultural reconstruction will remain individual and isolated. Although the absence or weakening of the shared culture is a necessary condition for attempts at cultural reconstruction, it is not yet a sufficient condition. There are some structural requisites for the emergence of attempts at cultural reconstruction. Hence, we must consider the empirical relationship between culture and structure.

In his *Thought and Change* Ernest Gellner advanced a speculative but useful hypothesis. He assumed a kind of inverse relationship between the importance of culture and structure: In a highly structured society, culture is not indispensable; but in loosely structured societies, culture or the communication system becomes the basis for relationships and encounters.[12] This is not to deny that some societies

10. Neil J. Smelser, *Theory of Collective Behavior* (New York: The Free Press, 1963), p. 327.

11. If the time-span is long enough, even elite revolutions can lead to major cultural reformations. The history of religious movements provide ample analogies: Buddhism was created from the top by Buddha, a Brahmin who was dissatisfied with the ways of his peers; but Buddhism became a major religion and as such a major agent for culture-building. See Max Weber, *The Sociology of Religion*, tr. Ephraim Fischoff (Boston: Beacon Press, 1963), pp. 267–268.

12. Ernest Gellner, *Thought and Change* (London: Weidenfeld & Nicolson, 1964), pp. 153–157.

have both a stable structure and a highly-developed shared culture. Small tribal societies, at least before their confrontation with foreign elements becomes too overpowering, often have both a highly developed structure and an elaborated shared culture. The society is a network of ascriptive solidarities and ascribed roles, and at the same time relationships are richly symbolized in rituals, dress, ornaments, etc. Accordingly, structure and culture are not incompatible.

On the other hand, in undifferentiated societies a shared culture is not a precondition of communication. Since the communities and the number of relationships are both small, people will know how to behave even if they don't have shared symbols and a common language. Gellner states that, in the stable relationship between lord and peasant, it matters little whether their symbol system is strongly shared, and he gives the example of a roving Brazilian Indian band in which two small groups had merged even without knowing each other's language. Similar examples can be found elsewhere. European armies in the past were often multilingual, apparently without any disastrous effects on their ability to carry on their military pursuits.

One may of course assume that, even in these cases, there exists some minimal amount of shared culture. On the whole, however, Gellner's hypothesis has much to recommend it. The point is that in a modern society in which a great number of encounters are not based on ascriptive roles the need for a shared culture and common symbols is extremely strong. Gellner admits that modern society hardly lacks structure, as is often assumed. Many bureaucratic relationships can be compared with the ascriptive relationships in a kinship system, but nevertheless the structure is clearly looser than in tribal societies. In modern societies people are bound to organizations within which the rigid ascription of roles takes place. Nevertheless, they are free to choose between organizations, and in the interaction across organizational boundaries a common set of symbols is strongly needed. Hence, culture becomes extremely important. In simple undifferentiated societies culture often reinforces the structure, but in modern societies culture rather replaces the structure.

In spite of the impressionistic character of Gellner's hypothesis, it provides many fruitful leads. Nationalism rose to provide a common bond, producing solidarity, in eighteenth century European societies simultaneously as the growing industrialization rapidly eroded the old systems of ascription. Many large empires in the past were bound together by belief systems, often religious. Many observers have pointed out how extreme is the stress on cultural revivalism in developing and modernizing nations. It has been said that nationalist leaders in emerging nations often direct almost all their attention to solidarity symbols without a similar emphasis on other aspects of modernization.[13] The interest in African history among the leaders of the new African nations is well known and often reported.[14] In all these cases we have situations in which old structures have been eroded and are unable to function as guides for expectations and predictions of behavior.

Conditions for the Need of Rapid Cultural Reconstruction

In today's advanced societies attempts at cultural reconstruction are expressed mainly through political ideologies often in opposition to the traditional culture and nationalism. In developing societies nationalism and political ideologies may exist both as competing and as merging forces. In any event, serious attempts at culture reconstruction presuppose both an incompleteness of structure and a lack of shared culture. The reasoning may be summed up and slightly elaborated in the following four-fold table:

| | Culture | |
	More Shared	Less Shared
Highly structured	1. Culture strongly reinforcing structure: no attempts at rapid cultural reconstruction Example: Tribal societies with rigid ascription of roles	3. As long as efficiency prevails the society functions without a shared culture: no attempts at rapid cultural reconstruction Examples: Feudal societies, armies. Societies or systems with rigid ascription of roles and a clearly defined power structure
Weakly or incompletely structured	2. Culture provides the uniting factor. Some instability but as long as all major groups have a share in the culture there is small likelihood for attempts at rapid cultural reconstruction Example: Modern national societies	4. Great likelihood for the rise of ideologies and other attempts at rapid cultural reconstruction Examples: Societies in transition

(left margin label: Structure)

13. E. g., S. N. Eisenstadt, "Sociological Aspects of Political Development in Underdeveloped Countries," *Economic Development and Cultural Change*, Vol. V (1957), pp. 289–307.

14. E.g., Immanuel Wallerstein, *Africa, Politics of Independence* (New York: Vintage Books, 1961), pp. 122–135.

The typology is not very revealing for two reasons. First, it is a truism to say that the absence or weakening of a shared culture is a necessary condition for attempts at rapid cultural reconstruction. Second, weak or incomplete structures that are empirically related to cultural reconstruction have not been differentiated and specified. In fact, the fourth type covers very different kinds of cases, of which the following three are particularly important: (a) the whole traditional structure has been eroded, as in some tribal societies after confrontation with Europeans; (b) the structure is intact in its traditional form, but new groups are left outside the structure, as were the working class in many European countries in the early Twentieth Century; and (c) the structure is coercive, but most people are unable to internalize the norms of the authorities, as in some conquered countries. These cases can be somewhat more fully described by discussing the structural conditions for the emergence of attempts at rapid cultural reconstruction.

Social Structure and Attempts at Cultural Reconstruction

To describe these conditions, some general structural variables are needed. One variable of utmost importance in almost any comparison of societies is the degree of differentiation, which is here defined by the number of structurally distinct and functionally specialized units in a society. A highly differentiated society has numerous specialized roles and collectivities performing specialized tasks in society.[15] Differentiation corresponds to the classical term "division of labor," when it is taken to mean the differentiation of the tasks not only of individuals but also of institutions. The second major variable is the degree of pressure toward uniformity existing in a society. The rationale for choosing these two variables, the degree of differentiation and the degree of the pressure toward uniformity, is that they can be identified in any collectivity, society, or group, and they can be related to other theoretical concepts in various ways. Pressure toward uniformity is a difficult concept to make operational, and finding an over-all indicator useful in different social systems is also difficult.[16] While differentiation here will be discussed as a

---

15. See, e.g., Robert M. Marsh, *Comparative Sociology* (New York: Harcourt, Brace & World, 1967), pp. 31–32.

16. It has been indicated by Veronica Stolte Heiskanen, *Social Structure, Family Patterns and Intrapersonal Influence* (Helsinki: Transactions of the Westermark Society, XIV, 1967), p. 17, that pressure toward uniformity always has to be specified according to the substantive system under investigation.

dichotomized variable, pressure towards uniformity will be discussed according to the following tripartite classification:

(1) Strong pressure toward uniformity. In undifferentiated societies, there are rigid rules of ascription. In differentiated societies with a surplus of material goods, there will also exist a rigid power structure. Most typical of the former example are *small tribal societies*, and most typical of the latter are *political dictatorships* demanding a commitment to a total ideology.

(2) Differentially strong pressures toward uniformity. The society is clearly divided into estates or classes, of which some have much more freedom of movement than others. Under conditions of low differentiation a typical case is represented by *agrarian feudal societies*, while under conditions of high differentiation the typical case would be a *modern society with a rigid class structure*.

(3) Weak pressure toward uniformity. Under conditions of low differentiation the most typical society in this category is one in which there has been a *rapid weakening of traditional structure*. We may speak of an anomic situation. Under conditions of high differentiation and weak pressure of uniformity we have the classical case of organic solidarity,[17] of which the *modern welfare-state* may stand as an example.

By cross-classifying the two variables we obtain the following table. The predictions about the existence and absence of attempts at cultural reconstruction are indicated in the cells.

It goes without saying that several societies are mixtures and only some societies can clearly be fitted into the typology. Furthermore, the typology is theoretical: that all factors in real life are accounted for is not assumed. The types in which revolutionary ideologies are developed and actual revolutions may occur are numbers 2, 3, 4, and 5. In all these cases we can assume with James C. Davies that actual revolutions need both a period of rising expectations and a succeeding period in which these expectations are frustrated.[18] In all these cases there are also attempts to create new beliefs and to discard old ones. They may all be labeled attempts at rapid cultural reconstruction, but the assumption is that these attempts are different under the different conditions described by the typology. The form

17. The rationale behind the typology is presented in E. Allardt, "A Theory on Solidarity and Legitimacy Conflicts," in W. J. Goode (ed.), *The Dynamics of Modern Society* (New York: Atherton, 1966), pp. 167–178.

18. James C. Davies, "Toward a Theory of Revolution," *American Sociological Review*, 27 (1962), pp. 5–18.

Differentiation

Pressure toward uniformity	Low	High
Strong	1. Situation of mechanical solidarity Tribal societies with rigid rules of ascription No attempts at rapid cultural reconstruction	4. Situation of coercion Ideologically-based political dictatorships Attempts to formulate ideology and programs for cultural reconstruction in secrecy Occasional revolutionary outbursts
Differentially strong	2. Situation of traditional domination Agrarian feudal societies Occasional outbursts of expressively oriented movements aimed at cultural reconstruction	5. Situation of hegemony Modern societies with a rigid class structure Great likelihood for the rise of ideologies and attempts at rapid cultural reconstruction
Weak	3. Situation of anomie Societies in which there has been a considerable weakening of the traditional structure Feverish attempts to find reference groups. Unsystematic but frantic attempts at rapid cultural reconstruction	6. Situation of organic solidarity The modern welfare state No mass attempts at rapid cultural reconstruction. A great number of individual attempts

of the attempts at cultural reconstruction within the different types can be described as follows:

1. *Situations of mechanical solidarity.* This is a situation in which culture is apt to reinforce an already highly developed and rigid structure. The prediction is that attempts at cultural reconstruction are lacking or very rare.

2. *Situations of traditional domination.* In this situation grievances are often conceived as caused by particular persons, and revolutionary outbursts are often directed toward specific persons and specific arrangements. Some beliefs that "explain" the grievances emerge, but they would not likely develop into systems of thought. This pattern was typical for many peasant rebellions in the European past.

3. *Situations of anomie.* These situations are thought to be common when the traditional structure has weakened considerably. Feelings of alienation and inferiority are rather easily evoked when new values and new techniques provided by alien forces are perceived and seen. The new values and new techniques weaken the traditional structure. Since the division of labor is still underdeveloped while old rules are being weakened, difficulties in forming expectations and predictions about the behavior of others will occur. The general attitude toward authority is that of deference. In this stage, hostile reactions will emerge when the representatives of the authorities do not meet the expectations. The millenarian movements in Medieval Europe were apparently often of this type. As Norman Cohn has shown, revolutionary messianism was particularly apt to arise when the Church failed to give the guidance the people longed for.[19] The hostile reactions are clearly of an expressive wish-fulfillment type. The Melanesian form is represented by the Cargo Cults with their beliefs in an imminent millenium that would bring the population all the material goods the whites possessed. As such movements are wish-fulfilling reactions without any definite implementation of new norms and values, they usually disappear or change in character rather soon after their occurrence. In Western societies many religious sects have been born under conditions defined by this developmental type.

As has been shown, there is, in New Guinea, a trend away from the Cargo Cults to politically organized movements.[20] Types 2 and 3 are becoming less important in the modern world, and the important systematic attempts at cultural reconstruction are now found more in types 4 and 5.

4. *Situations of coercion.* As long as the coercive forces are very strong, revolutionary thoughts are developed in secret groups. Revolutionary thinking is already systematized into general explanatory schemes, although fully developed ideologies usually will presuppose increased freedom in order to develop. The revolutionary spirit developing in Tsarist Russia before 1917 was nourished in several different and distinct groups. There was a common core of ideas about the evil of the Tsarist system and the need for drastic reforms, but the situation was one of many diverse ideas with a common element rather than of a culture-reconstructing ideology. Fully developed ideologies with systematic schemes for cultural reconstruction require

19. Norman Cohn, *The Pursuit of the Millenium* (New York: Harper Torch Books, 1961), pp. 307–319.

20. Peter Worsley, *The Trumpet Shall Sound* (London: MacGibbon & Kee, 1957), p. 281.

a certain freedom for development, and they are more likely to occur under the conditions in type 5 than in type 4. The systematic codification of Leninist ideology began under the Kerenski government, when the Tsar's absolute rule had already been crushed.

5. *Situations of hegemony*. The most far-reaching and systematic revolutionary ideologies are developed in this kind of society. Clearly, however, the systematic development of revolutionary ideologies often continues during the aftermath of a revolution that has already been won. This seems to be true for the Russian revolution, the Castroist Cuban Revolution, and the Maoist Chinese revolution. Nevertheless, under conditions of hegemony, revolutionary ideologies are developed into general explanatory schemes or theories. In the Leninist ideology everything is explained in terms of class struggle, and the party worker is supposed to be able to connect even the most trivial incidents with the general explanatory principles. The idea is to create a general theory by which all important phenomena can be interpreted.

The generality of the explanatory schemes and the ambition to create a completely new cognitive and evaluational model has seldom been expressed so clearly as in Mao Tse-Tung's famous essay on contradictions:

> Now we can make a few words to sum up. The law of contradiction in things, that is, the law of the unity of opposites, is the basic law of nature and society and therefore also the basic law of thought.... If, after study, we have really understood the essential points mentioned above, we shall be able to smash those doctrinaire ideas which run counter to the basic principles of Marxism-Leninism and are detrimental to our revolutionary cause, and also enable our experienced comrades to systematize their experience so as to impart them to the character of principle and avoid the mistakes of empiricism.[21]

Thus, the law of contradiction both explains the basic processes in nature and society and acts as a guide for practical action. It is, if anything, an attempt to present a complete cognitive and evaluational model.

6. *Situations of organic solidarity*. It is here assumed that highly differentiated societies containing weak pressures toward uniformity provide only meager soil for the growth of ideologies aimed at very rapid cultural reconstruction. It should, of course, be assumed that

21. Mao Tse-Tung, *An Anthology of His Writings*, ed. Anna Freemantle (New York: Mentor Books, 1962), pp. 240–241.

such societies are also efficient. In highly differentiated societies social exchange is rich and rewarding as long as it is not hindered either by the enforcement of strongly restricting rules or by external conditions.

Ideology and Cognitive Processes

In his paper about revitalization movements, Bo Anderson refers in many ways to the anticipatory and future-oriented character of both ideologies and the particular myths underlying them.[22] It is striking how many of his observations about the ideology of revitalizing movements can be said to rest on principles advanced in the psychology of cognition. Of particular interest is George Kelly's theory of personal constructs.[23] Kelly's theory is a kind of systematization of the basic principles of the "mazeway" of individuals.

Kelly's fundamental postulate is that an individual's processes are channeled by the ways he anticipates events. The manner in which an individual anticipates events is defined by his personal constructs, which are the modes by which an individual decides which events are similar and which events dissimilar. This definition implies, first, that individuals anticipate events by construing their replications and, second, that the constructs used and developed always involve both similarity and contrast. Thus, personal constructs are always bipolar, and similarity and contrast are, so to speak, intrinsic properties of the constructs. The bipolarity of the constructs has a strong similarity with the dialectic character of the main revolutionary ideologies in today's world. One could, however, advance the view that the dialectic mode of reasoning is not unique for Marxism and its different branches but rather a general trait in all revolutionary ideologies.

There are several corollaries to Kelly's basic postulate. He assumes that individuals differ in their anticipation of events and doubts that two persons ever can organize their systems of constructs into the same logical relationships. Another reasonable assumption, however, is that there are both shared constructs and shared systems of constructs. One may still assume individual differences but all depends on the degree of precision by which one prefers to scrutinize the constructs.

Another important corollary in the theory is that the constructs are bound together through a hierarchical system by which the relative

---

22. Bo Anderson, "Revitalization Movements," pp. 355–362.
23. George A. Kelly, *The Psychology of Personal Constructs*, I-II (New York: W. W. Norton, 1955).

importance of constructs and anticipations are defined. The same can be assumed about ideologies. Only by arranging the constructs in a certain hierarchical order can consistency in anticipations be gained. The number of constructs is not unlimited, but a construction system must be composed of a finite number of bipolar constructs. Thus, some aspects of reality as it may be seen by others simply have to be ignored. Of course, scientific theories and paradigms are also composed of a finite number of constructs. Even so, however, the strength of Marx's emphasis on just the bipolarity in combination with the finiteness of the number of constructs is striking. It has often been noted that Marx's theory about social class can be seen as a set of heuristic principles rather than a system of refutable sentences. More than two social classes can be observed almost everywhere but Marx assumes that only the two main opposites, the bourgeoisie and the proletariat, are of importance in studying and interpreting the historical development.[24] In the same way can construction systems be seen as sets of heuristic principles guiding the interpretation of new events.

A construct system is of course not completely automatic or foolproof. The individual has a choice between alternatives. According to Kelly's theorems, an individual chooses alternatives within the system of constructs in such a fashion that he gets the best basis for meeting and anticipating new events. Individuals also vary their construction system when they successively try to construe the replication of events. A rather common and general assumption would be that mature individuals are particularly capable of such a variation. Otherwise, a system of constructs becomes less and less realistic as time passes; and this point is a problem in ideologies that are shared systems of constructs.

The necessity of adjusting ideological construct systems to reality probably also explains the constant struggle against dogmatism and doctrinaire interpretations. Any construct system with chances to survive has to admit some form of modulation. However, as Kelly admits, people do not always change their ideas when there is negative evidence. He introduces the idea of the permeability of constructs, and he assumes that all adjustable systems of constructs contain permeable constructs into which new events can be subsumed. A good example of these principles of modulation and a permeable construct is the term "class struggle" in Marxist thought. According to the assump-

24. Ralf Dahrendorf, *Class and Class Conflict in Industrial Society* (Stanford: Stanford University Press, 1959), pp. 19–20.

tions, class struggle has always existed but manifests itself in different forms. It has ranged from the antagonism between slaves and their masters, feudal lords and serfs, capitalists and workers to the differences between rich and poor countries. Accordingly, new cases can be subsumed within a wide range of convenience.

Constructs exert a controlling influence on the individuals employing them. According to Kelly, this controlling influence becomes particularly interesting when individuals begin to see themselves in the context in which they are operating. When a person uses himself as a focal point for forming new constructs the controlling influence becomes especially great. For example, if a person sees himself in the context of the bipolar construct of powerful–weak, he binds himself to this dimension in his associations with others.[25]

The operation of this controlling influence is crucial for revolutionary ideologies. Successful revolutionary ideologies are underdog movements, and an important theme in them consists of definitions of the underdog status and the suffering connected with it. This theme is central in the ideologies of revitalization movements[26] as well as in the Marxist kind of political revolutionary movements. Furthermore, this kind of attempt to bind persons to constructs has frequently occurred in many of the recent student rebellions around the world. According to the revolutionary ideology the students fight not only for student power and improvements in academic life, but against the whole societal system. They are seen as joining all proletarians in their struggle against the capitalist or imperialist order. This is a bold attempt to bind persons to constructs, to say the least.

A Note on Mao's Cultural Revolution

It is almost amazing how Kelly's theory of personal constructs resembles some of the principles of philosophy advanced by Mao Tse-Tung. From this point of view some of Mao's basic principles can be seen as a theory specifically dealing with cognitive processes. There is, though, at least a superficial difference. Kelly explicitly regards the construct systems as interpretative schemes, which are imposed on the events, while, according to Mao, the constructs are intrinsic, in reality and in society. Whether construct systems can be

25. D. Bannister and J. M. M. Mair, *The Evaluation of Personal Constructs* (London and New York: Academic Press, 1968), pp. 12–28.

26. Bo Anderson, "Revitalization Movements,", pp. 360–362.

considered independent of the human mind and human intentions is dubious, but the matter may rest for awhile. Instead, some similarities between Kelly and Mao can be explicitly pointed out.

According to Mao, the basic principle of all construct systems is the "universality of contradiction":

> The basic cause of [the] development of things does not lie outside them but inside them, in their international contradictions. The movement and development of things arise because of the presence of such contradictions inside all of them.
>
> The interdependence of the contradictory aspects of a thing and the struggle between them determine the life and development of that thing. There is nothing that does not contain contradictions: without contradiction there would be no world.[27]

Man's whole conceptual apparatus evolves around this bipolarity or universal principle of contradiction:

> Every difference in man's concepts should be regarded as reflecting objective contradictions. Objective contradictions are reflected in subjective thought, constituting the movement in opposites of concepts, problems that arise in man's thinking.[28]

In addition to the universal contradiction, however, there are also particular contradictions. The principle of contradiction, or the universal bipolarity of the world, is the general principle that binds the different particular contradictions together into a gigantic system. In this way the constructs related to particular contradictions are combined into a general system of constructs:

> Of course, without recognizing the universality of contradiction, we can in no way discover the universal cause or universal basis of the development of motion in things: however, without studying the particularity of contradiction we can in no way determine the particular quality of a thing that differs from those of other things. . . .[29]

The difference between "universality of contradiction" and "particularity of contradiction" serves the requirement of modulation and permeability of the constructs. Another important distinction also makes for modulation in the Maoist construction system, however.

27. Mao Tse-Tung, *An Anthology of His Writings*, pp. 219–220
28. *Ibid.*, pp. 219–220.
29. *Ibid.*, p. 221.

He makes a distinction between the principal contradiction and the principal aspect of a contradiction. That is, some contradictions, such as between the productive forces and the relations of productions, between practice and theory, between the economic foundation and the superstructure, etc., are principal ones. However, "at certain times in the revolutionary struggle, difficulties outbalance advantages: then, difficulties constitute the principal aspect of the contradiction and advantages the secondary aspect."[30] Here, Mao means that at certain times it is more important for a revolutionary to concern himself with theory than with principle, more important to try to influence the superstructure than the economic base.

Here lies one of the peculiarities in Mao's writings. Although a Marxist, he often seems almost obsessed by culture, defined as a system of cognitive and evaluative principles. At least it is tempting to suggest that when he speaks about structure in the traditional Marxist fashion he is merely paying it lip service, while when speaking about culture he appears much more original.

The Chinese cultural revolution and particularly the events in 1966 have been rendered into different kinds of explanations. The cultural revolution can be regarded both as a phase in an internal power struggle as well an attempt to create a personality cult of gigantic proportions. Note, however, that the obsession with cultural forms, the struggle against the traditional culture, and the interest in creating models for thought and evaluation can still be connected with the more philosophical undertones in Mao's writings.

Mao makes his famous distinction between external and internal causes of change by labelling the external causes *conditions of change* and the internal causes the *basis of change*. His definitions are not always easy to understand, but the external causes are probably what we generally apply in causal analysis, in which the cause and effect are assumed, strictly speaking, to be logically independent of each other; in fact, a basic rule is that causes and effects in principle can be observed independently of each other. Mao, however, concerns himself primarily with the internal causes, with phenomena that belong together intrinsically.[31] There is, for instance, an internal relation between a motive and its corresponding action, between a rule and the observance of it. Inferences about motives or rules are usually made by observing the resulting social action. Thus, the relationship is not causal but conceptual and internal.

30. *Ibid.*, pp. 231–232.
31. *Ibid.*, p. 216.

Pinpointing what Mao means by internal relations is not so easy, since he gives many varying examples. Most examples, however, indicate that internal relations are interpretations imposed on social reality and therefore dependent on human intentions. Consider, for instance, the following passage:

> In war, offense and defense, advance and retreat, victory and defeat are all contradictory phenomena. Without the one the other can not exist. These two aspects struggle as well as unite with each other, constituting the totality of war, impelling the war's development and solving the war's problem.[32]

There is, one could argue against Mao, no need to interpret wars in this fashion. Wars can be described by counting the dead and calculating the material damage. Wars can be studied by assessing their influences on fertility, on migration, on the rate of inventions, etc. This would be to study external relations. Mao, however, is interested mainly in wars as results of human intention. To consider these events as a victory or a defeat one needs to impose an interpretative scheme upon them.

Mao's interest in internal relations is really an interest in culture, the culture being here models for cognition and evaluation. All major revolutions have been connected with some form of ideology and thereby with some attempts at cultural reconstruction. At least one is inclined to agree with Pareto and Mosca that all new rulers attempt to impose interpretation schemes, "political formulas" by which their rule can come to be considered legitimate.[33] The Chinese revolution, however, is in many respects unique in that a major stress is laid on cultural reconstruction. A systematic comparison of the Russian and Chinese revolutions is of course needed, but a reasonable hypothesis is that the Russian revolution was focused on changing culture to a degree much less than the Chinese has been.

Influence of Culture on Structure

At least implicitly, some of this presentation carries a skeptical undertone. The skepticism does not concern the belief that revolutionary ideologies have culture-building results, but rather the formulation of the problem. Ideologies are models of cognition and evaluation, and so is culture. It follows that there is a tautological element

32. *Ibid.*, p. 219.
33. Gaetano Mosca, *The Ruling Class* (New York: McGraw-Hill, 1965), pp. 71–72.

in statements about ideologies as culture-building. Parts of culture, of course, are not touched upon by ideologies, but this follows already from the content of the ideologies. Ideologies, however, often create cultural conflicts, and this stands out as a fruitful area of empirical investigation.

The bulk of this discussion has been concerned with the effects of different structural and psychological conditions on attempts at cultural reconstruction. The reverse effect, the influence of culture on structure, has been mentioned little, in a way, because, given the position taken, there is little to say about it. A reconstruction of culture, even a rapid one, does not in itself lead to structural changes or new institutions. Structural changes presuppose some use of actual power and deliberate planning. Social institutions have to be worked out or developed slowly, over time.

Yet, culture and ideologies, in the sense of models for cognition and evaluation, clearly can become important motive forces strongly influencing the paths of history. This influence can, of course, be made the object of serious and fruitful empirical work. Again, however, a philosophical point must be made. The ideologies in such explanations are viewed as motives, and as such their existence or importance as motive forces can be studied only by first knowing their results. In fact, inferences about ideologies as motives would be drawn on the basis of their results. Therefore, *explanans* and *explanandum* can not be considered as logically independent but conceptually related to each other. Explanations of structural changes in terms of ideologies tend to be teleological, and, although nothing is wrong with doing so, it means that no general hypotheses or nomological explanations can be advanced. If the *explanandum* already is contained in the *explanans,* no general law, hypothesis, or regularity is needed in order to connect them. Consequently, fruitful studies of the influence of ideologies on structural change have to be centered on unique cases and historical descriptions. The influences can be historically described and analyzed, but they can hardly be made the object of sociological studies aimed at the formulation of general propositions. Again, nothing is wrong with a research program focusing on unique cases, but, for example, if such a program had been described here, this paper should have been restricted to a particular ideology in a specific historical environment.

The reasoning here goes back to the basic distinction made earlier. The relationship between structure and man is external, while the relationship between culture and man is internal. Culture as well as an ideology get their sense or meaning from the role they play in a particular social system. It is different with structure. This term was assumed to denote stable patterns of interactions, and these patterns can certainly be analyzed externally without knowing the particular meaning attached to them.

To study the effects of culture is to study internal relations, to analyze how people conceptualize and symbolize their world. If culture changes, man's interpretation of the world changes, too. What is needed in studies of culture is in a sense primarily conceptual analysis. The relationship between culture and revolutionary ideologies is conceptual, whereas the relationship between structure and revolutionary ideologies is empirical and causal.

TOWARD A PRESSURE THEORY OF REVOLUTION

ROBERT C. NORTH, *Stanford University*

Energy, in a sense, is basic to man, his works and his behavior. It is shared by all other living systems: Each biological organism, including man, and each interpersonal organization or society of biological organisms must ingest energy in some form from the environment.[1] The progress of the evolution of all living systems, including man, seems to be associated with an "increase in the general energy or maintained level of vital processes."[2] Moreover, in all biological growth, "a mechanism must exist involving the breakdown of some energy-rich substrata to supply necessary energy."[3] This mechanism is basic to life.

White has asserted that "the principles and laws of thermodynamics are applicable to culture systems as they are to other material systems."[4] Indeed, the laws expressing the relationships between energy and matter "necessarily come first in order ... in the whole record of human experience, and they control, in the last resort, the rise and fall of political systems, the freedoms or bondage of nations, the movements of commerce and industry, the origin of wealth and poverty, and the general physical welfare of the race."[5]

1. Each individual can be viewed as an energy-producing, an energy-storing, and an energy-consuming organization or system.

1. Leslie A. White, *The Evolution of Culture* (New York: McGraw-Hill Book Company, 1959), pp. 47–50.
2. George G. Simpson, *The Meaning of Evolution* (New Haven: Yale University Press, 1949), pp. 256–257.
3. S. Spiegelman, "Physiological Competition as a Regulatory Mechanism in Morphogenesis," *The Quarterly Review of Biology*, 20, 2 (June, 1945), p. 123.
4. White, *Evolution of Culture*, p. 38.
5. Frederick Soddy, *Matter and Energy* (New York: Henry Holt and Company, Inc., 1912), pp. 10–11.

Human beings use four main types of energy: psychic energy, affective (emotional) energy, muscular energy, and energy unlocked from the environment through application of technology (knowledge and skills).

2. As biological organisms, human beings require such basic resources as air, food, water, and some amount of territory. The larger a given population, the greater the amount of resources demanded.

Man's ability to tap resources and harness energy for his own purposes depends upon his experience, his learning, and the general level of his knowledge and skills. These considerations discriminate the culture, the organizational characteristics, the institutions, and many of the customs and beliefs of human societies on various levels of development. Tools, weapons, and machines are indicators of the technological level (the level of knowledge and skills) a given society has achieved.

3. Human technology (knowledge and skills) also creates a demand for resources. The more advanced the level of technology among a given population, the greater will be the range and quantity of resources needed to sustain that technology and advance it further.

4. Within interpersonal systems (including nation-states and empires), population and technology combine multiplicatively to produce human demands for resources. These demands can be satisfied in whole or in part by the acquisition of resources, either directly from their origin or through trade. The scarcer the resources relative to the population and its level of knowledge and skills, the greater will be the level of (unsatisfied) demands.

In other words, the greater the number of people in any given environment, the greater the potential competition for available resources. Furthermore, the higher the level of technology the greater the possibilities for transforming resources into energy, the greater the demand for energy-yielding resources, and also, in many situations, the greater the possibilities for extracting energy out of a given substratum. Thus, "Energy is the key resource in technical advancement, not only in introducing industrial fabrication but also converting potential resources into employed ones."[6] Technical advancement is thus a key to extracting more energy from available resources than is possible at lower levels of knowledge and skills.

6. Edward A. Ackerman, "Population and Natural Resources," in Philip M. Hauser and Otis Dudley Duncan (eds.), *The Study of Population* (Chicago: The University of Chicago Press, 1959), p. 641.

Population growth may bring about either an increase or a decrease in the capabilities of a society.[7] Additional increments of population increase consumption and make heavier demands upon the resources and national product. These demands can be met through an increase of resources (discovery of new deposits, acquisition of new territory, and so forth), by advances in technology (the organization and application of knowledge and skills) for locating and harnessing existing resources, or by a combination of both.

If we know enough about the different levels and rates of change of population, resources, and knowledge and skills in the various major sectors of society we should be able to say something about the stability of that society and to assess the probabilities of revolution.

A General Systems Framework

The individual human being can be viewed as a system encompassing numbers of component sub-systems. Two or more human beings can organize into one or more interpersonal systems. Both nation-states (and empires) and revolutionary organizations can be viewed as interpersonal systems with component sub-systems, and they can also be considered sub-systems of larger, encompassing systems. A nation-state (or empire), for example, can be treated as a component of an alliance system or of the world-wide international system. And a revolutionary organization can be viewed as a (dissident) component of a national system or, possibly, as a unit in some international revolutionary movement.

As Parsons and Shils suggested, " . . . At every point, the scheme deals with at least *two* adjacent 'levels'—the level of unit and that of system. One must be clear whether the 'point of reference' of his concepts is the *unit* or the *system of units;* otherwise he is plagued with subtle semantic ambiguities that are extremely difficult to resolve."[8] The emphasis here is that

> with the system as the center of the analysis, the member is treated as a *unit,* that is, the unit is treated as *undifferentiated,* as if it were not a system, but as if it were a *particle,* and is described only in its relation to other particles or a system of particles. This is an extremely difficult point of view to maintain, unless "common sense" habits of thinking

7. Additional increments or power may be *attributed* to a country—such as China—on the basis of a large population, even though the per capita productivity is critically low.

8. Talcott Parsons, Robert F. Bales, and Edward A. Shils, *Working Papers in the Theory of Action* (Glencoe, Ill.: The Free Press, 1953), p. 172.

are overcome, since another of our fundamental postulates is that whatever one may choose to treat as a unit for a given analysis may, *by
the appropriate shift in point of reference,* be treated as a system, itself made
up of member units of some kind. It is upon this assumption that we
maintain that the conceptual scheme can be applied up and down a
wide range of microscopic and macroscopic systems. But when the scheme
is applied to a more microscopic or macroscopic system, *the point of
reference changes,* and hence the empirical referents of all the concepts
and variables also change. And from any vantage point, there will always
be member units which from *that* vantage point are not analyzed as
systems, but treated as units or particles, with certain given properties
that are not treated as problematic. The maintenance of this perspective
constitutes *one* of the principal differences between technical theoretical
analysis as we are attempting it here, and the "common sense" treatment
of the same empirical materials.[9]

In seeking to account for revolutions we shall, from time to time,
shift our point of reference from the nation as a system (with revolutionary movement as one component) to the revolutionary movement
as a system.

Since the decisions of interpersonal organizations are made by
individual human beings, their behavior can be partially accounted
for by considering the individual. The external environment of each
decision maker consists of two parts, one internal and one external.
The main levers of any organization are moved by individuals alone
(or by small groups of interacting individuals such as a cabinet coming
to agreement) in response to pressures and restraints from many
sources. The tendency of either a nation-state or empire, through
the nervous system of its leaders, is to test "input energies"—cognitions
of things as they are—against some criteria, some preferred state
of affairs, established by themselves, at least in part, and possibly
also by their advisors, by their predecessors, and sometimes by the
society at large and to respond if the result of the test is the revelation
of an incongruity.

Nation-state (and empire) behavior is thus identified as the outcome of a need felt by individual leaders—variously shared or not
shared by other members of the society—to solve "problems," to
reduce or close the gap between a real state of affairs (as perceived
by the leaders) and a preferred state of affairs. The existence of
such a gap or problem may be said to give rise to dissatisfaction
or tension within the decision and control apparatus of the state or

9. *Ibid.,* pp. 174–175.

empire (variously shared or not shared by other members of the society). Normally, the overriding criterion for national (or imperial) leaders involves the security and survival of the state (or empire)—though different leaders may differ markedly in the means they use to pursue these basic ends. Something similar can be said about organized revolutionary movements.

The nub of the matter is this: *the individual acting as decision maker for the state or for a revolutionary organization* (as well as, in fact, for himself) *represents a convergence or intersection of organizational and, hence, of behavioral levels.* In this context the individual decision maker and his milieu emerge as a potent entry way, so to speak, for the investigator's probe.

Decision-making Units

Individuals and nation-states (and empires) are decision and control units. Early manifestations of revolutionary activity may involve more or less unorganized or partially organized groups. Normally, however, a revolutionary movement becomes organized into a fairly complex decision and control unit before substantial successes are achieved. Such systems are capable of adapting or learning behavior.

Ashby discusses adapted or learned behavior in terms of ultra-stable systems in which

> two systems of continuous variables (that we called "environment" and "reacting part") interact, so that a primary feedback (through complex sensory and motor channels) exists between them. Another feedback, working intermittently and at a much slower order of speed, goes from the environment to certain continuous variables which in their turn affect some step-mechanisms, the effect being that the step-mechanisms change value when and only when these variables pass outside given limits. The step-mechanisms affect the reacting part; by acting as parameters to it they determine how it shall react to the environment.[10]

By feedback we refer to a method of controlling a system by reinserting into it the results of its past performance.[11] "The term *feedback* means that there exist two channels, carrying information, such that Channel B loops back from the output to the input of Channel B and transmits some portion of the signals emitted from

---

10. W. Ross Ashby, *Design for a Brain* (New York: John Wiley and Sons, Inc., 1960), p. 98.
11. Norbert Wiener, *The Human Use of Human Beings* (Garden City, New York: Doubleday and Company, Inc., 1956), p. 61.

Channel A. These are tell-tales or monitors of the outputs of Channel A."[12]

The activities of the individual human nervous system can be divided into two types of feedback process. The first is reflex behavior, which is inborn, genetically determined in detail, and not appreciably modified by individual experience. The second is learned behavior, which is not inborn nor genetically determined in detail, but is markedly modified by the organism's individual experiences.[13]

A feedback arrangement—whether operating in the nervous system of a biological organism, through the institutions of an interpersonal organization, or in a specialized, man-made machine—may be as simple as a common reflex, or sufficiently intricate to use past experience in regulating whole policies of behavior in terms of "learning!"[14] Simple feedback consists in the reinsertion of information for the relatively unsophisticated, short-term regulation and control of the system. "If, however, the information which proceeds backward from the performance is able to change the general method and pattern of performance, we have a process which may well be called learning."[15] This process amounts to the capacity for using information about the environment and operations upon the environment in order to deal with that environment more effectively.

There are two stages in the learning or adapting process. The first occurs when the organism or interpersonal organization initially "learns," that is, when it changes from a system that does not have an adapted mechanism to one that does. The second takes place when the developed mechanism, capacity, or skill operates, changing from inactivity to activity.[16]

Each individual human being is likely to maintain some perception of the universe, of man's role in it, and of his own particular position and interactions with his fellows. There will be habits, preferences, attitudes, expectations, perceptions of what is, what ought to be, and what can and cannot be. There will be expectations of "self" and of various "others." There will be identifications and loyalties. These phenomena will tend to be shaped by the experiences of each individual, including his memories of various kinds of interactions

12. James G. Miller, "Living Systems: Basic Concepts," *Behavioral Science*, X, 3 (July, 1965), p. 227.

13. Ashby, *Design for a Brain*, p. 2.

14. Wiener, *The Human Use of Human Beings*, p. 33.

15. *Ibid.*, p. 61.

16. Ashby, *Design for a Brain*, p. 64.

with other individuals, with various groups, and with the society as a whole. To the extent that some of these perceptions, values, preferences, expectations, identifications, loyalties, and habits are shared, reciprocated, or complemented by other individuals in the environment we have a foundation for community, for custom, for what Durkheim called the conscience collective, for law, and for institutions.[17] Indeed, we can go a long way toward explaining laws and institutions if we view them as expectations of interaction validated by more or less habitual responses. In any event, the behavior of the individual will be profoundly influenced by his perception of—and feelings about—such more or less shared phenomena. Each system has some number of variables that are related to its survival and "are closely linked dynamically so that marked changes in any one lead sooner or later to marked changes in the others."[18] Stability in a system implies the maintenance of some balance or equilibrium with the environment and also some coordination of the actions among its parts—a continuing steady state. Survival occurs when behavior takes no essential variable outside given limits. A system's behavior may be described as adaptive if it maintains the essential variables within these minimal limits.

The tendency of revolutionary movements is to test and, in the long run, seek to destroy the over-arching system. Revolutionary leaders normally try to exploit key variables or gain control of and manipulate them in ways calculated to challenge the system's survival.

Adaptive or learning behavior is equivalent to the behavior of a stable system. In these terms many living organisms—especially the higher living organisms—"modify their patterns of behavior on the basis of past experience in order to achieve specific antientropic ends."[19] Generally, organisms learn in order to survive, but there are certain complications, of course, such as suicidal behavior, which will be discussed below.

When the environment changes to a degree that alters the consequences of human values, habits, customs, beliefs, and ways of thinking, people need to recognize what has happened. They need to alter their thinking and behavior if they still wish to achieve basic purposes and goals. They need to search for new values, new institutions, and new ways of doing things in order not to work against

17. Emile Durkheim, *The Division of Labor in Society* (Glencoe, Ill.: The Free Press, 1960).

18. Ashby, *Design for a Brain*, p. 42.

19. Wiener, *The Human Use of Human Beings*, p. 48.

themselves, in order to prevent awesome consequences that they would not have sought in the first place. Revolutions tend to develop when some considerable part of the populace recognizes the need for change, but when social, economic, or political aspects of the system (or all three) remain relatively inflexible.

Stability in a system belongs only to the total combination and cannot be related solely to the environment, to the system itself, or to its components. Since feedback can be used to correct any deviation that emerges, the complexity of goal-seeking behavior a system may undertake is virtually unlimited. If it is displaced from a state of equilibrium and released, a stable system has the property to match its subsequent activity to the initial displacement to bring itself back to a state of equilibrium. "A variety of disturbances will therefore evoke a variety of matched reactions."[20] Leaders tend to respond to environmental events in ways that they perceive as contributing to the stability and survival of the system. Such perceptions may or may not have much in common with the "real" requirements of the situation. Also, short term advantages may be gained at long term cost, or vice versa.

5. National leaders can be viewed as operating to minimize or close one (or a combination) of three types of gaps. The most basic is a gap between resources that are demanded or "needed" and resources that are actually available.[21] The second is the gap between an expectation and the reality that materializes (as, for example, when climbing productivity begins to decline); and the third is a gap between the actor's level of resources or growth rate and that of a competitor or rival.[22] (Gaps in military and naval power, prestige, status, and other attributes may exacerbate other gaps or create new ones.) The leaders of organized revolutionary movements can be seen as operating to minimize or close similar types of gaps.

For conceptual purposes it is frequently convenient to postulate that gaps of these various kinds give rise to tension (stress, dissatisfaction) which, in turn, impels behavior. Tension is a relatively intangible concept, however, and one is often hard put to decide upon an appropriate indicator. In this paper, for the most part, we shall deal as much as possible with gaps or differences.

20. Ashby, *Design for a Brain*, p. 54.

21. This concept can be broadened to include social demands or "needs" and other benefactions.

22. See Alan Howard and Robert A. Scott, "A Proposed Framework for the Analysis of Stress in the Human Organism," *Behavioral Science*, X, 2 (April, 1965), pp. 141–159.

Developing Specialized Capabilities

Population, technology, and resources combine to produce energy on many organizational levels. This tendency is constrained, however, by the subsistence demands of the people. In order to be effective, national societies (and also revolutionary movements) require some surplus of energy above what is necessary for the minimal subsistence of the people. A combination of growing population and developing technology places rapidly increasing demands upon resources. Thus, inadequate resources will tend to increase competition and conflict among individuals and among interpersonal systems on various levels and to stimulate demands for further territory, by preemption or conquest, or for access to raw materials and markets, through enhanced trade. Some combination of these tendencies may also occur.

Against this background we would expect that increases in the numbers of a disadvantaged class or other group within a nation-state or empire together with an increase in the knowledge and skills of such a group will increase the potentials for acute dissidence and revolution to the extent that access to resources continues to be constrained. The rapid acquisition of knowledge and skills by the disadvantaged class or sector of society is likely to signal expressions of dissidence and the beginnings of a revolutionary movement—especially if access to resources or a share in decision-making power lags significantly behind other advances.

How much a given population is able to transform its environment and maximize resources depends upon the "hostility" or "friendliness" of the environment and also upon the knowledge and skills, and the total technology, of the people, e.g., upon the location of resources, the ease or difficulty with which they are reached, the ability to transform such resources, and the amount of energy required to transform and harness them.

Human beings—especially in environments that are neither too hostile nor too benign—increase their knowledge and skills over time by responding to the environment and operating upon it by cybernetic, more or less trial-and-error processes. Some of their knowledge and skills may be applied, in turn, to transforming and harnessing hitherto unused resources. Still people in areas where the resources are easy (but not *too* easy) to obtain and conveniently (but not *too* conveniently) distributed will probably be stimulated to greater organizational effort than people elsewhere. Furthermore, all these relationships are relative.

Clearly, the degree to which a given environment is hostile or benign depends somewhat upon the level and density of the population and their level of technology. Thus, a South Seas island may provide a benign environment until the population grows too large for the resources. On the other hand, the introduction of new technology—terraced farming, for example, or oil drilling equipment—may radically increase the benign quality of the environment for the numbers and density of population.

Maximum population refers to the greatest number of people that can subsist on the total product of a given environment provided that resources are distributed with some fairness among all. This maximum will depend upon the level of knowledge and skills, because a dense population with a highly developed technology can, in general, function more effectively than a dense population with a less developed technology. Some minimal number of people is needed to eliminate the risk of too much consanguinity or age disparity among martial partners. Depending upon the size and nature of the environment some minimal number is probably required in order to secure the basic necessities for survival. Sustaining life is not easy without some division of labor. In primitive bands and tribes such division is not highly developed, and a considerable amount of territory is needed to support a small number of people. The populace may be so scattered, on the other hand, that cohesion and cooperation are difficult to initiate or sustain. Estimates vary somewhat, but it seems probable that an isolated group requires five or six hundred people in order to function viably.

For any given level of knowledge and skills, marginal productivity is the increase in the production of a society by the addition of extra individuals, one by one, to the total population. As an outcome of the division of labor, marginal productivity rises initially but later peaks and slopes off through saturation and diminishing returns.

Frequently, when an environment is benign over-all, i.e., the combination of area, resources, numbers of people, and general level of knowledge and skills is favorable, certain classes or sectors or enclaves of the society can still be confined in one way or another to less favorable environments. Such circumstances are characteristic of slum dwellers, American blacks in the Deep South or in northern ghettos, American Indians living on certain reservations, and so forth. Often the "commerce" or "trade balance" between slum, ghetto, or reservation dwellers and the rest of society is grossly unfavorable, so that the disadvantaged must contribute more energy for the same return than he would expect, given the general norm of the society.

At both minimum and maximum extremes of population (a hunting and gathering band, or a huge "underdeveloped" country such as India or China) the tendency is toward a very low standard of living, a bare subsistence—except that, in either case, a high level of technology is likely to enhance possibilities for acquiring and transforming resources, harnessing energy, and thus increasing the society's effectiveness. Thus, "Low productivity may reflect either population pressure or backward technology"—or both.[23]

Between these two extremes at least one population size—in terms of environmental resources and the level of knowledge and skills—should maximize the capabilities of a given society. A nation or, within a national society, a class or sector of the populace may attempt to achieve such a favorable balance by a conscious strategy for acquiring new resources, by increasing the level of knowledge and skills, or both.

The way the leaders of a nation-state or other interpersonal system respond to perceived gaps between the actual state of affairs and the preferred state of affairs will depend to some considerable extent upon the absolute dimensions of the system at the time and also, in many instances, upon the rates of change of certain influential dimensions. Often, too, the leaders of an organization will re-allocate resources and re-direct efforts in order to develop the particular capabilities they believe are necessary to minimize or close salient gaps. The allocation of resources and human energy for specialized purposes is a major function of organizational leaders.

6. Absolute levels of population, technology, territory, resources, and trade affect a society's over-all capabilities, its power, prestige, and status. Rates of change along these dimensions (as well as absolute amounts of change) shape a nation's predispositions and behaviors.

7. In their efforts to close gaps between what is available and what is needed (or desired), individuals acting in their own interests and the leaders of interpersonal systems both tend to allocate certain proportions of the energy available to them for the development of specific capabilities. These special capabilities may involve methods of hunting, methods of trading, methods of agriculture, methods of warfare, industrial production, and so forth. Organizational techniques can be viewed as a specialized capability.

A national populace may be able to enhance its access to resources in various ways. "One is to utilize space within a country's boundaries

23. Hans Weigert, et al., Principles of Political Geography (New York: Appleton-Century-Crofts, 1957), p. 332.

which was hitherto unused. However, the possibilities of internal colonization are limited, unless the colonization is accompanied by technological progress and a corresponding expansion of communications. Internal colonization is therefore often possible only in connection with the second method, intensification of available space."[24]

The resources of a territory can be used more intensively by the application of a more advanced technology. An advance in knowledge and skills may give a society not only the power to convert potential resources into employed resources but also the ability to extend its reach to resources beyond its own immediate territory.[25]

Commerce offers a further possibility. "Trading relations, by extending the resources of a group of people, afford a substitute for size of political jurisdiction."[26] Frequently, however, nations and empires have seized upon still another alternative, "expanding their territories through war, by taking the land of their neighbors and expelling or exterminating the inhabitants or forcing them to work for their conquerors."[27]

The over-all ratios of population, resources, and technology may be generally favorable for the total society, but at the same time the relatively advantaged and disadvantaged sectors of the populace may have greatly different access to resources and knowledge and skills. In such instances, the disadvantaged may find ways to organize and enhance their access to resources and technology. The strategies used by disadvantaged classes within a society and by disadvantaged nations within the international environment are analogous. The disadvantaged class or group may be able to utilize resources that were not used before. By increasing their knowledge and skills, the hitherto disadvantaged may be able to gain new access to unused resources. Or a previously disadvantaged class or group may improve its commercial relations with other sectors of the populace.

If none of these possibilities is available or sufficiently successful in making new resources available, a disadvantaged class or group may organize for agitation and violence involving revolutionary efforts to disrupt the old system and replace it with a new order.

Like national systems, revolutionary movements, to be effective, require population, resources, and some level of knowledge and skills including an organizational decision and control apparatus. Without some level of these elements and without a more or less centralized

24. *Ibid.*, pp. 27–28.
25. Ackerman, *Population and Natural Resources*, p. 637.
26. *Ibid.*, p. 626.
27. Hans Weigert *et al.*, *Principles of Political Geography*, p. 28.

leadership, a revolutionary movement, whatever its long-range potential, is not likely to achieve much immediate effectiveness. A revolutionary movement thus emerges as an interpersonal energy-producing, energy-storing, and energy-consuming system. The major responsibilities of revolutionary leaders involve the management of energy and resources and their allocation or investment in the development of specialized capabilities such as political agitation against the "legitimate" decision and control system, economic disruption, mobilizing and training members, the mounting and supplying of guerrilla forces, and so forth.

Lateral Pressure, Conflict, Growth Rates, and Dominance

It is self-evident that two or more human beings cannot occupy the same space at the same time; nor can they consume the same unit of air or water or food or other resources at the same time except, in some instances, by special cooperative arrangement, as when two or more people warm themselves by the same fire or read by the same candle or are transported by the same vehicle drawn by the same beast or propelled by the same fuel. Even in these instances, the possibilities of sharing are finite and limited: the consumption of a resource by one cooperating group makes it impossible for any other individual or group to consume that resource. Any considerable expenditure of energy by two or more individuals (or interpersonal organizations) in close interaction is likely to generate some amount of conflict.

Traditionally, human beings have managed their conflicts over the occupancy of space and the consuming of resources in two major ways. (1) They have fought it out—often killing large numbers of each other; this method becomes what is sometimes called a zero-sum arrangement: each person (or group) perceives another's gain as his own loss. Or (2) they have organized in order to divide space and allocate, exchange, and optimize resources according to some plan; and also they have organized in order to transform the environment in various ways, maximizing resources so that there will be more to go around and benefits will be enhanced. To the extent that all the participants gain, this kind of arrangement is said to be positive sum.

But this statement is an over-simplification. Many interpersonal organizations and, indeed, whole societies, may be viewed as numbers of discrete human beings operating more or less cooperatively in efforts to extract, transform, and apply energy from the environment.

A political organization including—and especially—the decision and control apparatus of a state or empire tends to function as a mechanism for regulating, adjudicating, managing, containing, and resolving internal conflicts and also as a responsible nucleus for protecting and advancing external interests. These systems tend to invest a considerable portion of available energy and resources into activities or sets of activities. Thus in order to understand a system's past behavior and to predict its future behavior, we need to know something about its general level of energy and something also about the factors that seem to predispose it toward particular distributions and applications of energy and resources.

Human beings living in a generally favorable environment will be continually challenged by what appear to be the shortcomings or undesirable characteristics of the world immediately about them. Over the years and decades and centuries, they will invest certain amounts of energy and resources in efforts to "reorganize" the environment to suit their purposes, and these efforts, in turn, will stimulate them to devise more effective and efficient forms of self-organization. We may suppose, then, that for any given environment and any given level of technology there is an optimal population number and density for the potential survival of the society and for the development of further knowledge and skills. Similarly, for any given environment and any given population (numbers) and population density there is a minimum level of technology required for that society to survive.

If a population increases rapidly but technology and access to resources lag, the people will make strong demands, but the society will not have the capacity to bring about many changes. The pattern is likely to involve starvation, banditry, food riots, and other localized violence, but the disadvantaged will not have the knowledge and skills or surplus energy needed for effective organization and revolt.

To a considerable extent, as suggested above, the level and characteristics of a social-political organization appear to depend upon the nature of the environment (including the availability of critical resources), the numbers and density of population, and the level of technology, that is, the degree to which knowledge and skills are organized. But these factors tend to be intensely interactive, a change in one tending to bring about a change in the others. Given a small population, low density, low level of technology, and low level of political organization, the people involved will alter the environment only minimally. To the degree that the environment is altered, however, such alterations may facilitate an increase in population, an increase in population density, a rise in the level of technology, a particular specialization of technique, and an alteration in political level. Hence, the natural distribution of resources, the number of people, the broad level of technology (the organization and application of knowledge and skills), and the allocations by ruling elites of resources, access to knowledge and skills, and various benefactions are important factors in both conflict and most levels of human political organization.

Central to this thesis is that differential rates of population growth in combination with differential rates of technological growth contribute to conflict insofar as individual human beings (and societies) have differential—i.e., grossly unequal—access to food, housing, health, education, work, justice, and general influence or control over their environment. The roots of national and of domestic dissent and revolution seem to be closely associated with these basic differentials.

Against this background the dynamics of individual and group behavior can be identified in terms of population growth; muscular energy from animals and men; psychic and affective energy (attitudes, preferences, values, goals, aspirations, expectations, frustrations, fears, hostilities, decisions, and so forth); technological energy, which, as used here, is a particular aspect of psychic energy, namely, learning, knowledge, and skills; and non-animate energy and resources unlocked from the environment and harnessed for human purposes through the application of knowledge and skills.

8. Demands and specific capabilities combine multiplicatively to produce what might be called lateral pressure, which amounts to a tendency to invest energy and resources and acquire influence over a wider extent of space or among a larger number of other people or both. Specific capabilities yield particular types or modes of lateral pressure.

Differentiated demands give rise to interpersonal, inter-group, inter-societal, and international conflict. The object of demand may be material resources or social, political, or psychological resources such as status, prestige, influence, respect, or a greater share of power or decisions.

In general, a small number of people have fewer conflicts, absolutely, than a larger number of people. If they fight it out, they inflict fewer casualties. And if they organize, they require a smaller and generally less complex government and bureaucratic apparatus than do a large number of people when they organize.

We can postulate, then, that the greater the number of people, the closer their quarters and the more numerous and intense their interactions, the more conflicts will arise. A scarcity of resources will further the incidence and intensity of conflicts. Given a certain incidence and intensity of conflict, the higher the technology, the more lethal the modes of conflict are likely to be. But organization tends to contain, regulate, and resolve conflicts within its perimeter of control. And if conflicts are contained by organization, then the greater the number of people, the closer their quarters; and the more intense their interactions, the more differentiated, complex, and bureaucratic will be the organization.

In fact, the distinction between human conflict and human organization is not clear-cut, for the two phenomena are not mutually exclusive. There is organization in conflict, and conflict in organization. However, by organizing, human beings normally limit their conflicts, confining them and working them out within recognized, more or less agreed-upon channels. By organizing, they establish rules for governing conflicts, courts for deciding them, and legitimate instruments of force for compelling observance. To the extent that the rules are applied equally and fairly and individuals enjoy equal access to resources, privileges, benefactions, and influence over institutions of decision and control, the arrangement can be considered positive sum.

In nomadic societies there is generally little or no unused space in times of drought or when the soil has been exhausted or the population increases; and intensifying animal husbandry is frequently impossible on the nomadic level of civilization and technology.[28] Especially for a nomadic people, then, conquest as an alternative to starvation has often appeared to be the only solution.

Agricultural societies also create a pressure on land as populations grow or soil is depleted. Associated with them, moreover, is likely to be a newer and more imperative concept of stable territory and a formal, "legal" frontier. Also, agricultural technologies provided the basis for new standards of living and for institutional stability. A population increase within a given agricultural territory is likely to stimulate expansion by preemption, conquest, purchase, dynastic intermarriage, or other available means. In this way small kingdoms have tended to expand into vast empires.

A true state, however underdeveloped, is distinguished from bands and tribes in particular and all less comprehensive groups in

28. *Ibid.*

general by the presence of that special form of control, the constant threat or application of force by a body of persons "legitimately" constituted to use it. Force is a monopoly of certain offices; and personal, non-governmental force is outlawed (the occurrence of murder, feud, or riot signifies the absence of state power at that time and place). A political system is more or less stable according to the presence or absence and the functioning or non-functioning of these and other processes.

In general, the most effective integration of lesser units into states and empires has been achieved by able and ambitious kings or military chieftains who have enforced integration either by outright conquest or by what might be identified as aggressive and more or less coercive administration involving the imposition of taxes, the raising of troops, the enforcement of appeal to royal courts, the coinage of money, the maintenance of law and order, and so forth, on the basis of the exercise or threat of superior force.

Integration by conquest (William the Conquerer) and unification by coercive administration (Philip Augustus, Louis IX, the Muscovite princes, and other strong and ambitious rulers) appear, historically, to have been the most common procedures. Most great empires expanded by the one means or the other or, more frequently, by a combination of the two. Consensual integration has occurred only infrequently. Even the United States, whose genesis lay in the consensual integration of the Thirteen Colonies against British domination, expanded to the Pacific largely by conquest or coercive administration (at the expense of Indian tribes, Mexicans, and others who had lesser capabilities). Of the relatively few instances in which states or pre-state forms have combined successfully into a single, more or less permanent encompassing unit on a state level through negotiation and voluntary consent, four have been particularly notable—the Achaean Federation (c. 280 BC),[29] the Swiss Confederation (1291 AD), the seven United Provinces of the Netherlands (1579 AD–1795 AD), and the United States of North America prior to westward expansion (c. 1776–1800 AD).

9. Nation-states and empires with high lateral pressure (demands x capability) tend to extend their influence in search of resources (and often also because high levels of energy tend to seek some kind of investment or other expenditure). This tendency to expand may take the form of exploration, migration, conquest, commerce, financial

---

29. Edward A. Freeman, *History of Federal Government in Greece and Italy* (London: Macmillan and Co., 1893), p. 190.

investment, colonization, economic or military assistance to other countries, and so forth. The incorporation of territory and new populations (often with different cultures) within the state or empire extends sovereignty for the expanding power, but often sets in motion new developments in knowledge and skills among the encompassed populations and thus creates the initial conditions for subsequent dissent, increases in local capabilities, and possible revolution.

10. The higher the lateral pressure generated by a given state or empire, the greater will be its tendency to extend its influence into (and often domination over) territories and countries with a lower level of capability.

11. As a nation-state or empire extends its influence (and hence its interests) the leaders (and also often the rank and file citizens) tend to acquire the feeling that this influence and these interests ought to be protected. This tendency may give rise to the extension of military or naval forces, the development of a tendency to police areas beyond the legal boundaries of the state or empire, and a feeling of responsibility for regional or even world "law and order."

12. The desire to achieve and maintain law and order and protect national interests in far-off places may lead to wars against indigenous tribes, chiefdoms, and petty principalities and the effort to attract, equip, and partially finance client chiefs, princes, warlords, or other rulers or ruling groups. Often these groups constitute nuclei for subsequent discontent and possible (segmentary) revolution.

Anthropologists distinguish methods of integrating on five levels of social-political organization: (1) familistic bonds of kinship and marriage that integrate the relatively small and simple societies called bands; (2) pan-tribal sodalities, such as clans, that integrate several band-like societies into a single tribe; (3) functions of specialization, redistribution, and related centralization of authority that integrate still more complex societies into what are called chiefdoms; (4) the state, which is further integrated by a specialized bureaucracy[30] or decision-and-control system employing a monopoly of legitimate or legal force; and (5) a presumably emerging industrial society integrated not only by a state decision-and-control apparatus, but also by a complex network of specialized interdependent occupations. At any given junction such hierarchies (bands, tribes, chiefdoms, states,

---

30. Elman R. Service, *Primitive Social Organization* (New York: Random House, 1962), p. 181; Peter Farb, *Man's Rise to Civilization as Shown by the Indians of North America* (New York: E. P. Dutton and Co., Inc., 1968); and George Peter Murdock, "World Ethnographic Sample," *American Anthropologist*, Vol. 59, No. 4 (August, 1957), pp. 664–687.

coalitions of states, and so forth), together with the frequency and content of communications among them and among their components, are important features in the environmental configuration.[31]

The trend over the full range of man's history has been from band-like organizations of a few people with relatively ineffectual tools and weapons and minimal institutionalization of decision and control toward the vast, highly bureaucratic super-states of modern times with everything from computers to hydrogen bombs to work and fight with. For millennia the growth rates of population and technology were extremely low. From father to son to grandson, societies and the general environment did not change much. Now the rates of growth are very much faster, and keeping up with the implications of scientific and engineering developments and the larger and larger numbers of people is becoming increasingly difficult for both institutions and the individual. Yet we can trace some of the same basic behavioral elements almost from the beginning down to the present time. The generalized pattern of development has been repeated in many times and places through pre-history and history. Indeed, the phenomenon has been ubiquitous.[32]

The tribe, chiefdom, or state that became sufficiently strong tended to extend its influence and dominion over less capable neighbors.[33] "The most spectacular instance of this process in all history was the way in which the little tribes centered in Rome brought first Latium, and then gradually all Italy, and finally the whole Western world, together with the Near East, under the sway of their imperial city."[34] Further, the functions of head man, chief, king, emperor, president, or dictator have to increase "as the size of the community grows, as relationships with neighboring tribes become more difficult,"[35] and as the tasks of various segments of the society become more and more differentiated, specialized, and institutionalized.

There are constraints upon this kind of power, however: the logistic restrictions of space, time, availability of resources, and so

31. William H. Riker, *The Theory of Political Coalitions* (New Haven: Yale University Press, 1962); see also Karl W. Deutsch and J. David Singer, "Multipolar Power Systems and International Stability," *World Politics*, Vol. XVI, No. 3 (April, 1964), pp. 390–406.

32. See, for examples, K. Oberg, "The Kingdom of Ankole and Uganda," in M. Fortes and E. E. Evans-Pritchard (eds.), *African Political Systems* (London: Oxford University Press, 1940). pp. 127 ff. Cf. Freeman, *History of Federal Government in Greece and Italy*, p. 21.

33. John R. Swanton, *The Evolution of Nations* (Washington, D.C.: The Smithsonian Institution, 1942), p. 7.

34. R. M. MacIver, *The Web of Government* (New York: The Macmillan Company, 1947), pp. 35–36.

35. *Ibid.*, p. 33.

forth, and also the limitations imposed by allometry. Beyond a certain geographical obstacle or beyond a certain over-all distance from his center of power, the ruler's influence and control decline rapidly. Moreover, "If a king abuses his power, subordinate chiefs are liable to secede or lead a revolt against him,"[36] particularly if, by combining or achieving some particular source of capability, they see some possibility of out-matching him. On the other hand, if a subordinate chief seems to be getting too powerful and independent, the central authority may be supported by other subordinate chiefs in suppressing him.

An aggressive, ambitious, and powerful leader is likely to use his knowledge, skills, power, and prestige to favor the appointment of his son or other near-of-kin as his successor. "Thus, one family is singled out from all the rest, the ruling family. With this elevation the distinction between chief and subjects is developed ... with consequent new accretions of ceremony and ritual to corroborate the change."[37] The king's son may not have been as able a ruler as his parent, but habit, internalized loyalties, sense of duty, and the like may operate to preserve the dynasty for many generations. On the other hand, subordinated groups may bide their time until their capabilities have improved, relative to those of the ruling elite, and then stage a civil war or revolution.

The integration of components into a larger system tends to involve progressive centralization, e.g., increased centralized control among units, "so that a change in one is likely to influence process in many or all others."[38] The principle of progressive centralization pertinent to the emergence of organization in many contexts and on various levels means progressive individualization of the newly forming system. "An 'individual' can be defined as a centralized system"[39] and a state or empire takes shape as it behaves and is increasingly recognized by other actors as a single, independent, and more or less sovereign system. We would expect the progressive centralization of nation-states and empires to be associated with high rates of population and technological growth rates—at least on the part of the more active components in the unification.

Progressive centralization leads more or less at the same time to progressive segregation. As a system grows in population, extent

---

36. Fortes and Evans-Pritchard (eds.), *African Political Systems,* p. 11.

37. MacIver, *The Web of Government,* pp. 34–35.

38. James G. Miller, "Living Systems: Cross Level Hypotheses," *Behavioral Science,* X, 4 (October, 1965), p. 405.

39. Ludwig von Bertalanffy, "An Outline of General System Theory," *The British Journal for the Philosophy of Science,* Vol. 1, No. 2 (August, 1950), p. 136.

of territory,[40] or level of technology (organization and application of knowledge and skills), it is forced to reorganize, a more or less on-going process that achieves new divisions of labor. "Boundaries form where none existed before and semi-autonomous, decentralized subsystems, components, and echelons arise, acting on at least partly segregated information."[41] These are processes familiar to students of bureaucracy, social and economic classes, class struggle, and revolution and counter-revolution. Semi-autonomous decentralized components are likely to have population and technology growth rates which differ from subsystem to subsystem and which may induce both inter-component competitions and, in some instances, conflict and even (revolutionary) warfare between one or more components and the central system itself. Decaying nations and empires often exhibit these tendencies, and the Austro-Hungarian, Ottoman, and Chinese empires during the late nineteenth and early twentieth centuries are notable examples. Later, the overseas empires of England, France, Belgium, and the Netherlands suffered somewhat comparable disintegration.

Progressive segregation tends to mean progressive mechanization, which implies a lack of the ability to be regulated and an invitation for dissidence and revolution. Indeed, regulation becomes "progressively" restricted and finally impossible when the originally unitary system segregates into separate causal chains determined by fixed structures, that is to say, with progressive segregation. Again, the Austro-Hungarian, Ottoman, and Chinese empires and the overseas empires of the European imperial powers offer examples.

There tend to be two general restrictions on regulatory processes. "The first is the completeness of the open-system character of the organism [or interpersonal organization]. For instance, the growth regulations mentioned will not be possible if insufficient diet has caused lasting, irreversible disturbances, for example, in the ossification of bones." In a nation-state or empire, by crude analogy, growth regulation will be disturbed by a large population coupled with insufficient technological development. "The second limitation of regulation lies in the hierarchical order (cf. allometric growth), namely, in the progressive segregation of the organism into subordinate systems which gain a certain independence of each other."[42]

40. James Miller, "Living Systems: Cross Level Hypotheses," p. 405.

41. James Miller, "Living Systems: Structure and Process," *Behavioral Science*, X, 4 (October, 1965), p. 376.

42. Bertalanffy, "An Outline of General System Theory," p. 158.

Interpersonal systems, including states and empires, may be compared in terms of "coefficients derived by relating the amount of energy harnessed and expended in a given period of time to the number of human beings embraced in the system."[43] In these terms, one state or empire "may harness and use x units of energy per capita per year, and another, 3x or 10x." In human terms the significance of the coefficient resides in the relationship between the "amount of energy harnessed, on the one hand, and the number of human beings whose needs are to be served, on the other," and also in the nature and level of their aspirations and expectations.

Similar comparisons can be made in terms of the ability of one class, territorial, racial, or other component of a nation-state or empire to use x units of energy per capita per year and another 3x or 10x. In other words, the distributions among the national or imperial population at large of access to resources, technology, decision and control, and various benefactions will reveal useful information about the stability, adaptability, or probabilities of conflict within a system. The implications here are probabilistic, and not deterministic.

In non-living systems, the general trend of events, which obey the Second Law of Thermodynamics, is toward entropy, a state of maximum disorder. Biological organisms and interpersonal organizations or systems provide an appearance of violating a narrow interpretation of this law. Schrödinger asserted that the open, living organism "feeds"[44] from negative entropy, ingesting complex organic molecules, using energy extracted from them, and returning the simpler end products to the environment in the form of wastes. Strictly speaking, however, the Second Law is not violated: it holds for the system plus its environment but not for the system itself insofar as entropy tends to decrease within it.

Thus, entropy often decreases locally and temporarily. Human beings, other biological organisms, and also interpersonal organizations are enclaves, so to speak, of increasing organization and local—and temporary—buildups of information. These organisms and organizations[45] have certain characteristics in common. They are *en rapport* with their environments through sense organs (in interpersonal organizations, inputs of this kind must pass through the sense organs of individual human beings acting for or in the name of the

---

43. White, *The Evolution of Culture*, p. 41.

44. Erwin Schrödinger, *What is Life* (Garden City, N.Y.: Doubleday and Company, Inc., 1956), p. 71.

45. Norbert Wiener, *The Human Use of Human Beings*, p. 77.

system). They possess effector organs or institutions or mechanisms capable of performing tasks. They are capable of adjusting future conduct on the basis of past performance through feedback. Through these and other contributing functions, biological organisms and interpersonal organizations, by making decisions, produce around them local and temporary zones of organization, or negative entropy, in a universe whose general tendency is to run down.[46]

The final state in most physical systems is determined by the initial conditions. They thus exhibit finality. This is not true for living organisms, however, or for interpersonal systems, whose final state can frequently be reached from different initial conditions and in different ways. Such behavior is called equifinal.[47]

There is another important consideration. Summativity means that a complex can be achieved step by step by putting together the initially separate elements. Conversely, the complex and its characteristics can be analyzed completely into the separate elements. Biological and interpersonal systems are non-summative; the behavior of an element is different within the system from what it is in isolation. "You cannot sum up the behavior of the whole from the isolated parts, and you have to take into account the relation between the various subordinated systems and the systems which are superordinated to them in order to understand the behavior of the parts."[48]

Systems tend to grow or decline exponentially. "Growth in size, number, and complexity of components often compels a system to reorganize relationships among its parts. One reason for this is that, as its linear dimensions increase, its volume goes up as the cube of such distances and its surface as the square."[49] This rule of growth is known as the exponential law, which applies to money (compound interest), the decay of radium, the killing of bacteria by disinfectants or light, the loss of body substance in starving animals, the growth and decline of animal populations, and so forth. Human populations, interpersonal organizations, the body of knowledge and skills, inventions, and so forth tend to grow exponentially.

But such increases will also be limited by certain restricting or constraining conditions. Curves drawn to represent the growth rate and other behaviors of systems at various levels often show that activity

---

46. *Ibid.*, pp. 33–34.
47. Ludwig von Bertalanffy, "An Outline of General System Theory," p. 158.
48. *Ibid.*, p. 156.
49. James Miller, "Living Systems: Structure and Process," p. 373.

is initially slow, rises to a maximum, and then declines toward, or to, zero. This is known as the logistic, or sigmoid (S-shaped), curve.[50] In a general way, it describes, historically, the cycle of nations, empires, and even civilizations. But there are likely to be important variations within phases of an over-all, long-term cycle, depending upon interacting variables. Thus, "A population increases exponentially with the increasing numbers of individuals, but if space and food are limited, the amount of food available per individual decreases; therefore the increase in number cannot be unlimited, but must approach a steady state defined as the maximum population compatible with the resources available."[51] A population may also be constrained by disease.

Whenever human beings interact in a sustained way, we tend to observe the phenomenon of allometry, or hierarchical peaking, which seems to be characteristic of most organizations including states, empires, and international alliances. The principle of allometric growth, describing in biology the relative increase of chemical compounds, organs, cell groups, or physiological activities with respect to body size, is analogous to Pareto's law regarding the distribution of wealth within a nation. It suggests that many attributes—wealth, influence, decision-making power, access to knowledge and skills, and so forth—may be arranged within a system or among systems according to a distribution function. This tendency gives rise to inequalities among individuals and among classes, regional groups, nationalities, states, and empires.

The allometric, or parabolic, law is "an expression for competition within a system, each element taking its share according to its capacity as expressed by a specific constant."[52] With respect to a single biological organism, "two groups of cells transforming into the same structure and coexisting in the same physiological environment will compete for the energy-rich substrate."[53]

Each component part of the system takes, in the course of an increase in metabolism or rate of growth, a share proportionate to its size or activity within the larger system. A component capable of seizing more than its proportional share displays positive allometry—a characteristic of many elite groups. Conversely, a compo-

50. *Ibid.*

51. Bertalanffy, "An Outline of General System Theory," p. 136.

52. *Ibid.*, p. 138.

53. Spiegelman, "Physiological Competition as a Regulatory Mechanism in Morphogenesis," p. 123.

nent that acquires less than its proportional share, a depressed or exploited class or minority group, for example, displays negative allometry. In a sense, we can view each element as "a sort of imperialist, seeking to transform as much as possible of the environment into itself and its seed."[54] But some are more successful than others, and thus, to one degree or another, the less effective tend to be dominated.

Elite groups, political and military leaders, industrial tycoons, imperialist powers, and other dominating individuals and groups display positive allometry. Untouchables, slaves, serfs, depressed proletarians of the nineteenth century, and certain black and other minority groups in the United States and elsewhere are or have been examples of negative allometry. Other individuals and groups occupy space between such extremes.

Much the same kind of assertion can be made about two or more individual human beings, two or more bands, tribes, or chiefdoms, two or more nations or empires, and about two or more classes or other component subgroups within a larger organization or society. Revolutions can be viewed as re-arrangements of allometric distributions.

The relative growth rates of the parts of a system under consideration tend to stand in a constant proportion throughout the life of the system or at least during a phase or cycle for which the allometric equation seems to hold. A change in phase or cycle or the transformation of a system is likely to be signalled by a "revolutionary" or step-level change in some element or set of elements fundamental to the system and the subsequent establishment of some new pattern of distributions. Thus, under demands and pressures of interaction (and especially with pressure on scarce resources), individual human beings and also interpersonal groups (including states and empires) tend to become structured into something like a pecking order, or leadership hierarchy, each more effective individual (or organization) tending to inhibit the initiative of less effective individuals (and organizations) which tend, in turn, to contribute power to the more dominant one. In other words, when two (or more) individuals draw their sustenance (or influence, status, prestige, etc.) from the same source or substratum, the more effective will tend to dominate the less effective.

The more limited the substratum (the scarcer the resources), the stronger is likely to be the tendency of the more effective to dominate the less effective and the steeper the slope in the differen-

54. Bertrand Russell, *Philosophy* (New York: W. W. Norton and Company, Inc., 1927), p. 17.

tials. Again, something analogous can be said for interpersonal organizations including states and empires, and for classes or ethnic or other groups within a single state or empire.

Such tendencies appear both inside and outside various organizational structures and produce factions, interest groups, political parties, bureaucracies, and bureaucratic echelons (inside); and coalitions, alliances, or blocs (outside, as among relatively sovereign states and empires). Rank, hierarchy, power elites, interest groups, classes, imperial domination, colonial status, and the like all seem to be manifestations of these tendencies.

If we assume a gradient of effectiveness within two (or more) groups drawing their sustenance from the same substratum, the group with the higher rate of transformation (from less to more effectiveness) will tend to dominate the group with the lower rate of transformation (education, learning, technology, production). Among interpersonal organizations, including states and empires, we would expect, with allowance for differences in size and resources, that one with a higher rate of technological growth would tend, over the long run, to dominate another with a substantially lower rate of technological growth.

Revolutionary movements tend to emerge when a class or group with low effectiveness begins to achieve a much higher rate of transformation, and begins to overtake and threaten dominant classes or groups. Thus, as Crane Brinton pointed out, "Revolutionary movements seem to originate in the discontents of not unprosperous people who feel restraint, cramp, annoyance, rather than downright crushing oppression."[55] Such movements begin to achieve effectiveness to the extent that demands are combined with higher and higher levels of energy and specialized capabilities. Revolutions tend to be successful when mounting lateral pressure by the dissident class or group (or alliance of classes or groups) encounters a serious decline of capability and lateral pressure at the command of the ruling elite. Often, as the declining system becomes less and less effective, " ... the old ruling class—or rather, many individuals of the old ruling class—come to distrust themselves, or lose faith in the traditions and habits of their class, grow intellectual, humanitarian, or go over to the attacking groups."[56] Indeed, it is particularly characteristic of many successful revolutions that considerable elements of the dissident leadership have

---

55. Crane Brinton, *The Anatomy of Revolution* (New York: W. W. Norton and Company, Inc., 1938), p. 286.

56. *Ibid.*, p. 288.

defected from the ruling elite and thus contributed to the overthrow of the old regime by adding their knowledge and skills to the revolutionary cause.[57]

Under such circumstances, the governmental machinery becomes critically inefficient, "partly through neglect, through a failure to make changes in old institutions, partly because new conditions"—especially conditions arising from economic expansion and the growth of new monied classes, new ways of transportation, and new business methods—have "laid an intolerable strain on governmental machinery adapted to simpler more primitive conditions."[58] Beyond a certain threshold bureaucratic or police or military efforts to hold the aging system together may only hasten its demise. Essentially this is what happened as Balkan and East European nationalities broke away from the Austro-Hungarian and Ottoman Empires and as the Chinese Empire disintegrated into contending warlord regimes.

In these terms, we would expect the phenomenon of revolution to be associated with differential growth rates among components of certain types of nation-state and empire systems. On the one hand, we have the tendency toward separation or segmentation (which is descriptive of the "revolution" of the Thirteen Colonies in 1776, the Mexican revolution, various revolutions in South America, and others); and on the other hand we have the tendency toward sociopolitical upheavals such as the French revolution of 1789, the Russian revolution of 1917, and so forth, when a developing component class or other sector of the society produces an elite that challenges and overcomes the established elite and gains access to central decision and control.

For either type, a revolution would be expected to develop most rapidly not when the dominated group is most "depressed" but at the point where that group's level of knowledge and skills begins to rise rapidly. We would expect both types of revolution, each according to its own characteristics and pattern, to be associated with differential growth rates (component to component and component to overarching system) and to display progressive segregation (of components from the encompassing system) associated with progressive centralization (the overarching system in late stages, the component system in early, "vigorous" phases).

57. Alexander Groth, *Revolution and Elite Access: Some Hypotheses on Aspects of Political Change,* Institute of Governmental Affairs, University of California, Davis, 1966, p. 4.

58. Brinton, *The Anatomy of Revolution,* pp. 287–288.

The Influence of the Dominant Technology

To some considerable degree the institutions of a society tend to emerge as reflections, so to speak, of the prevailing or dominating technology of that society. Tasks that are performed with perseverance, that are deeply institutionalized, tend to have a profound effect upon the political, social, and economic forms of a society. Over centuries, agricultural societies—societies in which agriculture of one type or another has been the primary occupation—have displayed certain characteristic political, social, and economic forms. Such societies tend to exhibit minimal specialization of labor, combined or fused role functions, a two-class system of landed aristocracy and peasants or serfs (and petty traders), and a political community shared by only a small proportion of the populace. Most wealth is derived directly or indirectly from agriculture.[59]

Population increases within a predominantly agricultural society, as noted above, are likely to impel the acquisition of arable land by conquest, preemption, or other means. The tendency is to build large armies and an influential warrior class. As the population grows, provided technology is adequate to overcome geographical barriers and conquer neighboring peoples, state boundaries will be extended farther and farther from the original center. Contraction may take place, on the other hand, either because the population or the technology (or both) declines or because contact has been made with an enemy that is superior in population and technology.

An increase in population among the peasantry often leads to the division and subdivision of plots of land until the pieces are too small to support a family. Individual peasants are then forced to take up second occupations, such as home weaving, or abandon their land, becoming agricultural laborers, or go to the city to become industrial laborers.[60] Peasant discontent may give rise to riots, but it has seldom led directly to revolution. For the most part, peasants tend to remain unorganized and inarticulate about goals. Usually, rural unrest has to be linked to urban insurrection and intellectual leadership of one kind or another before it becomes a critical factor in a successful revolution.[61]

59. See George Modelski, "Agraria and Industria: Two Models of the International System," in Klaus Knorr and Sidney Verba (eds.), *The International System* (Princeton: Princeton University Press, 1961).

60. Jack Bloom, *Social Structure and Revolution*, Center for Research in Social Systems, The American University, Washington, D.C., 1966, p. 14.

61. *Ibid.*, pp. 14–15.

Commercially-based societies have been characterized by the exchange of goods as the major source of wealth. The division of labor has tended to be defined by the extent of the market which, in turn, is determined to a considerable degree by transportation costs. Status tends to be accorded to those who control money, commerce, or markets. Frequently there have been tendencies toward egalitarianism (at least among the commercial elite), elections, legislative bodies, and decisions by committee or other collegial body. Athens and other maritime city-states of the Greek archipelago and adjacent islands tended to be commercial in their outlook and institutions,[62] although agricultural elements were present.

Population increases in a predominantly commercial society such as characterized the Phoenician and Greek maritime city-states are likely to stimulate a search for raw materials and markets, the establishment or conquest of overseas colonies or spheres of trade, and, among sea powers, the building of a powerful navy.

Modern industrial states—as Almond and Verba's civic culture concept seems to suggest—have emerged, on the whole, from societies in which commercial elements have achieved great strength and have accomplished—often as an outcome of revolution—some workable, more or less institutionalized *modus vivendi* with a previously dominant agrarian-based ruling elite. Great Britain, the United States, and the Scandinavian countries have been relatively successful in this respect, France somewhat less so, perhaps, and other countries notably unsuccessful.[63] The struggle of commercial elements to achieve status and power in Russia has been long and influential, but often abortive. Japan stands out as an example of conscious, planned, calculated, and largely successful industrialization patterned after Western models.

Each of these types—those societies emerging with a predominantly agrarian base, those with a predominantly commercial economy, and those where powerful agrarian and commercial elites have achieved a workable *modus vivendi*—tends to display characteristic values, beliefs, customs, laws, institutions, and reciprocal expectations more or less appropriate to and reflecting the interactive patterns of the major technology. As a consequence, both leaders and rank

---

62. Cf Barrington Moore, Jr., *Social Origins of Dictatorship and Democracy* (Boston: Beacon Press, 1966); and John G. Corbett, "Phoenicia and Assyria: Integration and Economic Systems in the Middle East," Stanford University, June, 1966 (Mimeographed).

63. Gabriel A. Almond and Sidney Verba, *The Civic Culture* (Princeton: Princeton University Press, 1963); and Klaus Knorr and Sidney Verba (eds.), *The International System*.

and file citizens or subjects operating within one or another of these societies will be stimulated, influenced, and constrained by the modes of the prevailing technology and by mediating social phenomena.

It can thus be argued that the prevailing values, customs, laws, and institutions of a society tend to emerge from the more or less common or shared experiences of people interacting with the environment and with each other in similar or reciprocal ways. These critically important ties that bind societies together are what Emile Durkheim perceived as contributing to a conscience collective.[64] Major changes in interactive patterns may be expected to bring about changes in the value systems and habit patterns of at least some of a society's components.

Ruling elites often rely heavily on force or threat of force to induce compliance among the rank and file. Unless these sanctioned reciprocities are supported by values, customs, recognized law, and other social habits, however, the costs of enforcing compliance may become extremely high.

The conscience collective of a large, multi-national empire is not likely to be highly developed. Certainly, the European holdings of the Ottoman Empire had little in common with the central ruling elite or with each other. As national feelings and capabilities grew (and as the Empire's bureaucracy became increasingly weak and ineffective), the various national segments could break away without the inhibiting power of a strong conscience collective. We can make a similar assertion about the collapse of the Austro-Hungarian Empire. The Thirteen Colonies of North America were somewhat different in that they shared a wide range of values, beliefs, customs, laws, and institutions with England. On the other hand, however, the colonists (or their forebears) had emigrated out of dissatisfaction with many aspects of English society; they had lived a long time in a very different environment; and they had developed, from the early settlement days in Massachusetts, Pennsylvania, and Virginia, a deep sense of "American" commitment and identity. Over more than a century and a half they had developed their own conscience collective.

Profound social, economic, and political upheavals such as the French and Russian revolutions, on the other hand, are likely to confront the traditionally evolved conscience collective with a new, dissident, and challenging set of values, beliefs, customs, laws, institutions, and expectations. This challenge is the more likely to the extent that

---

64. Emile Durkheim, *The Division of Labor in Society.*

the conscience collective of the ruling elite amounts to a reflection of one prevailing technology and its interactions (agrarian, for example), while the revolutionary conscience collective has emerged from a new and rapidly developing technology (commercial or industrial) that is increasingly threatening the old patterns with sweeping innovations.

We can expect, then, that whatever greatly alters basic relationships will challenge prevailing values, beliefs, customs, institutions, and expectations. Revolutions begin to develop as such changes bring about serious dysfunctions in the old society. As Chalmers Johnson pointed out, the pressures that cause dysfunction also "compel the members of a substructure to do their work, or view their roles, or imagine their potentials differently from the way they did under equilibrium conditions."[65] Often these changes further exacerbate the revolutionary process.

13. A major change in the absolute ratios or in the comparative growth rates of population, knowledge and skills, territory, resources, and trade is likely to alter basic values, beliefs, customs, institutions, and reciprocal expectations to one degree or another. Also, a basic change in these ratios for a sizable class or other sector within a society is likely to alter and perhaps seriously challenge the conscience collective of the society as a whole.

14. Whereas the conscience collective is responsive to critical changes in the interaction patterns among members of a populace and also between the populace and the larger environment, alterations in the conscience collective (or the development of a new conscience collective) can bring about important changes in the patterns of interaction. The interdependency among all these factors is likely to be intense and somewhat circular.

The behavior of the head of state is thus constrained, limited, biased or skewed, and otherwise influenced (depending on how capabilities are distributed and perceived to be distributed) by perceptions and expectations held by other officers of government and by the citizenry about goals, means, roles, statuses, and reciprocities and about where the head of state ought to fit and how he ought to behave.

To the degree that these perceptions, expectations, and habitual reciprocities have been internalized by the head of state, by other

65. Chalmers Johnson, *Revolution and the Social System* (Stanford: The Hoover Institution on War, Revolution, and Peace, Stanford University, 1964), p. 5.

officers of government, and by the citizenry, they serve, in Parsonian terms, as stabilizers of behavior. They contribute to Durkheim's conscience collective. Since each head of state and those around him operate in a discrete and particular culture and society, differences in cultural and societal values will contribute to asymmetries in the interactions of nation-states.

National and empire systems tend to be stable according to the extent to which the conscience collective is widely and deeply shared. The well-springs of revolution may be located as increasingly large numbers of people begin questioning important elements of the conscience collective. A thorough-going social, economic, and political revolution seeks to destroy the old conscience collective and bring into being a new one reflecting new roles, hierarchies, interactions, and fundamental values and relationships.

The behavior of leaders will be influenced and constrained by public perceptions of and feelings about the characteristics of the system of which they are components (including its capabilities), the characteristics (including the capabilities) of other systems with which their system is interacting, and the characteristics of the encompassing supra-system of which all these systems are unit components. Among significant characteristics in each instance will be role structures, communications patterns, distributions of power, and the ways in which these phenomena are perceived and internalized by the actors.

In general, a leader from the ruling elite makes his assessments and decisions within the framework of the old conscience collective, whereas the revolutionary leader performs within the milieu of a new, revolutionary conscience collective. This crucial difference in context endows the words and actions of opposing leaders with quite different meanings, and dialogue is normally difficult, if not impossible.

Revolutionary Competition, Conflict, and Escalation

The emphasis so far has been upon differential levels and rates of change in population, knowledge and skills, and access to various types of resources. I have suggested that increases in population and resources give rise to increasing demands, which combine multiplicatively with specialized capabilities to produce lateral pressure, which, in turn, can be variously expressed. Differential capabilities among individuals and groups tend to produce hierarchies, the more effective elements dominating the less effective. Changes in relative capabilities produce the conditions for social and political change—sometimes by way of revolution.

It remains to connect these relatively impersonal considerations somewhat more explicitly with the values, beliefs, customs, expectations, and institutions of ruling elites, the rank and file, and revolutionary elites and with the types of behavior that tend to emerge as a revolutionary situation develops. As we have seen, human values, beliefs, customs, expectations, institutions, and similar phenomena can be viewed as reflections of the experiences of people as they interact with the physical environment, with each other, and with foreign or competing groups. Changes in technology and other basic factors bring about changes in beliefs, customs, expectations, and institutions. Large differentials in levels of knowledge and skills and in rates of acquisition of knowledge and skills, and also differentials in access to resources, bring about different interaction patterns and differences in beliefs, customs, expectations, and institutions. Such differences contribute to the formation of special interest groups and classes.[66]

Numerous revolutions have come about as a previously subordinate class such as the commercial bourgeoisie or the working class has increased its levels of knowledge and skill without commensurate increases in basic resources, without access to the decision and control apparatus of the state, or both. As their shares in the economy began to increase, for example, the urban bourgeoisie frequently demanded a larger and larger share of political power as well.[67] Often revolutionary elements of two or more classes have joined forces in order to overthrow the old system. Subsequently, the more effective of the revolutionary classes have tended to dominate the less effective.

The concept of class tends to be imprecise and is often difficult to operationalize empirically. Marx's concepts of class, of course, were over-simplified, and his predictions of proletarian behavior have generally not been validated. The role of a given class—whether revolutionary, counter-revolutionary, or more or less neutral—will depend upon the over-all relationship of the factors involved.

The rise of the bourgeoisie has been characterized by the technique of economic penetration abroad, and by a series of alliances with other social formations which have had some measure of influence on foreign

---

66. For a discussion of differing concepts of class, see Seymour Martin Lipset, *Revolution and Counterrevolution* (New York: Basic Books, Inc., 1968), pp. 121–176.

67. Bloom, *Social Structure and Revolution*, p. 7.

affairs. The bourgeoisie has at times combined with the monarch against the aristocracy; at other times with all the disaffected elements against the monarchy and the aristocracy. More recently, as the bourgeoisie has begun to suffer from insecurity feelings with the growth of the proletariat, it has combined with the older institutions and classes, often abandoning the forms of parliamentary democracy which were useful at an early state in its historical development.[68]

Like nation-states and other interpersonal systems, classes and revolutionary movements are composed of individual human beings; therefore, in the final analysis, it is the individual human being who serves as the basic unit—either as a leader or as a sub-leader or as a member of the rank and file. A class or a revolutionary movement—like a nation-state—achieves status and effectiveness as an operating system to the extent that values, symbols, expectations, goals, and institutions (or emerging institutions) including reciprocities between leaders and followers are shared and internalized. To the extent to which such a revolutionary movement becomes organized and takes shape as an effective system we may expect the emergence of new concepts and a new vocabulary, in keeping with the new values, goals, expectations, and institutions. According to Lasswell, "Revolutions rise after intense stresses have been built up in personalities; they run their course by taking revenge in the symbols which betrayed them; and they end by bowing to new authorities with new symbols and new modes of perpetuating themselves."[69]

Lasswell has thus defined a successful revolution in which the dissident system has replaced the old system as "rapid and extensive change in the composition and the vocabulary of the ruling few. . . ."[70] After a revolutionary movement has been in power for a time, many of the pre-revolutionary values, goals, expectations, and institutions may re-emerge and re-assert themselves—perhaps under the protective coloration of the revolutionary vocabulary.

Revolutionary conditions tend to emerge to the extent that gross incongruities emerge between the values, beliefs, customs, expectations, and institutions maintained and promulgated by the ruling elite and new realities of the environment. Anthropologist Alan Howard and sociologist Robert A. Scott suggested that, "In a given population the degree of deviation . . . will correlate directly with the degree to

68. Harold D. Lasswell, "World Politics and Personal Insecurity," *A Study of Power* (Glencoe, Illinois: The Free Press, 1950), p. 149.

69. *Ibid.*, p. 253.

70. *Ibid.*, p. 3.

which the problems confronting the people remain unsolved and the degree to which legitimate means of relieving the tension are blocked."[71] From city ghetto to the international system, then, we would anticipate that the greater the blockage—*through whatever circumstances*—the higher is likely to be the level of violence and other pathological phenomena. Conversely, we would expect a high level of violence to indicate a large degree of blockage on local, national, and world levels. Growing dissent and violence within a society amount to an alarm bell, a preliminary warning of ecological as well as political, social, and economic dislocation.

There comes a point in a severely dislocated society where the major problems cannot be alleviated by tinkering here and there. The probabilities mount that nothing less than sweeping changes will alleviate the growing crisis. In responding to various gaps, national (and imperial) leaders seek ways of maintaining and furthering the interests of the national (or imperial) system as they perceive it. Revolutionary leaders respond similarly to the gaps they perceive, except that their tendency is to maintain and strengthen the dissident movement and further its interests. In both situations, the major leaders tend to merge their personal interests with the interests of the system they are defending and promoting so that the two sets become difficult for the observer to distinguish.

The activity pattern of a system will be strongly influenced by the absolute levels of population, technology, and resources and by the rates of change of these factors. The system's behavior will also be influenced by the allocations for the development of specialized capabilities that have already been made.

In seeking to reduce or close one or another or a combination of perceived gaps between the actual situation and the preferred situation, heads of state and other responsible leaders may have to undertake certain activities and suffer some disagreeable or injurious consequences (costs, penalties, punishments, dissatisfactions) that they would rather avoid but are willing to undertake (or suffer) because they perceive such activities or consequences as to one degree or another prerequisite to the achievement of the over-ridingly preferred state of affairs. In other words, efforts to close one gap will tend to create or exacerbate other gaps. One of the basic problems of national leadership is how to determine what costs, penalties, punishments, or dissatisfactions are tolerable in the pursuit of the outcomes

71. Howard and Scott, "A Proposed Framework...", p. 159.

that are sought. Involved also is the asssessment of risk, that is, the calculation of the probability that the costs considered tolerable will yield the outcome desired. All these considerations, together with the network of environmental relationships, contribute to the values that national leaders (and to some extent the populace) are likely to invoke and the goals they are likely to pursue.

Depending upon national history and culture, upon their assessment of the international system of which their country is a part, and upon their assessments of their country's own relative capabilities and other attributes, the leaders of a nation-state will tend to pursue some general strategy or pattern of operation in order to move toward their goals. State strategies often differ considerably, two nations employing quite distinct means for pursuing the same or similar goals. As a general rule, we would expect leaders of a nation-state or empire to use those strategies, patterns, and styles that have been effective for them in the past. Tensions will be generated, however, to the extent that conditions have changed and formerly useful strategies, patterns, or styles are no longer effective. The Tsarist and Chinese empires at the turn of the century are clear examples of once powerful systems whose social, economic, and political institutions and patterns and styles of operation were essentially reflections and functions of an earlier, predominantly agricultural era. As Western technology impinged more and more upon these antiquated systems, the old patterns and styles of operation became increasingly inappropriate, irrelevant, and ineffective. Revolution in one form or another was all but inevitable. But the more the old system was challenged, the more defensive and rigid some of the leaders became in their efforts to preserve the old ways.

As a revolutionary movement becomes more and more organized as an operational system, its leaders, in seeking to reduce or close one or another or a combination of perceived gaps between the actual state of affairs and the preferred state of affairs, will—like their counterparts in the government they seek to overthrow—be forced to undertake certain activities and suffer some consequences that are disagreeable. In probabilistic terms, the mathematics of competition and conflict between a ruling elite (and the "status quo" system over which it presides) and a revolutionary leadership (and the system over which it presides) are almost precisely the mathematics of varying distances between race horses moving toward a finish tape (revolution).[72] The suggestion is that

72. These patterns are roughly analogous to competitions and conflicts between rival nation-states or empires.

15. A lessening of the difference (gap) in strength and effectiveness between the ruling elite (and the system it presides over) and the revolutionary system along any salient dimension will generate new demands (and anxieties and tensions) and a disposition among leaders of the ruling elite to increase capabilities (whether political, social, economic, police, or military) and regain their previous advantage.

16. A lessening of the difference (gap) in strength and effectiveness between the ruling elite (and the system it presides over) and the revolutionary system along any salient dimension will generate new demands (and tensions, expectations, anxieties, and fears) and a disposition among revolutionary leaders to increase appropriate capabilities.

17. A widening of the difference in strength and effectiveness between the ruling elite (and its system) and the revolutionary system along any salient dimension will tend to enhance the confidence of the ruling elite (lower its demands, tensions) but increase the anxieties, fears, and other tensions of the revolutionary leaders, who will experience a sense of "falling behind" and a tendency toward new demands (tension) and an effort to reduce or close the gap. Such competitions and conflicts are likely to become much more intense as revolutionary policies and actions become more and more threatening.

Among nation-states and empires, if State A—correctly or incorrectly—perceives itself threatened by State B, there is a probability that A will respond with threats or hostile action. As State B begins to perceive this activity seemingly directed toward itself, it is probable that B, too, will behave in a reciprocally hostile and defensive fashion. This threatening behavior by B will soon confirm A's original perceptions of danger and threat, and A will be inclined to increase its "defensive" activity. Thereafter, the exchanges between the two parties are likely to be caught up in an increasingly intense spiral of self-confirming hostile suspicions, actions, and expectations. This reaction, or Richardson process,[73] opens the possibility that Country A's defenses—undertaken for security, and not for aggressive purposes—may incite Country B to responses that will, in the long run, bring about the warfare that the defense system was designed to inhibit.[74] Similar processes operate when an organized revolutionary movement A begins to threaten or directly injure the old regime B.

73. Lewis F. Richardson, *Arms and Insecurity* (Chicago: Quadrangle Books, 1960).

74. Kenneth E. Boulding, *Conflict and Defense* (New York: Harper & Bros., 1962), p. 25; James G. Miller, "Living Systems: Cross Level Hypotheses," pp. 401–405.

Many responses de-escalate. As the Wohlstetters suggest in the context of escalating crises between nation-states or empires, "There are down-escalators as well as up-escalators, and there are landings between escalators where one can decide to get off or to get on, to go up or down, or to stay there; or to take the stairs."[75]

Conflicts and confrontations between a ruling elite and a revolutionary system are also subject to both escalations and de-escalations. Certain common predispositions, however, tend over the long run to intensify revolutionary processes. For example, the ruling elite, in responding to the challenge and threats of a revolutionary movement, frequently slows down rather than increases innovation and institutional change and thereby inhibits its own effectiveness; at the same time it also validates the public predictions made by the revolutionary leaders about what behavior can be expected of the "status quo" leadership. The tendency is toward police or military action rather than social, political, or economic transformation.

Also associated with the escalation is likely to be the extreme polarization of values, activities, and acceptable attitudes, so that all "middle ground" disappears and the rank and file are faced with only two, or at most three, choices: (1) supporting an outmoded and increasingly ineffective system, (2) joining the revolution, or, if possible, (3) withdrawing to their houses, so to speak, fastening their shutters, and avoiding all involvement whatsoever. Insofar as they are translated into policy and action by the ruling elite, these tendencies isolate the leaders, constrain their ability to identify alternatives, and deprive them of potential allies from among dissatisfied but less militant or less radical sectors of the society.

From conviction, or as a tactical move, or in response to the tensions and threats of escalation, or out of a combination of all three, revolutionary leaders are likely to raise divisive issues and put forward increasingly militant demands. This behavior is likely to stimulate the old regime to adopt increasingly restrictive and perhaps oppressive counter-measures: the constraint of civil rights and individual freedoms, the arrest of those expressing any kind of dissent, increasingly arbitrary powers assigned to police, possibly the imposition of martial law, and the infliction of casualties including (sometimes quite unavoidably) numbers of bystanders as well as revolutionaries. Such responses may be counted upon to alienate considerable numbers of the ruling

75. Albert Wohlstetter and Roberta Wohlstetter, "Controlling the Risks in Cuba," *Adelphi Papers*, 17 (London: Institute for Strategic Studies, 1965).

elite itself and impel them either into neutral withdrawal or into the ranks of the revolutionaries. To the extent that revolutionary forces avoid taking casualties or inflict them only on police or other recognizable agents of the regime, further support for dissent is likely to accrue. If this process continues long enough, it will contribute substantially to the weakening of the old regime and the strengthening of the revolutionaries' cause.

Whatever the other circumstances of a crisis escalation, the reaction coefficients tend to be high if either party feels itself to be misunderstood, that is, to the extent that A perceives a gap between its view of its own behavior and its perception of B's view of its own behavior, or to the extent that either party feels that it has been injured, or that its cause is just. Indeed, leaders and followers with a "great and just cause"—whether revolutionary or counter-revolutionary—are often prime candidates for participating in and helping to generate reaction processes.

18. In general, the higher the tension, anxieties, apprehensions, and fears felt by the leaders of a nation-state (and also, in many instances, by the status quo populace) or by the revolutionaries (or both), the stronger the tendency toward operating *as if* the game were zero sum, at least in response to those elements perceived by either set of leaders as antagonistic.

19. The higher the tension, anxieties, apprehensions, and fears in a revolutionary situation, the stronger the probability that some action attributed to one of the parties will be perceived by leaders of the other as threatening.

20. Once a reaction[76] process has set in, the higher the tension the stronger the probability that the issues of earlier competition and conflict will be obscured, that the actors will look for threats and respond with counter-threats, and that acts of violence or potential violence will increase.

21. The higher the tension—beyond a certain critical threshold—felt by the participants in a reaction process, the greater the probability that any aggressive activity—whatever, objectively, its likely consequences may be—will seem preferable to the leaders (and many of the followers) than the increasingly disagreeable tension itself; hence, the higher the tension generated by a reaction process the greater the probability of violence no matter what the consequences.

22. The higher the tension felt by one leadership (A) and the

---

76. In each case tensions may be assumed to include a wide range of negative affects.

more intense the hostile interaction with the other leadership (B), the higher the probability that the leaders of B will experience increasing tension and that interchanges between A and B will contain higher levels of threats or of actual violence.

23. As tension increases in the interaction process, time will be perceived by the leaders involved as an increasingly salient factor in decision making, and they will become increasingly concerned with elements of the immediate future rather than with more long-range considerations and possible outcomes.[77]

24. As tension increases, the leaders involved in an interaction process will perceive their own range of alternatives as becoming more restricted than those of their adversaries, and the range of alternatives for their allies will be seen as more restricted than the range available to their adversaries.[78] Even if leaders of one side perceive their own capabilities as less than those of the enemy, they may see large-scale violence as the only tolerable alternative.

25. The higher the tension in a reaction process, the heavier the overload upon channels of communication, the more stereotyped the information content of the messages, the greater the tendency to rely upon extraordinary or improvised channels of communication, and the higher the proportion of intra-coalition—as against inter-coalition—communication.[79] Members of each camp are likely to talk more and more to each other and less to the other side.

The Emergence of a Revolutionary Situation

Pre-revolutionary situations are marked by evidences of the advanced, progressive segregation of the old society and its regime. More and more the institutions of government encounter difficulties in performing their basic functions. The revenue system is likely to seem inadequate and to be more and more attacked. Army and Navy recruiters may encounter increased resistance. More demonstrations or riots are likely. The police will be resisted, increasing their numbers will be necessary, and special squads and secret intelligence units will likely be formed. Bombs will be used more and more. The conscience collective will come under attack from dissidents and from some of the sons and daughters of the ruling elite (as during the

77. Ole R. Holsti, "The 1914 Case," *American Political Science Review,* Vol. LIX, No. 2 (June, 1965), pp. 369–377.

78. *Ibid.*

79. *Ibid.*

Narodnik movement in Tsarist Russia). Substantial defections from the armed forces and mutinies are likely to mark the intensification of a pre-revolutionary situation.

At more or less the same time, disadvantaged elements in the society, gaining rapidly in vigor and knowledge and skills, will be improving communications among themselves and accomplishing the first uncertain stages of organization, concerted demand, and consistent protest.

In trying to recapture the regime's prior initiative, more moderate and innovative leaders will be caught more and more between the disruptions, threats, and civil disorders caused by the dissenters and counsels of repression and extreme counter-violence from ultra-conservative sectors of the old society. Reasonable alternatives put forward by responsible officers will be challenged and often blocked and flouted by both the pre-revolutionaries and the ultra-conservatives. More moderate and innovative leaders of the ruling elite will become more and more isolated and less and less capable of effective action. The ultra-conservative will be temporarily strengthened, and considerable numbers of the rank and file will support them on the assumption that, through defensive, repressive, ultra-conservative measures, the old society can be conserved.

As suggested by Howard and Scott,[80] severe deviations in the total society will serve as indicators of aggravated dislocations and more and more serious impediments to effective social, political, and economic renovation, innovation, and effective change. Wider and wider sectors of the population will become involved in demonstrations and counter-demonstrations, riots and counter-riots. Police budgets will increase and new police weapons will be used. Militia and later, perhaps, regular army troops will be used to reinforce the police against the pre-revolutionaries.

Revolutionary situations are developmental, and time is required for them to mature. The rate of development is likely to be determined in part, at least, by the speed and effectiveness of communication. The more rapid, diffused, and penetrating the means of communication, the more rapidly a society is likely to move through pre-revolutionary and revolutionary stages of development.

In many instances, however, a severe challenge or setback to the society is required to move it from a pre-revolutionary to a revolutionary situation. According to Lasswell,

80. Howard and Scott, "A Proposed Framework . . . ," p. 52.

> During the last century, every curtailment of the flow of credit from capital-exporting countries (an incident of depression) lit the fuse of discontent in capital-importing countries; but in many, if not most, of these instances, the spread of social revolution was hindered by the older social formations which were often able to reassert themselves against the rising industrial mercantile and commerical agrarian elements which had been weakened or partially discredited by the collapse of values.[81]

It is a mistake, however, to assume that revolution is necessarily associated with a decline in national productivity. By 1914 Tsarist Russia was overtaking France for fourth place in industrial production. The vulnerability was more in the systems of allocation and distribution than in basic production.

Prolonged warfare, stalemates, or defeat in war often lead directly into a revolutionary situation, as happened in Russia in 1917. An outmoded, acutely segregated regime may collapse more or less under its own weight, so to speak, as the Chinese Empire collapsed in 1911–12. For the establishment of a successful revolutionary government, on the other hand, dissident forces must develop some measure of social and political cohesiveness, a conscience collective, and a decision and control system (government) at least embryonically comparable to the decision and control system being replaced; that is, it must be capable of energy and resource accumulation and allocation, information receiving and processing, alternative recognition, priority setting, decision making, policy implementation, and other functions including external defense, domestic (intra-movement) cohesion maintenance, and so forth. If no such system emerges from among dissident forces, the society is likely to disintegrate somewhat as China did during the rule of the warlords.

As soon as a revolutionary regime emerges and achieves control, however, its progress toward progressive centralization will be accompanied by the germinal tendencies of progressive segregation. For some period of time—perhaps generations or even centuries—the balance between these two processes may be such that the system will grow in vigor, influence, and power. Sooner or later, however, we can expect the combination of progressive centralization and progressive segregation to produce its own inflexibilities and its own dissident, pre-revolutionary groups—unless the society and its leaders can embark upon some type of vigorous renewal program. In the long

---

81. Lasswell, "World Politics and Personal Insecurity," p. 161.

run, old regimes can best renew themselves by making radical adjustments peacefully—anticipating the impatient, militant, and possibly violent challenges of the dissidents and potential revolutionaries.

THE REVOLUTIONARY PARTY AS AN AGENCY OF SOCIAL CHANGE
(or *The Politics of Mah jong*)

PETER WORSLEY, *University of Manchester*

A few decades ago, political science was the despair of sociologists. It had two major divisions, "ideas" and "institutions." The ideas were in fact the political ideas of philosophers from Plato and Aristotle through Locke, Hobbes, and Burke down to minor figures like T. H. Green; and the "institutions" were mainly constitutional arrangements, typified, for Britain, by Sir Ivor Jennings' works on *Cabinet Government* and *The British Constitution*.[1] The comparative, cross-cultural dimension was virtually non-existent. "Colonial" studies were built around the introduction of installments of Westminsterial constitutions.[2]

Apart from the new note of *realpolitik* struck in works like Lasswell's *Politics: Who Gets What, When, How* (1936), it took a world war and several revolutions to direct political scientists toward a more authentically sociological approach. Gradually, we have come to recognise that ordinary people as well as political philosophers, political elites, political activists, and political scientists have ideas, too, and the final nails in the coffin of the old "history of ideas" are being hammered home now by those intellectual descendents of Alfred Schutz, the contemporary phenomenologists, with their emphasis upon the primordial nature of "commonsense" knowledge.[3]

---

1. Sir Ivor Jennings, *Cabinet Government* (Cambridge: Cambridge University Press, 1936); and Jennings, *The British Constitution* (Cambridge: Cambridge University Press, 1946).

2. For example, J. W. Davidson, *The Northern Rhodesian Legislative Council* (London: Faber, 1948).

3. See Peter L. Berger and Thomas Luckmann, *The Social Construction of Reality* (London: Allen Lane; Penguin Press, 1967).

As for "institutions," we long ago discovered that political power is not restricted to parties and governments, but that other "interest-aggregates" and "pressure groups" also exercise effective power. Such a realisation—obvious enough to the man in the street—was nevertheless a breakthrough, achieved, naturally enough, in this country, where the activities of lobbies were more visible, institutionalised, and also more decisive in that they affected the actions of the world's most powerful State. Following this lead, researchers, notably those of neo-Machiavellian persuasion such as S. E. Finer,[4] soon discovered pressure groups in Britain.

Politics was by now infinitely wider than the study of governments and parties. It concerned all matters of public significance about which people contended. Of course, many groups contend about questions that governments regard as closed, or as unproblematic "non-questions"; these matters are usually also non-negotiable. I have in mind the way in which the basic assumptions about what we in Britain call "The Establishment" are not only scarcely ever questioned or challenged, but scarcely ever even raised for discussion. For Britain, the two decisive planks of foreign policy underpinning the general policies of both major parties are the commitment to the North American alliance and the commitment to a nuclear strategy. Formally, Britain's membership in the North American Treaty Organization has to be renewed this year [1969]. Far from there being any debate on the question, however, Mr. Healey, Minister of Defense, simply announced that the Treaty automatically renewed itself unless either party offered to withdraw. Neither did. On the nuclear issue, Paul Watkins, maker of the film on nuclear warfare, *The War Game,* recently observed that, in the year following the public showing of his film, the number of hours British television devoted to nuclear weapons was around five (a decline), and these programmes usually ended by concluding that the Bomb was a regrettable necessity.

This kind of uninspected agreement on cardinal planks of policy is what used to be called "consensus politics." In theoretical terms, however, that label is inadequate because it contains built-in elitist assumptions. It assumes that consensus among the controllers of politics equals general consensus. This assumption may be valid empirically, for one can often demonstrate large-scale general public support for official policies, but consensus amongst elites is not necessarily

---

4. S. E. Finer, *Anonymous Empire: A Study of the Lobby in Great Britain* (London: Pall Mall, 1958).

accompanied by general consensus. At its height, the Campaign for Nuclear Disarmament had the sympathies of nearly one-quarter of the British population. and it now seems ironic, for example, after the years of turmoil over civil rights, Vietnam, urban renewal, and student protest in the U.S.A., that the political science of the fifties was dominated by the assumption that consensus was not simply an elite, but a mass, phenomenon. We had moved beyond ideology,[5] and the only meaningful running debate was about means, not ends; there was no utopian society to be achieved, for the debate itself was the "good society" (democracy) in operation.[6]

Dissensus as between political elite and the rest of the population may take two forms. There may be dissensus about those issues that are on the public agenda, or about what should even be on that agenda. What blacks in the U.S.A. have done in recent years is to inscribe themselves on the agenda, just as students have "written in" questions about a war in Vietnam that seemed at one time very popular.

Men close to the central workings of the greatest state in history should naturally be susceptible to the notion that all that matters, when the chips are down, is what goes on in Washington, and that those who occupy the top positions in the structure of institutionalised power will prevail. Yet, of course, there are other institutionalised sources of power than these "constitutionalised" powers of administration, public service, and parties. Within developed countries, we have come to realize how complex structures like modern cities and industrial plants can be brought to a halt by the withdrawal of cooperation, not just by large masses, but even by tiny, but strategically-located, groups whose participation—as disposers of garbage, stitchers of upholstery and automobile-seats, as dock-workers (to mention only some recent striking cases)—is necessary to the ongoing of other sections of society.[7] And, of course, we have not yet seriously witnessed militant action deliberately aimed at disrupting city life—the urban guerrilla. Potentially, then, power in modern, urbanised, industrial civilisation is by no means unequivocally in the hands of those who control central and local governments. This power, too, depends essentially, as political theory tells us, on "ideal" elements: the withdrawal

5. For example, Daniel Bell, *The End of Ideology: On the Exhaustion of Political Ideas in the Fifties* (Glencoe: The Free Press, 1960).

6. S. M. Lipset, *Political Man* (London: Heinemann, 1960), p. 403.

7. E. P. Thompson, "At the Point of Decay," in E. P. Thompson (ed.), *Out of Apathy* (London: Stevens, 1960), pp. 6–7.

of consent, the shaking-off of so-called apathy, the loss of legitimacy, the questioning of the accepted, can lead to instant transformations even if the guns and the dollars remain in exactly the same hands.

Outside the developed world, these transformations are much more visible and much more rapid. For the striking feature of politics in the twentieth century is that a category that embraces just about the most powerless people on earth—the peasantry of underdeveloped countries—has been transformed into one of the most powerful forces on the world's political stage. Because this category—only potentially a group by virtue of occupying a common life-situation—has been provided with the institutional and ideological requisites, it has become changed into an organised entity disposing of enough power, in the case of Vietnam, an overwhelmingly agrarian country, to fight the richest and most powerful nation on earth to a standstill, with a little help from their friends.

The power of the powerless is thus actualised through political mobilisation. For such mobilisation to occur an agency of mobilisation is required. This agency is the revolutionary party.

It is very difficult to grasp this process of transformation using the categories that inform so much of contemporary political theory. For the long-awaited junction of sociology with political theory has produced a singularly unsatisfactory synthesis. What political science has borrowed from sociology has been a set of concepts that, paradoxically, has long been subjected to a withering "internal" critique from within sociology itself, that is, the theoretical apparatus of functionalism.

The first inadequacy has been the separation of something called "political behaviour" from social action in general. As we have already noted, the central, theoretical assumption that politics is a specialised type of social relationship, a "sub-system" within the over-all social system, leads inexorably to a logical chain of false deductions. At one simple level, of course, we can, empirically, identify institutions that directly control the central decision-making process. Parties and government and administrative machinery clearly do so, and it would be perverse to deny this obvious specialisation of function. Obviously, central and local government can command resources of unique power and do so over a range of issues with which more specialised interest-aggregates do not concern themselves. Indeed, these more specialised groups commonly exercise their influence by bringing it to bear precisely upon these governmental organs. This argument has been most skilfully expounded, perhaps, in Ralf Dahrendorf's analysis, *Class and*

Class Conflict in Industrial Society, in which he concludes that industrial power, whether wielded by business or by organised labour, is merely a special case of power in general, and, in the end, ultimate power lies with government and its executive agency, the Public Service.[8]

Yet equally clear empirically is that power is pluralistically diffused, that governments and administrative machines respond to the pressures of extra-governmental interest-aggregates, that "reciprocity" and "feedback" operate not only directly but also indirectly in that those in office anticipate what the reaction of these interests will be (so-called non-decision-making), that representatives of these interests are directly ensconced within governmental apparatuses, and that such interest-aggregates themselves have power to make decisions, legitimately or otherwise, that may at times be as conclusive, or even more so, as any decisions governments may make themselves. Thus, an organised group occupying a strategic position in the economy, such as the motor-industry in Britain (which brings in fifteen percent of foreign earnings) or, say, the cotton-producing Gezira Board in the Sudan, is a force that cannot easily be trifled with by any government. Or the interest-aggregate represented by the electorally-significant automobile-using population (not all of whom are actually organised as members of the Automobile Association and the Royal Automobile Club, the two major associations of car-owners) constitutes a grouping that any government would hesitate to press too far—for example, by increased motor-taxation—lest they activate an opposition that might expose the offending party to defeat at the polls. Such exceptionally powerful groups and categories are thus in a position to preclude certain issues from adaption as governmental policy, and, to do so, they do not necessarily have to take action; their mere existence, and the potential of activating their latent power, is enough, normally, to ensure that policies seriously inimical to their interest are not enacted.

Here, then, is the great stumbling-block in studies of community power, which attempt to measure power simply by analysing its mobilisation and application in situations where confrontation arises. Latent power, of course, may never materialise in the form of overt clashes ("social dramas"), because these clashes are avoided. The result is that the process of political bargaining takes place within rules of the game that take the continued power-positions of both parties

---

8. Ralf Dahrendorf, *Class and Class Conflict in Industrial Society* (London: Routledge & Kegan Paul, 1959), Chapter 8.

for granted. Hence, full mobilisation, actualisation, and confrontation are never called for. Pressure-group studies in Britain have shown an inverse correlation, for example, between overt lobbying and effective political influence. Stewart showed, for the fifties, how the British Communist Party and its associated organisations have been the most prominent and visible organisers of deputations to Parliament, of meetings, of campaigns to pressure M.P.s by means of letters, etc., yet, at the same time, they remain politically very much minority groups.[9] Conversely, the very powerful interest-aggregates have no need of such public demonstration, both because their positions are fully taken into account by government in anticipation, and because of the growth of informal consultation and, increasingly, of institutionalised machinery designed for this very end. Finer noted that the Trades Union Congress, in 1958, was represented on sixty governmental committees and named a further score on which the then Federation of British Industry was represented.[10] Such bodies have no need to resort to public agitation, i.e., the attempt to mobilise public opinion, because the channels of communication between the "constituency," to use Selznick's term,[11] and its appropriate matching segment within Government are always in use. The need to by-pass such channels, to call up additional reserves of support, is rare. So powerful influence can be singularly invisible. Such simple structural characteristics are thus perfectly comprehensible in sociological terms, and the more emotive formulations usually dubbed "conspiracy theory" are unnecessary.

Elsewhere,[12] I have labelled the distinction between the politics that goes on in the specialised political sub-system "Politics I," and the politics that goes on extra-governmentally "Politics II." "Politics I" is what is usually called "the political sub-system." But significantly, we have no such label for "Politics II," and the area where the two intermesh constitutes the most problematic area for political analysis: the area of "linkages," "gatekeepers," and the like.

9. J. D. Stewart, *British Pressure Groups: Their Role in Relation to the House of Commons* (London: Oxford University Press, 1958). See also Finer, *Anonymous Empire:* "It may even be stated as a rule: that the stronger an organisation's relations with M.P.'s, the less public notice it arouses; and, conversely, that fuss, noise, mass lobbying, and similar demonstrations are often an indication of the failure of an organisation to achieve effective Parliamentary relations" (p. 54).

10. Finer, *Anonymous Empire*, pp. 31–32.

11. Philip Selznick, *TVA, and the Grass Roots: A Study in the Sociology of Formal Organization* (Berkeley & Los Angeles: University of California Press, 1949), p. 145.

12. P. M. Worsley, "The Distribution of Power in Industrial Society," *Sociological Review*, Monograph No. 8 (1964), pp. 15–34.

Indeed, I would go further and suggest that it is a mistake not only to restrict "politics" to the study of "Politics I," but even to restrict it to "Politics II," for, as most modern theory recognises, politics is the study of the process by which we induce others to behave in the way we wish. This is the widest possible definition of politics. Its implications are that politics is a dimension of all social action, not a special kind of social action. For all social action has either intended or unintended effects on the behaviour of others, i.e., it has political effects, since it induces responses in others. (By "behaviour" I do not mean just overtly visible acts, for to affect the thinking of others is to affect their subsequent acts, since men behave in accordance with mental [or "ideal"] orientations of action-beliefs, values, norms, ideals, ideologies.)

If this is so, all behaviour has a political dimension or aspect. "Politics II," then, the intended mobilisation and application of power by groups outside government and party, is itself only a further species of organised political action. For the actions of people pursuing their collective and private goals are all "political" insofar as they are "end-oriented" and not purposeless. Such behaviour may intentionally seek to affect governments or parties, in which case we all instantly label it "political." But even if it is not aimed at such bodies, the pursuit of such goals has implications for both governments and parties, and for other interest-groups in the political community as well. We should probably, then, reserve a third category—Politics III—for that most inclusive form of political action that occurs in everyday social intercourse whenever we exchange ideas, express opinions, even sometimes deliberately aim at changing the thinking and behaviour of those we interact with. When we act like this, we may think of our behaviour as, say, "conversation," as "gossip," we may categorize it as "religious," "social," "business," or whatever, but it all has a political dimension. Such unstructured political interaction becomes transmuted into Politics II when we deliberately co-ordinate our personal activities with those of like-minded fellows; it becomes "Politics I" when we co-ordinate our actions so as to influence governments and parties.

At this point, I would like to dissent from the use of the term "parapolitical," which might seem to be equivalent to Politics III and which is a term approved of even by Swartz, Turner, and Tuden.[13] Politics III is not specialised politics, true; it is a by-product, incidental,

13. Marc J. Swartz, Victor W. Turner, and Arthur Tuden (eds.), *Political Anthropology* (Chicago: Aldine, 1966).

an accompaniment, a dimension, aspect, or attribute of social action in general. In this sense, it is not specialised political behaviour. But I insist that it is political behaviour, not para-political, the prefix of which implies something "beside" or "beyond" politics, even "wrong" or "irregular," according to my dictionary. Politics III is not "other than" politics—something akin, or apparently (?pseudo, ? mistaken for) politics—it *is* politics. Thus, although Swartz et al. recognise that politics is not a special type of behaviour, they remark that "we might want to call a religious ceremony 'political' " (i.e., politics is a dimension of religious behaviour); but they erroneously label "low-level" decision-making and conflict "para-political" because it deals only with relations within parts of a system, not with the "boundary-maintaining mechanisms of whole societies." Behaviour within "sub-systems," segments, or parts is, I repeat, political behaviour, not "parapolitical." If we do not understand that Politics III is politics, then we will be unable to understand revolutionary mobilisation—what I call below "the politics of mah jong."

We can thus conceive of a set of ranges of political behaviour, from the most diffuse type of political behaviour (Politics III)—those political effects that all behaviour has on others, but particularly that intended as such—through the more restricted range of "Politics II," where we combine our actions with those of like mind to form "interest-aggregates," to the most restricted range of "Politics I," where we bring this organised action to bear on the specialised authorities. But even at the most restricted range of Politics III, political behaviour is not just the sum of individual actions. Even here there are patterns of behaviour, since whole categories of people tend to behave in similar ways. The category becomes transformed into a group, however, only with organisation. The useful term "interest-aggregate" embraces both categorical and group behaviour under one rubric.

Secondly, we need to use the concept of *level*, as distinct from *range*. Range is a formal-analytical concept; level a substantive one. When Swartz and his colleagues write of "local-*level* politics," they are thinking in terms of levels of social structure, in which face-to-face relationships constitute the lowest level, national or societal politics the highest level (except insofar as they, in turn, are part of an international or inter-societal world political order), and the politics of groups, categories, and associations at district, regional, or other similar levels as together constituting an "intermediate" level.

Now much of local-level politics is indeed Politics III in my use of that term. But Politics I also exists at the lowest level: thus, government agencies and national political parties have branches and representatives in the villages, and government policies are carried out at the village level. Conversely, Politics III also occurs at the highest levels of social organisation: cliques, cabals, and "factions" are to be found in Cabinets, board rooms, and national committees. The concept of range, then, is quite distinct from that of level, even though it is common to speak as though the widest range of political behaviour necessarily coincided with the lowest substantive level of social organisation or structure.

Political science classically used to deal almost exclusively with high-level entities (parties, governments, etc.). Later, "grass-roots" studies began to examine low-level politics. Finally, attention was given to intermediate levels—to pressure groups, regional organisations, and so forth. Political sociology, indeed, came into existence because it was seen as required in order to explain how politics at the national level was connected to politics at the local level. Then a whole literature on "brokers," "gatekeepers," "mediators," "patrons," etc., grew up, since it was found that the meaning of party membership to the member or voter was very different from the significance of the party to the party elite. In the extreme, it was discovered, party members did not even know what the party programme was! The processes by which people nevertheless became part of a political organisation and the ways in which "loyalty" was maintained, especially when switches of policy occurred, plainly required special attention. The weakness of political science models that failed to pay attention to this area has been reflected in the almost universal failure of those U.S. social scientists who wrote about the "end of ideology" in the 1950s to anticipate the severe conflicts that were to emerge in the form of protest against the Vietnam war, student unrest, and black militancy. Similarly, in Britain, no one foresaw that immigration and student unrest would become major issues in the late 1960s. Political communication, for one thing, had been too much conceived of as a *downward* flow, from the elite, in a series of vulgar "mass society" and elite theory models.

The conventional and necessary distinctions between "political" behaviour and social action in general, and between "political" organisations and organisations in general, are also relative rather than absolute distinctions, and attempts to distinguish the pursuit of "economic" objectives from "political" ones in, say, labour union activities are bound to be unsuccessful.

No doubt, too, similar distinctions of range are needed in other contexts. Thus, Blau distinguished the "organisation" we observe in the patterned regularities in all social behaviour we take as the subject

matter of social science from those special institutionalised arrangements we normally call "organisations."[14] Again, "cooperation" is a
Politics III dimension of social action simply equivalent to the social
division of labour in any form; cooperative organisations are a special
institutionalised form of this coordination of social functions within
systematic structures.

We have arrived at the second cardinal assumption informing
contemporary political sociology, an assumption borrowed largely
from functionalist theory and hence over-systematised. This is the
concept of "system" itself. The concept long antedates functionalism,
of course. It was intrinsic to the emergence of a science of society,
since it implies that a society is an entity whose component parts
are so connected that change in one part induces change in the rest.
The "over-determined" view of social system, however, postulates too
direct a relationship between the parts, and Merton long ago demonstrated that the connectedness may be so oblique or mediated that
the repercussions of change in one part may be very slight in its
effect on the rest of the system.[15] Moreover, all the parts are not
of equal weight, for power is unequally distributed. Merton showed,
too, that nineteenth-century conceptions of the "systematic-ness" of
social systems—e.g., Herbert Spencer's—and later functionalist conceptions (Malinowski, Radcliffe-Brown) were over-influenced by
biological analogies that were not even valid in Nature. Yet political
science has imported from sociology precisely the categories rejected
over twenty years ago by Merton.

One of the most unfortunate consequences of this over-
systematisation is the insistence, fundamental to most modern "systems
theory," that a social system is essentially a bounded entity. So we
have models of the political system that conceive of it as analytically
isolated. Yet we would have great difficulty analysing the political
system of South Vietnam as a "boundary-maintaining" entity when
the persistence of that system depends upon its incorporation within
a wider set of relationships. The United States, that is, is an intrinsic
part of the Vietnamese political system even though it is, in one sense,
"outside" its boundaries. Similarly, Czechoslovakia does not constitute

14. Peter M. Blau, *Exchange and Power in Social Life* (New York: John Wiley & Sons, 1967),
p. 199.

15. Robert K. Merton, "Manifest and Latent Functions," in Merton (ed.), *Social Theory and Social
Structure* (Glencoe: The Free Press, 1957), pp. 19–84. [Original essay published in 1949.]

a bounded political system. It is both part of a wider field of political relationships, in which the Soviet Union is the most directly effective "constituency," and of a yet wider field, which is the world polity. Furthermore, not just in analytical but also in real terms, the U.S.S.R. and the U.S.A. are not "outside" the boundaries of the politics of Vietnam and Czechoslovakia—they are political actors within those societies.

I have argued elsewhere that today the only inclusive social system is world society, a qualitatively new, emergent development in human society engendered by the establishment of global political, economic, and communications networks. In this light, the concept of a boundary-maintaining system is singularly inadequate as the intellectual cornerstone of political theory. As we can see, then, attempting to apply bounded-system concepts to the analysis of student unrest would also be unrewarding, since the sources of this unrest are by no means derived from the internal political culture of the universities as social systems, but patently arise from the concern of students about "external" national and international issues.

You will no doubt have noticed that, in order to speak meaningfully about these ideas, I have been obliged to use much more relativist and situational language than that provided by systems theory: terms like "range," "field," and "network." For in analysing given situations, we are always involved in analysing a succession of *both* ranges of inclusiveness *and* levels of organisation, not with one system with neat internal divisions of level and fixed boundaries. One attempt to grasp this relativity of structure and range that offers promise is provided in the aforementioned work by Swartz, Turner, and Tuden, wherein these authors have also abandoned the language of system and opt instead for the concept of "social field." This concept does not imply that organisations, with organised hierarchical structures and vertical internal divisions, are analytically dismissed (and there is a danger that, as with modern phenomenology, a purely situational analysis can distract us from the awareness that structures do exist). Still, anthropologists have naturally reacted to the over-systematisation of politics, for they have had to deal with "acephalous" societies in which there were no specialised political structures—no kings, chiefs, courts of justice empowered to act on behalf of society—but rather political cultures in which decisions were reached and executed in a much more "collective" way or, more accurately, in a way that allowed for and normally involved participation—not by all, but by all eligible, which usually means adult males.[16] Moreover, although there were agencies and offices through which decisions were taken, personnel were not necessarily recruited on the basis of ascription. The usual label, "traditionalistic," entirely misses the point, for acceptance as a leader, a decision-maker, an arbitrator in disputes, was open to men who achieved leadership by virtue of their wisdom, their preeminence in farming, in hunting, in war, or as ritual specialists—areas open to all, even if often qualified by some countervailing elements of ascription, such as belonging to a particular lineage, being the son of a leader, having privileged access to more productive land, etc.

In such societies, there is no Politics I: there is politics, but no specialised government. There is political influence and political authority, but no political sub-system, for a man's influence was a function of his occupancy of other roles. People listened to him because he had exhibited competence through his achievements in other fields, or because he occupied ascribed roles that were not specialised political roles—because he was head of the lineage, an elder, etc. The operation of politics was thus an aspect, or by-product, of general social action, and decision-making usually occurred within the framework of other social units: the family, the lineage, the clan, the cult-community. Here, the community rarely meets as a whole, rarely delegates authority, and generally solves its disputes by means of individual self-help, by the mobilisation of political support within these social units—as when disputes are resolved by resorting, not to the courts, but to one's kin-group. Community-wide action is usually reserved only for persistent and aggravating major issues that cannot be resolved at these lower levels; it usually entails wide participation and is thus only intermittent, not continuous, government.

To study politics in such societies, one studies social action in general and the operation of all the basic social units. Thus, anthropology makes us sensitive to the notion that politics is co-extensive with social action, that it exists everywhere and is not a private property of elites. Politics, from this perspective, is situational, too, for the social units involved vary according to the gravity of the issue. The boundaries of the relevant "social system" shift; what social field is disturbed[17] by a dispute depends on what the nature

16. E. E. Evans-Pritchard and M. Fortes (eds.), *African Political Systems* (London: Oxford University Press, 1940).

17. For an early, and classic, statement of the concept of "social field," see Max Gluckman, "Analysis of a Social Situation in Modern Zululand," *Bantu Studies*, Vol. XIV (1940), pp. 1–20, 147–174.

of the dispute is and the relationship of the social groups to which the disputants belong. The process has been classically analysed by Evans-Pritchard, for the Nuer, as one of "segmentary opposition."[18]

There is not even a hard-and-fast distinction between legal and political action, but only disputes, that originate between individuals, so that we would normally call them "legal" disputes, except that they require for their resolution the mobilisation of what we would also call "political" support.[19] Thus, to exact compensation, a group of kinsmen may seize property belonging to the group of the offender. If the issue is minor, it may be resolved at this level. If not, attached lineage-segments become involved on each side, allies are mobilised, and escalation occurs upwards through the successive involvement of sub-lineage, lineage, clan, and tribe. What begins as a dispute between individuals can end as warfare between groups, because individuals belong to kin-groups and cannot appeal to a non-existent State.

Escalation and the mobilisation of allies are processes equally familiar to State societies. But plainly, the existence of a specialised State apparatus—policemen, judges, armies, militia—constitutes a structural difference so basic that it might seem that modes of analysis relevant for acephalous societies must end there. I think not.

Let us test the relevance of these ways of thinking about politics by applying them to modern revolutions. Plainly, the flexible structures that regulate political life among the highly autonomous Nuer lineage-groups contrast severely with the centralised and hierarchical control exercised by a modern revolutionary party. Yet in the revolutionary emphasis on equality—despite hierarchical differences of function, and indeed in the emphasis placed in party ideology upon the creation of an egalitarian, participant society—there is resemblance.

More important than such analogies, however, is the way in which revolutionary politics begins as Politics III and becomes successively transformed into Politics II and Politics I, just as a Nuer dispute can escalate to the level of wars involving groups of tribes or even the whole Nuer "nation" if the enemy is non-Nuer.

---

18. E. E. Evans-Pritchard, *The Nuer: A Description of the Modes of Livelihood and Political Insititutions of a Nilotic People* (Oxford: At the Clarendon Press, 1940).

19. See A. R. Radcliffe-Brown, "Preface," to Evans-Pritchard and Fortes (eds.) *African Political Systems*, pp. xi–xxiii. For a classic case study of the operation of this system of social control, see E. Colson, "Social Control and Vengeance in Plateau Tonga Society," *Africa*, Vol. XXIII (1953), pp. 199–211.

In 1926, Mao Tse-tung went to Hunan, the centre of massive peasant disturbances. We all know that he carried out his famous survey of the class situation in the countryside that formed the basis for subsequent policy regarding the peasant. Though its political importance cannot be over-emphasised, it is, for the most part, orthodoxly Leninist and thus not particularly novel. (Its novelty—revolutionary indeed—consisted in applying Lenin to China.)

Alongside this, however, Mao reported to the Party on "The Peasant Movement in Hunan"[20] in much wider human terms, in what is surely one of the most fascinating and crucial documents of this century's history. In the very first paragraph, he emphasises that he found *"many strange things . . . that I had never seen or heard of before,"* and proceeds to describe the results of these pioneer ethnographic researches.

The peasantry, he found, had created new peasant associations that had grown from three- or four hundred thousand to two million in less than a year and embraced half the total peasantry, nearly all of them in many counties. The main targets were local bullies, bad gentry, and lawless landlords. These groups (plus "corrupt officials in the cities") were the main categories of people under attack, but the principal cultural features under attack were "patriarchal ideologies and institutions" and "evil customs in the rural areas." His list of the "Fourteen Great Deeds" these revolutionary peasants had accomplished begins, naturally enough, with the organisation of the peasants into the peasant associations and the organisation of political, economic, and military attacks on the landlords. But it also involved fining them, shaming them in paper hats, banishing them; controlling rents, leases, interest-rates, and grain-movements; arming "spear corps" of tens of thousands; burning the idols in the clan-temples, etc.; and breaking the legal, religious, and feudal "customary" power of the landlords: in other words, their total culture of social control.

It is interesting to see the things the peasant associations did once they had replaced the landlords' authority with that of their own peasants' associations. I mention them in the order Mao lists them. Firstly, they outlawed gambling and opium-smoking (mah jong sets were burned, literally by the basketful). Then the "flower drum" entertainment is forbidden. Then sedan-chairs are smashed (until this action hurt the carriers, so that carrying-rates were raised instead).

---

20. Mao Tse Tung, "Report of an Investigation into the Peasant Movement in Hunan," Vol. I of *Selected Works* (London: Lawrence and Wishart, 1954), pp. 21–59.

Then wine-making and sugar-refining, the keeping of pigs, chickens, and ducks, and sumptuous feasts are forbidden, for all these are ways of wasting the food that should go to the people. Conversely, the slaughter of cattle was prohibited, because of their value as draught-animals (which the poor had often had to sell). As well as bandits, vagabonds, people who hung around temples and bullied the citizenry, were eliminated. Chanting New Year greetings to the accompaniment of castanets, praising the local deities and singing lotus rhymes, paying New Year calls (a "foolish custom"), festival processions in honour of the god of pestilence, the purchase of pastry and fruit for ritual presents, the burning of paper clothing during the festival of the Spirits, the pasting up of posters for good luck in the New Year, the smoking of water-pipes, the letting off of fire-crackers and firing of shotguns, Taoist and Buddhist services for the dead, gifts of money at funerals—all were forbidden. And Mao correctly concludes that these and other prohibitions, "too many to enumerate, are of great significance in two respects: First, they represent a revolt against bad social customs . . . [associated with] . . . the landlord class. . . . Secondly, they are a form of peasants' self-protection against exploitation by the city merchants . . . [against whom] . . . the peasants have to cultivate frugality." He then goes on to observe that these are only primitive and negative modes of self-protection. "To protect themselves economically, the peasants should build up cooperatives for collective purchasing as consumers," just as they were building up roads and embankments. Finally, the peasants were establishing their own "peasant schools" with curricula suitable to their modern needs, in contradistinction to both the "old-style" Chinese schools and the "foreign-style" schools that used textbooks designed for the city. The peasants' ideas of their own educational needs were thus sounder than that of the "so-called 'educators' for 'popular education,' which for all their hullabaloo has remained an idle phrase."

It is interesting to see Mao as an anthropologist, for, though a Party worker of experience by this time, he was an outsider. His position symbolises the gulf between the revolutionary party at that time and the revolution going on all round it. The day-to-day conflicts of Politics III, mah jong, sedan chairs, ducks, firecrackers, and wine, have "jelled," as it were. The peasant associations represent the transformation of these uncoordinated and discrete resentments of a whole category—the peasantry—into organised action. This is the crucial area of mobilisation, the point in time at which the repudiation of mah jong becomes part of revolutionary culture, the point at which, in Marx's classic formulation, the peasants become a class-for-themselves. This is what I mean by "the politics of mah jong," not some new variety of games theory. But their political achievement —the peasant association—remains localised (though "localities" are pretty massive in China) and their objectives limited to traditional grievances. The style of the movement is negative and destructive; there is less certainty about how to innovate.

Despite Mao's tributes to the self-movement of the peasantry, his (and his Party's) being outside this revolutionary turmoil mean that he had first of all to find out what was going on before he could hope to win control of the situation. In the absence of reliable data, he had to accomplish his initial analysis through anthropological field-work. In Tsarist Russia, Lenin had at his disposal the vast documentation of the so-called Zemtsvo statisticians.[21] His initial analysis, therefore, took the form of library research based on survey material.[22] Indeed, the Bolsheviks scarcely penetrated the village until the mid-twenties. Lenin's analysis also had serious defects; his successors compounded his analytical mistakes and were finally forced into total and violent confrontation with the peasantry during collectivisation, a policy emerging out of a severe, practical need for grain, however, rather than Marxist theoretics. Fortunately for the Bolsheviks, the key to Russia was the town, not the countryside. (It will remain a wry speculation that, if Lenin or someone had done a little rural fieldwork, collectivisation might have been avoided.)

Lenin's mentors provided him with initial analyses of the urban industrial capitalist society much more thorough than their agrarian ones. Marx's *Capital* and *Grundrisse* were library studies, indeed. But Frederick Engels combined the anthropological approach of first-hand participant observation of life in Manchester with the rich data provided by the classical governmental Blue Books of the time to find out what life was like in the ethnic ghettoes such as "Irish Town" and "Little Ireland" and the "planless, knotted chaos of houses, more or less on the verge of uninhabitableness," which so resemble the shanty-towns of the contemporary Third World. As a member of the Cotton Exchange, Engels knew that research into the lives of "a race wholly apart from the English bourgeoisie" was vital. He had to forsake "the company and the dinner-parties, the port-wine and

---

21. See Teodor Shanin, *The Awkward Class: Political Sociology of Peasantry in a Developing Society: Russia, 1910–1925* (London: Oxford University Press, 1972).

22. V. I. Lenin, "Theory of the Agrarian Question," Vol XII of *Selected Works*, (London: Lawrence and Wishard, 1939).

champagne of the middle-classes" to gain first-hand knowledge of working men—"I wanted to see you in your own homes, to observe you in your every-day life, to chat with you on your condition and grievances, to witness your struggles. . . ."[23] For Mao, too, culturally distant from the "strange ways of the peasant, and living in a society ill-studied and subject anyhow to massive change," observation and participation, not recourse to the British Museum, were the order of the day.

But Mao was able to work so effectively only because he had the intellectual tools of analysis forged by Marx as given, ready at hand. Moreover, he was living in an era not just of mass politics but of mass revolutionary politics. Marx spent a lot of time in the British Museum because there was precious little communist revolutionism about in his day. After World War I, both Marxism and revolutionism were institutionalised and diffused across the globe.

Yet it is important, even today, to distinguish the two. Revolution is the inclusive term, communist revolution a special case. We have already seen Mao watching the revolution and pondering how to infuse it with a communist content. And, of course, violent political upheaval had been occurring for nearly half a century before Communism had ever been heard of in a China that had witnessed the biggest revolutionary upheaval in modern history—the Taiping Revolution.

Even today, when Marxism is readily available in instant form, when Communism is not merely a theoretical utopia but an institutionalised reality, revolution is by no means co-extensive with communism. In a book written shortly after Castro's conquest of power, Jean-Paul Sartre showed that the Cuban Revolution was a broadly populist one, in which the dominant emphases were a synthesis of liberal-humanism and a kind of *"socialisme sans doctrines."*[24] The classic speech "History Will Absolve Me" reflects this notion well: there are passages from Martí, of course, from John of Salisbury, Aquinas, Luther, Knox, Locke, Rousseau, Paine, the Declaration of Independence, the French Declaration of the Rights of Man, and some quite obscure thinkers, too, but not one from Marx, from any Marxist, or from any modern revolutionary.[25] Castro's differences

---

23. Frederick Engels, "The Condition of the Working Class in England," in *Marx and Engels in Britain* (Moscow: Foreign Languages Publishing House, 1953), p. 334.

24. Jean-Paul Sartre, *Huracán sobre el azúcar* (Republic of Cuba: Ministry of State, 1960).

25. Fidel Castro, "History Will Absolve Me," in *On Trial* (London: Lorrimer Publishing Co., 1968), pp. 9–67.

with institutionalised Marxism—the Cuban Communist Party—are equally well known. Yet Cuba quickly found its way to Marxism after the Revolution. Régis Debray recently observed that the U.S.A. learned more, faster, from Cuba than the revolutionaries.[26] One might invert this idea for the earlier phase of the new revolutionary regime, however, for it would seem to be the intransigence—leading to invasion ultimately—of the United States that drove the Cubans into the arms of the Russians: the counter-revolution revolutionised the revolution, to invert Debray. But a plurality of causes was probably at work, and the sheer logic of being a revolutionary lighthouse, plus the preeminence of an erstwhile revolutionary country oriented to Marxism as the chief source of support, would have made for at least some degree of Marxist influence.

But I do not wish to debate this point, but, rather, to observe that revolutions, even today, continue to be made without much benefit of Marxism, even without much theory at all. For, basically, you do not need elaborate theory—what you need is enough theory. This is not to preach American pragmatism, for the theory has to be relevant and accurate and will normally depend on a more or less elaborated and evaluated wider body of thinking. Marx wrote much of his theory in a highly intellectual and systematised way; Mao was too busy with revolution to do so: his major theoretical works ("On Practice," "On Contradiction") are brief: his theory is constantly and directly about revolutionary action. With Castro, the action becomes primary, the furious thinking—undoubtedly there—not committed to paper until after victory.

The construction of an elaborate corpus of theory, of course, does not need re-doing if it is already available. All that remains is to take out what is relevant and apply it. And, of course, there is a functional division of labour here. Despite Mao's evident respect for the peasants' self-movement, he does not hesitate to decide what they need to do. They need, for instance, to form cooperatives fast, to arm themselves, etc. Mao enunciated these ideas with the confidence of one who knows, and who knows because he is confident both that he has the right theory and that he has done his homework. Given this assumption that he is equipped to lead, to bring order into what everyone around him described as an "awful mess," he is able to sum up what needs to be done in a few simple slogans. He does

26. "The revolution has revolutionized the counter-revolution.... Cuba has raised the material and ideological level of imperialist reaction in less time than that of the revolutionary vanguard." "Problems of Revolutionary Strategy in Latin America," *New Left Review*, Vol. 45 (September-October, 1967), pp. 13–41.

not, then, solely learn from the peasants: he brings them aims, goals, models, and answers.

Before a population is ready to respond to messages of this kind, the people obviously need to be receptive. Given that the life of the mass of mankind throughout human history has been nasty, brutish, and short, the major problem is why people have put up with it for so long, or, in more functionalist language, "the problem of order." We can, I think, discount the charge that functionalism is not concerned with change: it is, insofar as a concern with persistence, with asking the question "Why do structures persist?" is the positive mode of the question "Why do they not change?" It is true that functionalists pay inadequate attention to macro-change and rapid change of structure and focus their attention too much on secular change, on "reintegrative" processes that occur within persisting structures, on the restoration of "normality" where conflict has broken out, and so on. Thus, although functionalism does handle process and repetitive processes in "stationary" (very slowly-changing) societies reasonably well, it is poor when it comes to massive, swift, and disintegrative change.

As others have noted, Parsons has very little to say about rebellion or revolution, but very much on how societies persist. Again, after their excellent stress on process, dynamics, and on social field, Swartz, Turner, and Tuden end their ideal-typical analysis of the phases of the political struggle—mobilisation of political capital, encounter or "showdown" (by means of "breach of the peace," "crisis," "the operation of countervailing tendencies," and the "deployment of adjustive or repressive mechanisms")—with the "restoration of peace." Empirically, most of the societies they examine in their volume are free from major revolutionary dislocations (except for Mexico, in Paul Friedrich's study). Yet such macro-changes as those involved in moving from colonial status to independence, even if accomplished peacefully, can hardly be handled simply in terms of restoration.

A more inclusive theory would have to have a place for situations in which the outcome of the political struggle might well be the victory of one party and defeat of the other, their being subjugated, rendered powerless, or even—in the extreme—eliminated. Moreover, even if "peace" is established, it is a peace on new terms, not the old peace, not the restoration of the *status quo ante*. Again, the polity may persist at one level, while the power distributed among subordinate components, segments, or elements shifts significantly, as we saw when the peasant associations were taking over from landlords, even though the then Republic continued.

These processes are, indeed, well discussed by our authors: "If the [political field] . . . is now analysed . . . and . . . compared with the political field that preceded the power struggle, many changes will usually be visible. As likely as not, the scope and range of the field will have altered, the number of its parts will be different, and their size will be different.

"More importantly, the nature and intensity of the relations between parts, and the structure of the total field, will have changed. Oppositions will have become alliances, and vice versa. Asymmetric relations will have become symmetric relations. High status will have become low status, and vice versa. New power will have become channelled into new authority. . . ."[27]

Yet they go on to insist—in a general typological model of the political process—that "certain crucial norms and relationships . . . will persist," and admit deviation from the model only where the full sequence of phases is cut short by the evidence of encounter or by the calling in of outside (e.g., central government) agents. They envisage only one specific situation departing from this model of equilibrium restored—that in which conflict becomes endemic, with one general set of conditions under which the full sequence of phases does not occur. That is, when "recourse is made to new types of machinery." Those eight words are the only theoretical recognition of those major actualities of the twentieth century—rebellion and revolution. What begins as revolt against functionalism ends in a convergence with it.

The difficulty they are having is in handling emergence, and here the Parsonian language of the market is very misleading. Parsons has compared force in politics with gold in the monetary system:

> Both have great effectiveness, and both may operate within a high degree of independence from their institutional contexts, but excessive dependence on either leads to rigidity and a reduction in the number and types of things the systems can do. A monetary system that relies heavily on gold in its day-to-day transactions would be primitive and clumsy, and the same would be true of a political system that is heavily dependent on force.[28]

But force itself "must rely on relationships based on something other than force," ideological commitment, loyalty, obedience, etc.—some kind of value-orientation. The instruments of violence

27. Swartz, Turner, and Tuden, *Political Anthropology*, p. 37.

28. Talcott Parsons, "Some Reflections on the Place and Force in Social Process," in Harry Eckstein (ed.), *Internal War: Problems and Approaches* (New York: The Free Press, 1964), pp. 33–70.

are of no avail if the commitment to use them is shaken, if new commitments emerge to displace the older deference to authority, if legitimacy dissolves.

In his *History of the Russian Revolution*, Trotsky pens a picture of the crucial event in the Revolution of 1905, the moment on February 24th when the Cossacks withdrew their allegiance and could no longer be relied on:

> ... A whole mass, 2,500 of them, ran into the Cossacks. Cutting their way with the breasts of their horses, the officers first charged the crowd. Behind them ... galloped the Cossacks. Decisive moment! But the horsemen, cautiously, in a long ribbon, rode through the corridor just made by the officers. "Some of them smiled," one of the workers' leaders recalls, "and one of them gave the workers a good wink ... ".
>
> ... The break in the army first appeared among the Cossacks.... They were always being pulled around, sent everywhere, or kept in suspense.... They were sick of it, and wanted to go home. Therefore they winked: "Do it, boys, if you know how—we won't bother you!"[29]

Trotsky's revolutionary colleague, Lenin, phrased his definition of a revolutionary situation as one in which the ruling class could not continue to rule in the way that they were used to and in which the ruled would no longer go on living in the same way either. This apparently simple characterisation is much more profound than it may seem. It contains two elements: the revolt of the masses, and the disintegration of the apparatus of domination. Both are required for a revolutionary conjuncture. A country with a resolute government and a united and supportive ruling class, such as those in South Africa, Greece, or France in May, 1968, can weather severe challenges, especially if the revolutionaries, however numerous, exist within a situation in which the lives of the majority are not seriously threatened.

If one were to continue the Parsonian metaphor of force as gold and money as power (i.e., authority resting not just on force but on some "ideal" element of trust–legitimacy), then it becomes difficult to think of innovation. For the political capital is not fixed in the way that the supplies of gold or money are. Or, more exactly, political capital can be generated, not merely mobilised where it already exists in penny packets, but actually brought into being. (Of course gold, too, can be produced, mined, and marketed, and capital accumulated.) Political mobilisation in the sense of the harnessing of energy is only

29. Leon Trotsky, *The Russian Revolution*, tr. Max Eastman (Garden City: Doubleday Anchor Books, 1959), pp. 100–101.

one aspect of the process. Simply to coordinate certainly raises the level of effectiveness. It even recommends itself to such constitutionally anti-organisation people as anarchists:

> ... On one occasion, when Bakunin was travelling from Paris to Prague, he had happened upon a revolt of German peasants, who were "making an uproar around the castle," not knowing what to do. Bakunin got out of his conveyance, and without wasting any time to find out what the dispute was about, formed the peasants into ranks and instructed them so skillfully (he had been an artillery officer in Russia) that, by the time he resumed his seat to continue his journey, the castle was burning on all four sides.[30]

This is political mobilisation with a vengeance! It displays, too, that decisiveness of the successful revolutionary, that readiness, not so much to "learn from the peasant," as to tell him, very firmly, what to do. But "mobilisation," nevertheless, is too mechanical a concept, for, over and above more coordinations, new energies, which never existed before, are released. But the process of energising peasants who have always kept quiet and respected the landlord releases or creates, brings into being, a political resource. Money-market metaphors scarcely capture this process adequately.

One could take the Parsonian metaphor a little further by thinking of the mobiliser of capital and the entrepreneur who takes risks and opens up opportunities. These people deliberately set out to innovate, to play the market. In the process, they, deliberately or otherwise, produce reactions among their competitors—say counter-bids in a take-over challenge. They are not simply passive hoarders or rentiers: they seek to maximise their profits, to enlarge their operations, not merely consolidate or maintain them. They are expansive and organising. This, indeed, is what constitutes leadership: participation in "development" situations, not the endorsement and preservation of the status quo.

I am sure that revolutionaries would not thank me for comparing them with expansive capitalists. They might not object if we changed the language and said that the generation of this kind of "emergent" political support resembled the creation of value by the activity of labour in Marx's political economy. Let me now drop the metaphors, for the political energy the revolutionary party seeks to mobilise is

---

30. Edmund Wilson, *To the Finland Station: A Study in the Writing and Acting of History* (Garden City: Doubleday Anchor Books, 1959).

political energy of the Politics III type—everybody has some of it, no matter how little. It is not confined to the wealthy or those in public office. And it cannot be purchased; it can only be won.

The (probably complex) initial analysis made, the message can be simply put. The increasing separation of the popular culture from that of the rulers, which the peasants express by rejecting sumptuary landlord-style customs and by promulgating an egalitarian, rather puritanical code, and which Mao reads primarily in direct political and economic terms, as revolt against the landlord and as economic self-protection, is surely of much wider significance. It represents an affirmation of a separate and renovated sub-cultural identity, in the same way as Black Power does in the contemporary U.S.A., with its various sources of legitimation—Islam, an independent Christianity, in Pan-Africanism, etc.—and the converse denunciation of the dominant culture.

Not all is head-on confrontation, however. Revolutionaries handle deeply-entrenched popular beliefs gently, but firmly. Here is Mao dissolving the traditional authority of millennial religions in the simplest, yet mocking and oblique, fashion:

> One who believes in the Eight Characters hopes for good luck; one who believes in geomancy hopes for the beneficial influence of the burial ground. This year the local bullies, bad gentry, and corrupt officials all collapsed within a few months. Is it possible that till a few months ago they were all in good luck and all under the beneficial influence of their burial grounds, while in the last few months they have all of a sudden been in bad luck and their burial grounds all ceased to exert any beneficial influence on them? . . .
>
> The gods? They may quite deserve our worship. But if we had no peasant association, but only the Emperor Kuan and the Goddess of Mercy, could we have knocked down the local bullies and bad gentry? The gods and goddesses are indeed pitiful; worshipped for hundreds of years, they have not knocked down for you a single local bully or a single one of the bad gentry!
>
> Now you want to have your rent reduced. I would like to ask: How will you go about it? Believe in the gods, or believe in the peasant association?[31]

"These words of mine," Mao says, "made the peasants roar with laughter." "Simple slogans, cartoons, and speeches have achieved unusually great and quick results . . .". And they need be only simple slogans, no matter how sophisticated the underlying philosophy.

31. Mao Tse Tung, "Report of an Investigation . . . ," pp. 48–49.

"Land," "Bread," "Freedom," "Independence," are enough: peasants do not die willingly because they are philosophically attracted by dialectical materialism. One of the few social-revolutionary movements in Africa, the so-called Mau Mau, had only these basic ideas, plus elements of indigenous and Christian religious beliefs. Such simple themes may, of course, be highly elaborated: they can become encrusted with "complicated" accretions, to use Gluckman's term, but they are not "complex."[32] They remain simple—and that is all that is needed, for the simple things are basic and primordial, surviving, eating, not being beaten or robbed.

To coin the slogans that will register, one must comprehend popular needs. This kind of involvement in peasant life, the absorption of the popular culture, is the root of the guerrilla success. It can never be achieved by outsiders. Even the anthropologist lives there only for a year or two. In order to transform type III politics into types II and I, identification of this kind is a necessity. It is not easy to achieve where the guerrillas are highly mobile all the time, as Che Guevara found out.

Guerrilla war is not all good knockabout fun about the gods. "To put it bluntly, it was necessary to bring about a reign of terror in every rural area," terror directed against the gentry, says Mao. When their economic and political power is broken and they are humiliated, fearing them is no longer necessary. Confidence, decisiveness, and commitment are now bred in the recruits. Their positive collective power heartens them. The Hunan peasants had mostly just spears, but twenty million spears, Mao points out, is no mean armed force. Men are welded together now in strong organisations and by powerful symbolical identifications, a unification reflected in shifts of language. The popular idiom Mao uses in talking to raw peasants is different from the "Party jargon" that the trained cadre use as their everyday mode of speech. Such an idiom is at once an identification and a commitment. It marks off the politically conscious from the rest. Even in much less "demo-centralist" revolutionary movements, where elitism is a heresy, this function of language is apparent. Here is Hans-Jürgen Krahl, German SDS leader, on Czechoslovakia, 1968:

> In that phase of [bourgeois society's] historical dynamic, the institutionalised fiction of the autonomous, self-sufficient juridical per-

32. Max Gluckman, *The Judical Process among the Barotse of Northern Rhodesia* (Manchester: Manchester University Press, 1955), pp. 19–20. See also Ronald Frankenberg, *Communities in Britain: Social Life in Town and Country* (Harmondsworth: Penguin Books, 1966), p. 288.

son—embodiment of bourgeois individuality—revealed itself as a pure abstraction of the socially necessary outward appearance of commodity exchange. . . . This idea has been transformed in the heads of Yugoslav and Czechoslovak philosophers of reform into, at best, the mutilated form of diluted, existential, ontological, or phenomenological versions of Marx's theory of alienation . . .".[33]

This language is light-years removed from that in Mao's lecture. It is not language calculated to move the average West German metal-worker into action. Nor was it intended to. It is the language of revolutionaries, and highly intellectual revolutionaries, talking to each other.

The creation of this specialised revolutionary sub-culture is what the Party accomplishes (where successful). It does so, however, not because it isolates itself, but as part of the process of training and organising, while at the same time it remains oriented outward. Since it has no traditional, constitutional, or other established legitimacy, it can achieve leadership only by doing real things, by meeting popular needs: by attacking landlords or foreign occupation troops, by land and other reform measures, etc. (although these measures are fully possible only in liberated areas). Leadership has to be earned, too, by leaders who themselves suffer and take risks, but also produce results.[34] I have argued elsewhere[35] that the fashionable theory of charisma is a non-sociological and inadequate substitute for a theory of leadership. Unless it is based simply on force, leadership implies a relationship of reciprocity between leaders and led. Of course, force may be used, too: directly, to eliminate enemies of the revolution in the first place; but also indirectly, to show that a return to normalcy is impossible, by disrupting everyday life. The intended lesson here is that no one can contract out. This is what 'terror' is about: it is not just blind destructiveness.

Recruitment by participation, training and transformation by organisation. The next crucial step for the party is to provide a cognitive map of the world and of the individual's place in it: to link biography and history, as Mills put it.[36] He is provided with an explanation of the world, how it works, its composition, who does what, and where

33. Hans-Jürgan Krahl, "Class Struggle in Czechoslovakia," *New Left Review*, Vol. 53 (1968). pp. 3–12.

34. William H. Friedland, "For a Sociological Concept of Charisma," *Social Forces*, Vol. XLIII, No. 1 (October, 1964), pp. 23–24.

35. Peter Worsley, *The Trumpet Shall Sound: A Study of "Cargo" Cults in Melanesia* (New York: Schocken Books, 1968), Preface to the 2nd edition.

36. C. Wright Mills, *The Sociological Imagination* (New York: Oxford University Press, 1959), Ch. 1.

he stands within this world. The little world of the village is thus linked, albeit simply, to world society and to world history. The individual is thus provided with explanation, location, and orientation at one blow: the effects are a transformation of personality because the meaning of his life has been transformed. Much recent psychological research has concentrated on the study of the breakdown of the personality. More should be done on how it can be powerfully transformed as a prelude to massively increased activity. Emphasis on the central significance of meaning is, of course, Weber's great contribution to sociology. Any child of Weber, as we all are, has probably been similarly affected by Mannheim, too.[37] For the revolutionary party provides not simply an existential explanation—even less an "ideological" justification or endorsement of the world; it provides a critique and alternative—a "utopia," in his sense. There is one special attribute of these utopias, however. That is that they are not "ideal," but institutionalised, realities. Communism is not a speculation, a dream, or a micro-experiment, but exists in the shape of powerful states that have "taken off" where other societies have not. The "utopias" are thus derived from actual models, so the pure utopianism, which has to rely on dreams of possible societies, gives way to the more compelling utopias of the present—the "demonstration effect" of actual models such as the U.S.S.R. or China. The diffusion of these models, of course, is immensely accelerated with the growth of modern communications. Thus Tanzanian villages are now linked together and with the world outside that country by hundreds of thousands of transistors.[38]

Finally, the revolutionary party is not just out to help people "understand." It is out "to change the world." It itself is the agency of this change, the vehicle or channel through which the free-floating political energy, the static electricity of Politics III, is harnessed, transformed, and put to work. But there is one crucial condition: the politicians are not going to do the changing for you. You are. To effect the changes, you have to be prepared even to die. That calls for a very special kind of commitment and very special ways of inducing that commitment.

The revolutionary party is thus quintessentially mass politics. Politics ceased to be a privileged pursuit of the few in Britain in the

37. Karl Mannheim, *Ideology and Utopia: An Introduction to the Sociology of Knowledge* (London: Routledge and Kegan Paul, 1936).

38. Göran Hyden, *TANU Yajenga Nchi: Political Development in Rural Tanzania* (Lund: UNISKOL, 1968).

middle of the nineteenth century with the formation of new mass parties, notably the Liberal Party in Birmingham under Joseph Chamberlain, who invented caucus machine politics, and the "Tory Democracy" of Disraeli and Lord Randolph Churchill.[39] These masses were successfully mobilised for parliamentary electoral politics. But revolutionary parties mobilise people for other ends: parliamentarism is either forbidden, "decorative," or ineffective. Revolutionary mobilisation is not tied to electoral rhythms; it is a continuous process, *"une mobilisation,"* to modify Renan's phrase, *"de tous les jours."* By contrast, even the mass politics of the electoral machines seems feeble organisationally. Participation in political life in Britain, except for General Elections, even in "mass" political organisations, is minimal[40]—one percent is the norm—and the situation is similar for voluntary associations (.5 percent of the ordinary members attend cooperative meetings).[41] Despite the undoubted solidity of the "bedrock" allegiance to each of the parties, General Elections turn on less than 10 percent of the votes; and the degree of indeterminacy over-all is surprising. Blondel calculates that "as many as a quarter of the electors are in some sense floating voters, from one election to the next."[42] Kennedy's close win over Nixon was followed by the massive defeat of Goldwater. Nor does mass allegiance or identification necessarily mean a developed and differentiated political consciousness. As noted earlier, study after study has shown that the loyalists commonly have no idea what their party's programme is,[43] or are opposed to their party's policy.

This can scarcely be said of revolutionary mass parties, but with their effective socialisation procedures, we should not be surprised. American studies of "political socialisation," which have been summarised by Hyman,[44] are in fact not about political socialisation, but about political socialisation in America in the last decade or two. The conclusion that political attitudes and attachments are transmitted primarily by the family and cluster around party identification as distinct from policy seems well-documented for the U.S.A. in this

39. Robert Mackenzie, *British Political Parties* (London: Heinemann, 1955), Ch. IV.

40. See, e.g., A. H. Birch, *Small Town Politics: A Study of Political Life in Glossop* (London: Oxford University Press, 1959).

41. G. N. Ostergaard and A. H. Halsey, *Power in Cooperatives* (Oxford: Blackwell, 1965), p. 73.

42. Jean Blondel, *Voters, Parties, and Leaders* (London: Penguin Books, 1966), p. 71.

43. For example, Birch, *Small Town Politics,* pp. 82–85.

44. H. H. Hyman, *Political Socialization: A Study in the Psychology of Political Behavior* (Glencoe: The Free Press, 1959).

period. As a general theory of socialisation, of course, it would be ludicrous were one to try and apply it to, say, China. Even though Hyman sets out to analyse only U.S. data, his work should remind us that most of our political theorising is very ethnocentric, even where it is not more crudely informed by unexamined value judgments. The most ideological and least-questioned typological division, it seems to me, is the use as a general framework of the dichotomy "totalitarian/democratic." I hope that I have at least shown the poverty of such categories, which seem to me an ideological reflex rather than an adequate specification of the more differentiated categories we need in order to understand revolution, or, for that matter, political action in general.

The effectiveness of the revolutionary party—the successful revolutionary party during the "heroic" phase, that is—is more than the sum of its parts. It provides more than organisation or leadership, more than just explanation or orientation, more than a mobilising agency or a reference-group, more than all these and the other attributes described. For it does all these things taken together, and thus constitutes a special kind of institution, one that can provide a sense of total identity, purpose, and belonging for the individual. It can also constitute a "society within a society."[45]

This totality was well appreciated by the father of modern revolutionary organisation, Lenin. It was the crux, indeed, of his classic battle with Martov over party membership. This furious debate between two microscopic groupings within an insignificant body might seem to have all the hallmarks of sectarian ideological and exile politics. Yet, we now see, with hindsight, that it was world-historic, for the issue at stake was commitment. Could one be a party member just by carrying a card and paying dues? Lenin's answer was "No." One had to work, as maximally as possible, in order to be numbered amongst the "vanguard." The faction he gathered around him built a party that carried out the first major revolution of the twentieth century. All subsequent revolutions have been influenced by that model.

Yet Lenin worked under the strictly clandestine conditions in Tsarist Russia. The Bolshevik party was microscopic. Subsequent revolutionary communist movements have shown that mass revolutionary parties can be built up before the revolution—especially

45. Peter Nettl, "The German Social Democratic Party, 1890–1914 as a Political Model," *Past and Present*, Vol. 30 (April, 1965), pp. 65–95.

in liberated zones, where, indeed, the nucleus of the future is estab-lished.[46] The "vanguard" today, therefore, can be very large, and the chances of the operation of the "iron law of oligarchy" resulting in new Stalinisms are probably less where power is more widely dif-fused, where participation is high, and where, in the extreme, anti-elitism is itself actually institutionalised in forms ranging from the rather limited "workers' control" of Poland or even Yugoslavia to the thoroughgoing upheaval of the "Cultural Revolution." Debray's theories, however, and the practice of *focismo,* seem much closer to the Leninist model of a small, activistic elite vanguard, and not surpris-ingly, since the guerrillas are here operating in conditions of illegality and intensive counter-revolutionary activity much more analogous to the underground conditions in which revolutionaries operated in Tsarist Russia. Since, despite their disclaimers, all revolutions export their recipes, it is not surprising that we have two different models for armed revolution today—Cuban and Chinese.

46. Edgar Snow, *Red Star Over China* (London: Gollanz, 1937).